OIL, ISLAM AND CONFLICT

CONTEMPORARY WORLDS explores the present and recent past.
Books in the series take a distinctive theme, geo-political entity
or cultural group and explore their developments over a period
ranging usually over the last fifty years. The impact of current
events and developments are accounted for by rapid but clear
interpretation in order to unveil the cultural, political, religious
and technological forces that are reshaping today's worlds.

SERIES EDITOR
Jeremy Black

In the same series

Britain since the Seventies
Jeremy Black

Sky Wars: A History of Military Aerospace Power
David Gates

War since 1945
Jeremy Black

The Global Economic System since 1945
Larry Allen

A Region in Turmoil:
South Asian Conflicts since 1947
Rob Johnson

Altered States:
America since the Sixties
Jeremy Black

The Contemporary Caribbean
Olwyn M. Blouet

OIL, ISLAM AND CONFLICT

Central Asia since 1945

ROB JOHNSON

REAKTION BOOKS

Mark Fawcett, 'Semper Fidelis'.

Published by Reaktion Books Ltd
33 Great Sutton Street
London EC1V ODX
www.reaktionbooks.co.uk

First published 2007

Printed and bound in Great Britain
by Cromwell Press, Trowbridge, Wiltshire

British Library Cataloguing in Publication Data
Johnson, Robert, 1967–
    Oil, Islam and conflict: Central Asia since 1945. – (Contemporary worlds)
    1. Asia, Central – Politics and government
    I. Title
    958.042

ISBN-13: 978 1 86189 339 0
ISBN-10: 1 86189 339 6

Contents

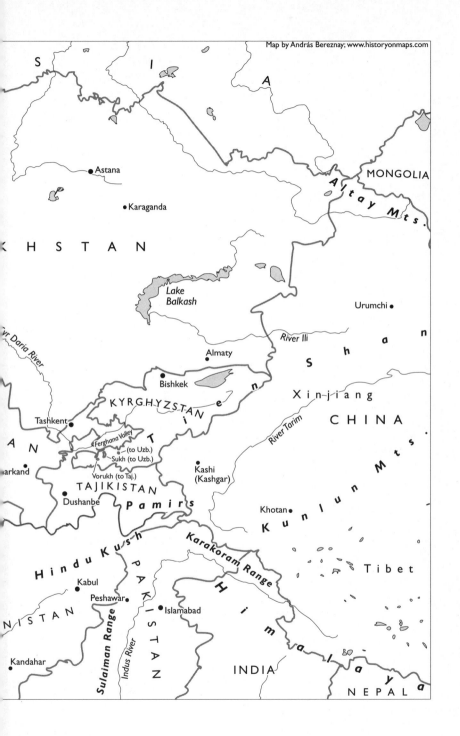

Map by András Bereznay; www.historyonmaps.com

S

I

A

MONGOLIA

Astana

Karaganda

K H S T A N

Altay Mts.

Lake
Balkash

Urumchi

River Ili

T i e n

S h a n

Almaty

vr Daria River

Bishkek

KYRGHYZSTAN

X i n j i a n g

CHINA

Tashkent

River Tarim

Ferghand Valley

(to Uzb.)

Sukh (to Uzb.)

Vorukh (to Taj.)

arkand

Kashi
(Kashgar)

TAJIKISTAN

Khotan

Dushanbe

P a m i r s

K u n l u n   M t s.

Hindu Kush

Karakoram Range

T i b e t

Kabul

P
A
K
I
S
T
A
N

H
i
m
a
l
a
y
a

Peshawar

Sulaiman Range

NISTAN

Islamabad

Indus River

Kandahar

INDIA

N E P A L

Preface

This book, part of the Contemporary Worlds series edited by Professor Jeremy Black, is designed to complement *A Region in Turmoil* (2005), a study of conflict in South Asia since 1947, and forthcoming studies of South-west Asia. This is a thematic and comparative study of the new battlefields in Central Asia. Though barely understood in the West, Central Asia has long been the crossroads of civilizations and conquests. Nevertheless, it is in the post-Soviet era that perhaps the most dramatic changes are taking place. A regional perspective allows us to gather together and analyse a range of current issues in their historical perspective, including the future of Central Asian hydrocarbons, the problem of security and stability in the republics and the themes of representation, repression and resistance.

This region is likely to become a new arena of international interest in the 21st century, not least because of its cocktail of abundant oil and gas, Islamic jihadist groups, dictatorial regimes, and rivalry between Russia, China, Pakistan, the US and Iran. Indeed, it could become the 'new Middle East' in the sense of being a battleground for access to precious resources, for religious fundamentalism and for sectarianism and authoritarian-vs-democratic politics. Narcotics, ethnic tensions and impoverished states with, or seeking, weapons of mass destruction (WMD) further add to the instability.

Instead of looking at individual states or separating the issues, we are able to examine the activities of pan-Islamic jihadist groups, such as the Islamic Movement of Turkestan (IMT, formerly known as the Islamic Movement of Uzbekistan, or IMU), which operates across national borders. Likewise, it allows us to trace the Islamic Renaissance Party, Hizb ut-Tahrir (HT), 'Arab-Afghans' and the Chechen fighters who have participated in one way or another in conflicts from Afghanistan to Iraq. A regional study also enables us to make comparative assessments of the 'oil pipeline' politics of the great powers and the Central Asian leaders. Above all, this work attempts to combine the *context* of recent history, the oil and gas industry, endemic economic weaknesses and the rise of militant Islam but also stresses the importance of the *policy line* being taken by the Central Asian regimes – which Olivier Roy, Ahmed Rashid and other specialist observers have suggested are the cause of many current problems. This book also offers a perspective on the 'war on terror' from a particular region in light of the West's experiences (Russia is included as a 'Western' power in this sense) in Afghanistan, Chechnya and Iraq. This is particularly relevant given the West's interest in Iran's nuclear programme and in China's apparently burgeoning power. Finally, it gives us a fresh perspective on problems which feature frequently in the media, especially Afghanistan, the rise of religious extremism and anxiety about WMD.

Given that contemporary definitions of Islam are 'loaded' with particular meanings which have political overtones, it is necessary to offer some explanation of the terms used in this work. I make a distinction between Islam – the established religion of the Muslim world – and Islamism – a radical, politicized ideology. Islamists believe that their faith is superior and that action is required to assert its pre-eminence. This can take the form of justifications for direct action or popular protest, such as 'the defence' of the religion, the 'protection' of fellow Muslims regardless of their nationality, or a desire to expunge a 'humiliation' of Islam. Islamism can take the form of peaceful, if vocal and strident, protest, but it can also mean support for underground organizations, sympathy for 'resistance' (or terrorist) groups, and even more active participation. In a storm of protest about the publication of cartoons allegedly depicting the Prophet Muhammad, Islamists staged demonstrations around the world. One took place in London, where, in fact, the cartoons were not published. That did not prevent some protestors calling for the beheading of those who insult Islam (however they decided to interpret an insult), the killing of British servicemen and -women, and threats of terrorism on the streets of the capital. In Pakistan, there were riots in several cities and two people died, although it must be made clear that the majority of Pakistanis did not participate and were genuinely shocked by the levels of violence and vandalism. Islamists tend to blame a variety of groups for their plight. They criticize secular regimes in countries where the majority are Muslim; they point to Jewish and Christian-Western capitalist conspiracies; above all, they blame the US, its foreign policy, its espionage, and its military and economic power. Islamists seek to mobilize Muslims, to move populations towards mass resistance, be that passive or more violent in form.

Another distinction must be made, however, between Islamists and jihadists. Jihadists are the 'active service units' of the Islamist phenomenon. They are highly committed and often fearless of death. Many are veterans of recent conflicts in Afghanistan, Kashmir, Chechnya or Iraq; almost all are idealists but a number are simply criminals. They fight using terrorist or guerrilla tactics, ambushing, raiding, hostage-taking for ransom or detonating explosives. They intimidate, extort, traffic in drugs and people, smuggle arms and murder. They justify their activities in elaborate, romanticized notions of honour, serving the cause of Allah and the faith, and protecting the people. But the reality is that they kill, mutilate, terrorize and destroy. They are not interested in compromise or negotiation, and they see their life's mission as waging 'holy' war. Many are men in their twenties, angry with the world and eager for power. These values have been imported into Central Asia from the Middle East, Pakistan and Afghanistan. Today, the inequalities of wealth, external influences, clan loyalties, and repressive security policies of the Central Asian republics have begun to blur the boundaries between the followers of Islam, Islamists and jihadists.

Acknowledgements

In the research and writing of this book, I incurred debts of gratitude to many people, but specifically I would like to mention my hosts in Kyrgyzstan, Pakistan and Uzbekistan for their hospitality and protection, and Exeter University and World Challenge Expeditions for making my visits possible; Peter Hopkirk for his inspiration, encouragement and support; Professor Jeremy Black for his warm friendship and advice; Hugh Leach, Norman Cameron and many friends in the Royal Society for Asian Affairs for their support; colleagues and students in the History Department of the University of Warwick for their stimulating and correcting ideas; colleagues and friends on the 'War and the Muslim World' course at Warwick; my Iranian friends, including Faraj Ahmadi and Bijan Omani; and the many friends I have met on courses at Dillington House in Somerset, including Dr Paul Macdonald and Susan Farrington. I would like to pay special tribute to the staff of Radio Free Europe (Radio Liberty), who have taken considerable risks to obtain and report accurately in Central Asia.

Rob Johnson

2007

Chapter 1

Regional Issues and Contemporary History

On 13 May 2005, there was a mass demonstration in Andijan, the east-ernmost city of Uzbekistan. The crowd, numbering several thousand, expressed their anger at their deteriorating economic situation, and at the government's arrest of 23 businessmen accused of Islamic extrem-ism. According to the Uzbek government, the demonstration had been sparked by the violent jailbreak of the defendants in which unspecified numbers of security personnel were kidnapped or killed.[1] Whatever the circumstances of the demonstration, that May the crowds consisted of unarmed men, women and children. Yet, apparently without issu-ing a warning, the marshalling troops, backed by their Soviet-built armoured personnel carriers, opened fire.

The number of those who died is much disputed. The government argues that of the 187 dead, almost all were killed by Islamist terrorists in the gun battle. Human Rights Watch believe that more than 500 were murdered by the security forces, and perhaps as many as a thou-sand were killed in the crackdown that followed. In September 2005, fifteen extremist suspects were put on trial; two months later they were convicted for terms between fourteen and twenty years. Allison Gill, head of Human Rights Watch in Moscow, described the legal process as little more than 'show trials'[2] and believes that confessions were extracted after torture. In December 2005, a further 58 people were convicted. Despite American and European calls for an inde-pendent enquiry, the Uzbek government, led by the hard liner Islam

Karimov has refused to consider one. The details of what has come to known as the Andijan Massacre will, for the time being, remain a mystery.

Andijan lies at the heart of the Ferghana Valley, a fertile plain 300 kilometres long and just 100 kilometres wide but home to 10,000,000 people – that is, 20 per cent of the population of Central Asia. Divided between Uzbekistan, Tajikistan and Kyrgyzstan, the valley has become the focal point of a pan-Islamic renaissance in the region and the seat of jihadist terrorism. At Namangan, in December 1997, an Uzbek army captain was kidnapped and beheaded – his head being put on display outside his office by his killers.[3] In the same month, a collective-farm chairman and his wife were also murdered in this way, and just a week later, three policemen were gunned down. Hundreds were arrested without effect. In May 1998, the Uzbek parliament passed the Law on Freedom of Conscience and Religious Organisations, banning all unregistered mosques and religious leadership. Karimov demanded that terrorists 'must be shot in the head', adding, 'If necessary I will shoot them myself.'[4] When six car bombs were detonated in the city centre of Tashkent in 1999, in what seemed to be an attempt to kill Karimov and members of his administration, the Uzbek government launched an even harder crackdown. In the immediate aftermath, Karimov exhibited his characteristic defiance by visiting the very heart of the city and issuing stern warnings against his opponents. In a matter of days, 2,000 people had been arrested. By April 1999, Karimov had extended his threats by stating that any father of a militant would be arrested. He was reported as stating, 'If my child chose such a path, I myself would rip off his head.'[5]

The militants claim that they themselves are responding to the arbitrary violence of the state. Tohir Abdouhalilovitch Yuldeshev, a mullah and spiritual leader of the militant IMU, argued that 'the goals of the IMU activities are firstly fighting against oppression within our country, against bribery, against the inequalities and also the freeing of our Muslim brothers from prison [and] we do not repent our declaration of jihad against the Uzbek government. God willing, we will carry out this jihad to its conclusion.'[6] Yuldeshev specified the establishment of an Islamic theocratic state and the imposition of Sharia law as the longer-term objectives of the armed struggle. Yet, despite all the rhetoric about Islamism on both sides, the real struggle is the one for naked power in the wake of the collapse of the Soviet Union.

The conflicts had begun even before the demise of Gorbachev. Economic deterioration, high unemployment, ethnic rivalry and a wave of anti-Russian anger led to the outbreak of serious riots in Ashgabat in Turkmenistan in May 1988. The following summer, sectarian riots over housing and land rights between Uzbeks and Meskhetian Turks turned into gun battles in the Ferghana Valley. Similar causes led to riots between Tajiks and Armenians in Dushanbe in Tajikistan in February 1990; that summer there were bloody battles between Kyrgyz and Uzbeks in the eastern end of the Ferghana Valley in which Uzbek farmers were butchered and hung up on meat hooks in Osh. With Soviet troops restoring order there, more fighting broke out in 1991 against the Uzbek government further down the valley. And in the Caucasus, Georgia faced separatist violence in Abkhazia and South Ossetia, while Armenia and Azerbaijan fought pitched battles for the control of Karabakh and 30,000 died in the conflict there.

But nowhere was this battle for power more bloody than Tajikistan. In a civil war that raged for five years, from 1992 to 1997, and that cost a staggering 50,000 lives, this divided state was hit particularly hard by the severance of Russian-Soviet backing and was subsequently plunged into a struggle for the resources that remained. In the autumn of 1992, weeks of rioting had not been stemmed by the Tajik authorities or the Russian troops flown in to support them. An opposition was formed, clustered around the Islamic Renaissance Party (IRP), but clan groups in rural areas split away from the state altogether. When the government was overthrown in December of that year, clan warlords inflicted a reign of terror over their areas of jurisdiction, murdering ethnic rivals and clashing with each other and the IRP. Russian contingents were joined by detachments from neighbouring Central Asian states, anxious to prevent the fighting from spreading across the region. The fall of the Central Asian government there reinforced the resolve of the other republics' leaders to cling on to power by any means.

At the other end of the region, an equally dramatic and bitter conflict was unfolding. Amid the ruins of Grozny separatists fought two protracted wars with Russia. Moscow was determined to ensure that a strategically vital region, particularly its lucrative oil resources, were not lost in the collapse of a failing state. Concerned by rising lawlessness, mafia crime and antagonism to their directives, the Russians felt compelled to deploy troops, just as they had done elsewhere in the Caucasus when their interests were threatened. For the Chechens, there were long memories of Stalinist brutality and new aspirations to independence. However, the nationalists' agenda was complicated by clan rivalry and by the involvement of foreign jihadists. Russia believed it was fighting a nest of terrorists and 'bandits', a view reinforced by the tactics and techniques of certain groups. As a result, Russian coercion grew ever more extreme. Russian commanders wanted to level Grozny and drive out the separatists using the full weight of their military power. Yet, despite greater progress in the second of the two Chechen Wars (that is, since 1999–2000), Russia still faces desultory terrorist campaigns. These have spilled into the rest of Russia, the most notorious episodes being the Moscow Theatre Siege and the massacre at Beslan in 2004.

But it should not be forgotten that the storm centre that had done so much to shake the Soviet regime and perhaps to precipitate the reform, and fall, of the USSR was Afghanistan. Here, not only had the people endured the bloody reprisals of the Afghan Communist regime and its Soviet allies for ten years, but they had then been subject to a protracted civil war fought between warlords, ethnic groups and their foreign backers. As the last shreds of legitimacy of any central authority were shot away in street battles in Kabul, the Pakistani Pushtun protégés, the Taliban, seized power in 1996 and imposed an authoritarianism that surpassed even the brutalities of Najibullah, the last Communist dictator of the country. Resistance, though, never ceased, and was strongly focused in the Shia heartland of Hazarajat, and in the northern provinces. With 5,000,000 Afghans in exile and untold numbers internally displaced, the Taliban and their enemies conducted an exhausted, broken-backed struggle until, in 2001, American and Coalition forces swept the United Front (known in the West as the Northern Alliance) back to Kabul. Noor Ahmed Khalidi believes that the number who died in the Soviet war was 876,000, with a further 1.5

million permanently disabled.[7] Another 10,000 died in the most intense phase of the civil war between 1992 and 1995, but, other than the well-documented Taliban massacres in Hazarajat and Mazar-i-Sharif, the final death toll under the Taliban is not known. Afghanistan was left in ruins, its infrastructure destroyed, and its people traumatized and impoverished.

Central Asia's recent, and much of its historic, past has been shaped by state terror, authoritarianism, and conflict. Many civilizations and conquerors have swept through a region that offers few definable borders. Indeed, Central Asia is characterized by its vast spaces. Nomadic peoples found only a few areas for permanent settlement in mountain valleys, in oases and alongside rivers in between the relentless deserts and great ranges. These small areas of population provided a ribbon of service centres for the caravans of the Silk Route, which is, in fact, a trade artery of greater antiquity than the commerce in silks. The khanate kingdoms that emerged in the region were governed in authoritarian style, but the jurisdiction they claimed was only really authentic in those areas outside the cities where they could enforce taxation. Nomads continued to roam the steppes, mountains and deserts, and, across the region, old clan loyalties have persisted to the present day.

It was the physical distances and the vast barriers of deserts and mountains that kept out or delayed so many invaders, but the rivers acted as corridors for the movements of armies, migrants and commerce. The great Syr Daria and Amu Daria (Oxus), like the Caspian Sea, acted as conduits as much as boundaries. In antiquity, Central Asia was divided roughly between Persians to the south and Turkic nomads to the north, the latter thought to have emerged from Siberia or perhaps further east.[8] Between 339 and 327 BC, Alexander and his Macedonians conquered Sogdiana and Bactria (which spanned present-day Afghanistan, Tajikistan and Uzbekistan), but Alexander, like his successors, ruled through local intermediaries. Parthians dominated western Central Asia (today's Turkmenistan and Caucasus) until they were defeated by the Persians, while the north fell under the Sakas, peoples displaced from the north-east by the Hsiung-nu (Huns) from the Gobi. The Huns continued to push westwards, subjugating the Uighurs (in modern Xianjiang) and then pushing on to Europe. In their wake, Turkic nomads again reclaimed northern Central Asia. In the first and second centuries AD, the Kushan Empire emerged, stretching from India to Iran, promoting Buddhism as its faith. Nevertheless, contests for the fertile Ferghana Valley were unceasing until the hundred-year campaign of the Arabs and their legions of Muslim converts. The Chinese were checked at Talas (Kyrgyzstan) in 751, although the Arabs failed to put down roots in the region at all, and it was left to local Islamic leaders to establish kingdoms of their own. Situated around the oases, the Persian Saminids, for example, established a lasting linguistic and cultural heritage. The Ghaznavids of Afghanistan and other successor regimes took over until the Seljuks poured in from the north to capture the whole of Central Asia and Turkey from the eleventh to the thirteenth centuries.[9]

Seljuk rule was destroyed, along with much of Central Asia, by the Mongols. In 1220, it was said that 30,000 were slain at Bokhara and that pyramids of severed heads were built along the bloody route of the invaders. Yet, after the wave of murder had passed, the Mongols re-established the Silk Route caravans and set up their characteristic mounted-courier service. In the 1300s, Timur, a Barlas Turk who had established his kingdom around Samarkand, embarked on a new period of expansion and accumulated considerable wealth. Seizing artisans from Persia and other conquered territories, Central Asia enjoyed a cultural flowering – which helps to explain Uzbekistan's eagerness to downplay Timur's brutal tactics and promote him as the national hero of the Uzbek people. In Shakrisabz, where his palace stood, an enormous effigy of 'Tamerlane' now towers – his face in a suitably disapproving grimace.

The Timurids were defeated in 1500 by the Shaybani Uzbeks, who, with their capital at Bokhara, re-established Turkic culture and language. But the Silk Route was in decline, thanks, in part, to the rise of Western sea-borne commerce. The decline in revenue meant it was harder to maintain the route, protect the caravans or pay for the old standing armies. Petty rulers sought to carve out their own power in weakened khanates, while the conservative ulema (Islamic teachers) suppressed innovation in science, education and culture. By the seventeenth century, Central Asia was a shadow of its former glory. Impoverished, it was a backwater of the Islamic world, and, crucially, it was bitterly divided on the eve of the era of European imperial expansion.

The greatest political transformation came with the Russian annexations. Starting in the seventeenth century with parts of Kazakhstan, the Russians seized the Caucasus after decades of struggle in the 1850s.[10] In the 1860s, Tashkent was taken and Bokhara was proclaimed a protectorate, while Khiva fell after a swift military campaign in 1873. The Turcoman nomads were crushed in fighting between 1879 and 1881, when the last stronghold at Geok (Gokdepe) Tepe was captured. In the 1880s, Merv (Mary) and the northern Pamirs were absorbed, and the pressure southwards was concluded in the 1890s with the settlement of the southern borders with Britain. Britain, for its part, established a protectorate over Afghanistan by dictating its foreign policy, while China was prompted to reassert its control of Sinkiang (Xinjiang) Province in 1877. The Russian imperial governors established borders for the new dominions – and crushed any unrest.

The motives for this expansion are somewhat contested. The contemporary argument, expressed by Prince Gorkachov in his Circular of 1864, was that since nomadic or weak states had ill-defined borders and created turbulence on the frontiers, the difficulty for a strong power like Russia was 'knowing where to stop' in its annexations.[11] The British, anxious about the relentless advance of the Tsar's forces towards their Indian border, suspected that all this was a smokescreen for military ambition. There is some evidence to suggest that the Russian army and the Asiatic Section of the Imperial Foreign Ministry did indeed harbour grandiose ideas about defeating the British on the borders of India, although this may have been no more than a game to ensure Britain's compliance with Russian ambitions in Europe and the Near East. Some argue that it was the 'Cotton Famine' caused by the American Civil War which prompted the Russians to look to Central Asia, although commercial reasons for exploiting the region tended to come after the conquests. Perhaps the best explanation is that these impulses coincided in an era where Russia enjoyed a military advantage and when a culture of imperialism made such ventures justifiable.

The Russians altered the landscape of Central Asia. Millions of Russian peasants were settled in Kazakhstan and further south. Russian workers were brought in to staff the new industries. Vast irrigation schemes watered the cotton fields, and a railway network was developed with a military and commercial focus. But there was still unrest, and the 1916 uprising in what is today Uzbekistan was the most serious. Already the area was badly affected by a famine, Moscow's decision to conscript Central Asians to fight in the First World War sparked resistance from Kazakhs and Kyrgyz nomads, and quickly spread across the region. The reprisals were as severe as they were comprehensive. Tens of thousands were killed, and tsarist troops pursued Kyrgyz fugitives from their burning villages right up to the border with China. It is estimated that as much as a quarter of the Kyrgyz population was uprooted or massacred. By the time of the Revolution in 1917, the Russians were detested.

However, despite the Revolution, the disparate agencies of Central Asia failed to prevent the Bolsheviks from establishing Communist rule, and foreign interventionist forces, notably the Turks (Caucasus) and the British (Trans-Caspia), were unable to sustain their influence because of costs and commitments elsewhere. A revolt by the Basmachis, despite lasting ten years, also failed to stem the Bolshevik armies.[12] The Basmachis were Central Asians who were committed to expelling the Communists. After the sacking of Khokhand following a rebellion in 1918, many were unconvinced by Bolshevik claims that they were the liberators of the region. Up to 20,000 men, many of whom were farmers by day, became fighters by night. Like the mujahedin and the Taliban in the late twentieth century, their dual identity was a perfect camouflage. The Basmachi had the advantage of knowing their own territory too, but they were often divided along clan lines and there was no co-ordinated strategy. There were, for example, assassinations of Bolshevik personnel but no plans to seize power. Preoccupied by the Russian Civil War, the Bolshevik detachments could barely contain the insurgency. Worse, their officers were inexperienced and the rank and file were incapacitated by malaria and local diseases. In 1920, as the civil war was drawing to its conclusion, Mikhail Frunze launched a new offensive, making use of Muslim units recruited from the Caucasus. Bokhara was taken, but this did not quell the rebellion, and Frunze was forced to make some political concessions. Lenin appointed the former Turkish military dictator Enver Pasha to govern, but he misjudged the choice: as soon as Enver arrived, he defected and became the leader of the Basmachi revolt.

Enver's aim was to create a Pan-Turkic empire from Constantinople to Mongolia, and he believed the Basmachi would provide the core of a new Islamic army for that purpose. He quickly obtained the approval of the exiled Emir of Bokhara and sent messengers to each of the Basmachi factions, hoping to unite them. He made deliberate references to the aspiration to found a new caliphate and addressed himself as a kinsman of the Caliph and a representative of the Prophet. This had a very positive effect on the morale of the rebels. On 14 February 1922, Enver captured Dushanbe, subsequently raiding Bokhara. Some 7,000 more recruits came in. As his force grew, he remodelled his headquarters on the Turkish army staff and obtained arms from Amir Amanullah in neighbouring Afghanistan. Many Afghan 'volunteers' also crossed the Oxus to join the rebellion. Faced with this growing insurrection, the Bolsheviks made new overtures to negotiate an end to the fighting, but when this failed, they deployed 100,000 men to overwhelm the rebels. Enver was forced to withdraw his smaller force to the Pamirs. On 14 June 1922, 3,000 Basmachi tried to ambush a force almost three times their strength, but they suffered heavily under Bolshevik artillery. As the Bolsheviks swept eastwards across the mountains, some of the rebels gave up, and the Basmachi began to fragment once again. As the Bolsheviks seized village after village in their progress up the valleys, they offered concessions to win the hearts and minds of the population. Many responded positively, fearing the Communists' retribution if they did not comply. Amanullah, seeing the end, withdrew his volunteers and matériel. The remaining Basmachi, low on supplies and with dwindling support, were forced to become bandits, a situation in which the IMT found itself during its campaigns of 1999–2000. Finally, on 4 August 1922, Enver was cornered at Abiderya and died leading a cavalry charge against Bolshevik machine guns.

In consolidating their rule, the Communists established a party apparatus designed to minimize the influence of local ethnic groups.

Stalin redesigned the borders of the Central Asian states in such a way that ethnic groups were divided and would become rivals. Yet, ironically, it was the supranational nature of the Soviet Union, and the illusion that it was a free association of states, that necessitated the artificial creation of 'national' identities for the Central Asian republics. When the USSR collapsed, there was a decisive moment when it was unclear whether the old Soviet republics would survive or whether new states based on ethnic identities would emerge. The outcome was not unlike Africa after decolonization: artificial states, plagued with poverty and ethnic division, consisting of competing groups who, all too often, took up arms against each other for control of the resources that remained.

ISLAM AND GOVERNMENT

The dominant form of Islam traditionally practised in Central Asia was Sufism, although most of the population are Hannafi Sunnis. Sufis followed a mystic ideology according to which an inner knowledge of God could be revealed through meditation, ritual and dancing. Emerging as a separate sect from the late tenth century, the Sufis represented an ascetic reaction to the formalism and legalism of Sunni Islam. Named after their rough woollen cloaks and borrowing from Christian, Buddhist and neo-Platonic ideas as well as pre-Islamic symbolism, the Sufi brotherhood emphasized direct communion with the divine. It was this absence of intermediaries and the missionary work of its advocates, the *tariqas* (orders), that helped to spread Sufi ideas among the peoples of Central Asia. Since some Sunnis and Shias regarded Sufism as a heretical sect, especially as it seemed to embody opposition to authority (particularly that of the mullahs), Sufis developed clandestine groups which often evolved their own forms of prayer and ritual. After the Mongol onslaught, then under the tsarist regime and later under Soviet oppression, these secretive networks helped the Sufis to maintain the faith among the people. The Naqshbandis, for example, named after their fourteenth-century founder Mohammed ibn Baha ad-Din Naqshband, regarded their own authority as eternal and therefore more important than that of any temporal tyrant. They led a revolt against the Russians in Andijan in 1898. More importantly, this tradition of clandestine belief has survived into the independence period. Despite the new governments' attempts to suppress an Islamic revival, the older approach to worship has assisted in the popularization of both religion and religious opposition.

Sufis were nevertheless the most tolerant of all the Islamic groups. In Kazakhstan, the last regional state to be converted to Islam (in the seventeenth century), elements of folk culture and shamanism survived within the Sufi orders. This degree of toleration and corruption among Sufi families in power led to the Jadid reform movement in the nineteenth century. Jadidism, advocated by intellectuals like Ismail Gasprinski, tried to reconcile Western influence with religious reform, faith, education and scientific research in a quest for an Islamic renaissance. Yet despite these and other sectarian disputes, pilgrimages to the shrines of Sufi saints, especially in Bokhara, were important symbolic acts which reconnected the people of Central Asia with their religion and identity.

However, aside from the small enclave of Ismaili Shi'ism in cities like Samarkand and Bokhara (and the branch of Islam often, wrongly, attributed to Shia belief in Tajikistan), the key division throughout much of Central Asia's history was between orthodox, conservative Sunni Islam and the Sufis. The conversion of Persia to Shi'ism under the Safavids from the 1500s had reduced their Shi'ite influence in Central Asia, but the Russians' decision to endorse an ultra-conservative 'official' Islam under their occupation, along with their aggressive secularization programme in the Soviet era, tended to distance, if not alienate, many Central Asians from Islam altogether. The Jadids, who had sided with the modernizing Communists after 1917, were banned and then steadily wiped out in Stalinist purges. In 1991, despite the efforts of underground Sufis, Central Asians were so cut off that they were remarkably unaware of events in the Muslim world – particularly the deep humiliation felt by Palestinians after the creation of Israel in 1948, the Islamic Revolution in Iran in 1979, and the emergence of suicide terrorism from the 1980s. The one conflict that was known about, including the Islamic fighters' part in it, was Afghanistan's struggle with the Soviet Union. That conflict was to have profound repercussions for the region's politics in the 1990s.

Traditions of governance in Central Asia also help to explain the current political dispensation. Using the conservative ulema as the legitimizing voice of their authority, the nineteenth-century khans ruled with an astonishing severity. Emir Nasrullah of Bokhara, for example, ruled as an authoritarian despot, executing those even suspected of subversion and espionage. Infamously, it was Nasrullah who decided to execute two British officers in 1842, believing they were orchestrating neighbouring states – Khiva and Tashkent – against him.[13] Yakub Beg was a freebooter who seized power in Kashgar in the later nineteenth century and ruled equally harshly with a ubiquitous and plentiful organization of informers.[14] In Afghanistan, local chieftains behaved brutally towards the people until the country was unified under the Durranis in the nineteenth century. Abdur Rahman, an exile who had been invited to take the throne by the British in 1880, exercised power without restraint. Faced with rebellions on the periphery of his country, he forced populations to move into the remote north-west, and had criminals or insurgents boiled alive, turned into human icicles, blown from cannons and ripped apart from tensioned tree trunks. He carried out a repression so thorough against the pagans of Nafiristan and the Shias of the Hazarajat that the British referred to it as a policy of extermination.[15]

Nor were the mountain or nomadic leaders any more tolerant. Imam Shamil, long celebrated as the heroic resistance fighter against the Russians in the Caucasus, was as tough on the people of Chechnya as his enemies. The Turcomans, who once roamed what is today Turkmenistan, were feared as slavers across the region, and their demise at the hands of the Russian army was celebrated. They had a tradition of cutting off the feet of those they could not carry off as prisoners, condemning their victims to a slow death in the desert. The Pathans on Afghanistan's western border were also notorious for mutilating their enemies with knives or beheading those who incurred their displeasure. In the twentieth century, brutal tortures did not disappear. In the Soviet–Afghan War, the prison at Kabul run by the KHAD secret police earned a terrible reputation. Torture was routine and included confining prisoners alongside dismembered body parts or corpses.[16] It is not known how many were murdered by the Soviet–Afghan authorities, but their deadly tactics certainly continued under the Taliban, being augmented with staged trials and public executions. Whether radicalized by war or not, Central Asia has had a long tradition of unaccountable governance with regimes exercising power without checks or balances. For most of the republics, the judiciary has long served the interests of the state, and the executive still governs without much concern for parliamentary bodies. Such systems are vulnerable to abuse by political élites.

The governments of the Central Asian republics have been quick to condemn the activities of Islamist groups which oppose them. They argue that their opponents are jihadists and that efforts to curtail them are part of the American-led 'Global War on Terror'. It was always going to be the weakness of such an ideology that a worldwide struggle against terrorism could be used as camouflage for government crackdowns. That said, there is no doubt that Islam has been politicized, radicalized and even militarized since the 1970s. In Central Asia, the Soviet tradition of repression against Islam was continued by the republics' governments into independence, precisely as the more militant varieties of Islam were being introduced to the people after a gap of seventy years. Millions have embraced Islam more openly, and radical anti-government groups have enjoyed unprecedented growth. The results have been explosive.

The Soviet techniques for dealing with Islamic resistance developed as soon as the Bolsheviks seized power but reached extremes under Stalin. Having divided the republics into antagonized ethnic groups in 1936, and having established a Russian political élite (almost all of the Turkmenistan leaders were Russian, for example), Stalin imposed collectivization to break the nomadic culture of the region. About 1.5 million Kazakhs died through murder, death during migration, and starvation, representing one third of the population. The Kyrgyz were also repressed, driven into China and massacred; they lost a quarter of their population. Progressive reforms were also designed to destroy older cultures: mass education, new industries to 'proletarianize' the people, mechanized farming and housing schemes to 'settle' nomadic populations. The resources of Central Asia – cotton, oil and minerals – flowed back into Russia while Russian migrants were relocated among the indigenous peoples.

Islam was regarded as a bourgeois decadence, reactionary and 'backward'. It was also, the Russians knew, a potent mobilizing ideology that threatened the regime with civil unrest. There had been a brief attempt to ignite the Muslim world against all the European empires at a conference in Baku in 1920, but, despite all the fiery rhetoric and apparent solidarity, the Central Asian Muslims present, who were under Communist rule, were conspicuously unenthusiastic. This is partly explained by the fact that Lenin's followers generally portrayed the mullahs as counter-revolutionaries and enemies of the people, and there were hints that religious leaders had links with foreign intelligence services. Consequently, religious observance and ritual was banned in Central Asia. Mosques were closed and converted into workshops. Women were forbidden to wear a hijab. Children could not read the Koran at school. By the mid-1930s, there were sixty mosques left in Uzbekistan, twenty in Kyrgyzstan and just four in Turkmenistan.[17] During the war, Stalin needed to mobilize the Muslims of Central Asia against the Nazi invasion, and an approved Islamic Directorate for Central Asia and Kazakhstan was established with offices at Tashkent, Baku, Buinaksk (Daghestan) and Ufa (Russia). While this marked the birth of 'official Islam' with leaders carefully chosen to convey support for the regime, Stalin continued to deport peoples he suspected of pro-German sympathies, including half a million of the Chechen population (one third of whom died en route to Siberia). Despite some liberalization under Khrushchev between 1955 and 1958, the Soviet regime continued to suppress Islam.[18]

In the 1960s, at the height of the Cold War, 'Official Islam' was given greater recognition in an attempt to win over Muslim countries. Two official seminaries were opened in Tashkent and Bokhara although the syllabus still included Soviet Studies. Nevertheless, trained and approved mullahs were permitted to open mosques, holy days were observed, and a few were able to travel on the hadj to the Al-Azhar University in Cairo and to shrines in South-west Asia. However, in the final years of the Soviet Union, this façade of approval was exposed.

Gorbachev regarded Islam as an enemy of modernization, while, ironically, Central Asian political leaders feared that Moscow's programme
of perestroika would encourage an Islamic revival, calls for greater
freedom, and therefore resistance to their control of the region.

In fact, Islam had never been fully suppressed: it had gone underground. And it was these underground networks that enabled moderate
and radical versions of Islam to revive so quickly after independence.
When mosques were closed down, many had run religious instruction
in their homes, meeting at night and in secret for rituals and worship.
Communist holidays became the opportunities to visit Muslim shrines.
In Tajikistan, thousands would meet at each of the 500 shrines minis-
tered by 700 unregistered and unofficial mullahs. Women played a
particularly important role in maintaining the shrines. In addition,
visiting mullahs crossed the region holding services, including Islamic
weddings. The Ferghana Valley was host to a particularly strong concentration of them. Sufi networks published religious materials in secret
and used their underground contacts to circulate them. Even officials
within the Party apparatus gave their tacit approval by quietly attending ceremonies, perhaps using the activity as a form of defiance to the
Moscow regime.

While perestroika had the unforeseen effect of allowing Islam to
resurface publicly, building on its underground foundations, there
were changes in Islam wrought by external forces too. Militant ideas,
which originated in South-west Asia, were the means to give expression to widespread anger with the old systems of governance.
Religious identity was also the badge of political dissent. The first
development of this feeling was the Soviet War in Afghanistan. As
news of the mujahedin resistance spread across Central Asia, many
were forced to question their long-held assumptions about Soviet
power. Rumours and myths emerged, in keeping with the ancient
craft of story-telling typical of the region. Some Central Asian troops
defected to the mujahedin, but all of them were noticeably more
sympathetic to the Afghan people than the Russians. Hundreds of
young men from Uzbekistan and Tajikistan began to slip across the
border to join the fighters or escape to madrassahs in Saudi Arabia and
Pakistan. More than 40,000 Muslims from some 43 countries eventually

joined the struggle against the Soviets, providing significant contact with the men of Central Asia.

It was this 'foreign' contact that exposed Central Asians to the radical agenda of Islamism. In Pakistan, the ultra-conservative Deobandi branch of Islam favoured the strict adherence to Sharia law, the restriction of women, antipathy towards Shi'ism and, most significantly, a military jihad. Allocating free places to Central Asian scholars, they inculcated the idea that Afghanistan was only the first step in a grander plan to bring down all the republics in the region. Uzbek students were increasingly drawn to this model, especially when, at the latter end of the Afghan Civil War, the Pushtun-dominated Taliban, sponsored by Pakistan's intelligence services, established their jurisdiction over much of Afghanistan. Nevertheless, Tajiks tended to gravitate towards the Aghan-Tajik leader Ahmad Shah Masoud, whose version of Islamic resistance was closely tied to Tajik nationalism. During the civil war, Masoud found himself opposed by Gulbuddin Hekmatyar, Pakistan's protégé, and then by the Taliban. Tajik–Uzbek tensions were thus increased as their respective allies in Afghanistan were at war, and this partly explains the ideological-religious dimension of the contemporaneous Tajik Civil War.

The Afghan Civil War was complicated by two other interpretations of militant Islam which had implications for Central Asia. Shia Afghans tended to look to the Iranians for their material and ideological support, and consequently clashed with the Taliban from the mid-1990s. When the Taliban took power, they were able to make much of the need to suppress rival, 'heretical' forms of Islam in favour of an exclusive world-view. This intolerance was in tune with the third militant interpretation of Islam: the Salafest Wahhabis from Saudi Arabia and Yemen. Although Wahhabis had established a small presence in the Ferghana Valley from 1912, their austerity was unpopular, so it was not until Saudi funds began to support the mujahedin, and Saudi madrassahs trained and indoctrinated some of the fighters, that there was any support for them. In essence, Wahhabis called for the complete transformation of Islam back to its original, seventh-century form. Favouring literal interpretations of the Koran, even if the choice of sura, verse and lines are highly selective, Arabic Islam has an authority because it appears to be closest geographically, linguistically and spiritually to the original faith.[19] Despite this, the strict observances and haughty manner of the Arab fighters alienated many Afghans, while most Central Asians are suspicious of a creed that rejects a toleration so long part of the region's culture. Wahhabis favour the disciplined imposition of Sharia law, the virtual imprisonment of women, and the enthusiastic, self-sacrificial pursuit of a military jihad.

The real jihad is the struggle to live out one's faith in an imperfect world, *jihad a' nafs*, but historically the concept has been corrupted to mean a holy war against unbelievers, *jihad bi al saif*. Obligated by the *fard'ayn* – the duty to serve in defence of fellow Muslims in the *umma* (universal community), militant Islamists have altered the concept to embrace a military counter-offensive. Jihadists often now subscribe to an exclusive world-view. They dream of a united caliphate or empire ruled by one pious leader and supported by a *shura* (council) of oligarchs whose sole job is to advise on the interpretation of Islam so that the Caliph might govern. Ignoring the fact that the Islamic world has been divided since the demise of the Umayyad dynasty, and that Islam was spread as much by peaceful means as by the sword, jihadists see solutions in simplistic, aggressive and binary terms. However, few of them are able to articulate the form of government they want, or even the type of society they favour (beyond a call for the imposition of Sharia law and certain social disciplines). The impression given is that the holy war is a lifelong struggle, an end in itself, which gives meaning, pride and identity to disaffected young men and women. Persecution and repression actually serve to reinforce the sense of identity they seek as risk-takers, the oppressed and honourable warriors who sacrifice themselves, sometimes literally, for a greater cause. They believe the religious calling they serve elevates them above ordinary society, legitimizes their violence and places them beyond worldly criticism. There is no room for reform, *ijtihad* (consensual interpretation and application to the modern era) or a scientific renaissance. Nor is there much of a role for women, unbelievers or 'ordinary Muslims'. As Ahmed Rashid noted, 'The new Islamic order for these Jihadi groups is reduced to a harsh, repressive penal code for their citizens that strips Islam of its values, humanism and spirituality.'[20]

Yet, curiously, it is the very repressive nature of the Central Asian governments that makes the popularization of these militants all the more likely. Already there are absurd but popular myths about them.[21] The advanced guard of the IMT is said to consist of beautiful female snipers who either shoot down their opponents effortlessly at long range or else seduce them. The fighters' rucksacks are said to be packed with cash which is distributed freely to sympathetic or helpful farmers. Two fighters are said to have pinned down a battalion of Uzbek regulars, while others claim that saints have blessed the fighters' bodies to make them impervious to bullets or sweet-smelling after death. Simplistic theology and folklore make for good propaganda. Such stories also lend the militants a popular legitimacy. The militants themselves believe they are waging their war in the tradition of the Basmachis of the 1920s or the mujahedin of Afghanistan.

The IMT, formed in 1998 as the IMU following heavy-handedness by the Karimov government and the failure of moderate groups to make any headway, has launched terrorist and guerrilla operations from bases in Afghanistan, Tajikistan and within the Ferghana Valley. Nevertheless, its objectives are far greater than toppling the Karimov regime as its subscribes to the jihadist 'imperial' agenda. Tajikistan, Uzbekistan and Kyrgyzstan have all increased their military spending and taken political steps to deal with the threat they face, and they have attracted financial backing from Russia, the US and China in this endeavour. The threat is certainly serious. The ethnic, clan and political rivalries that divided Tajikistan in 1991 were militarized by the presence of jihadist groups, and the five-year civil war between warlords, Tajik democrats and jihadists left 50,000 dead and millions displaced. Despite the inclusion of Islamist parties in coalition governments, jihadist groups continue to destabilize the country, even while it groans under an economic downturn. The IMT is in the forefront of this effort, drawing recruits from disaffected unemployed men or foreign fighters in search of the jihadist cause (such as Chechens, Uighurs and Daghestanis), and generating funds from foreign sponsors (much of whom are Arab) and from narcotics. Although smashed and scattered in 2001, the IMT appears to be slowly regrouping.

Equally idealistic, but even more vague about its vision for the future, is Hizb ut-Tahrir (HT). Popular among students with a strong sense of mission and utopianism, HT barely addresses the issues that confront Central Asian politics – lack of civil rights, inequality, economic weakness and high unemployment. Instead it is more concerned with events in Palestine and other world regions. But, in a sense, this is its appeal. Vague rather than detailed policies are attractive to those in search of a better, more ideal future. The means are irrelevant and the propaganda is simple fare, but it is highly popular.

Another factor that has fostered greater militancy is the fact that many Central Asian governments have fallen back on old Communist techniques of coercion. Uzbekistan, Azerbaijan and the authorities in the Caucasus have been the most obvious offenders, but heavy-handed policing has also been a hallmark in Chinese Xinjiang, Kazakhstan, Kyrgystan, Tajikistan and Turkmenistan. Afghanistan is still gripped by an insurgency. Many other issues beset the region. Drug-smuggling is a problem closely linked to terrorism. Afghanistan is still the main producer in the region and its heroin crop is the cause of local corruption and the source of funding for terrorist groups. However, since exports to the West are very lucrative, the UN estimated in the summer of 2006 that there had been a 59 per cent increase in production since 2001. Poverty and a gross inequality of wealth have also been causes of unrest, and there is now an endemic problem in human trafficking. New ecological problems, the most infamous of which is the death of the Aral Sea but which include urban pollution, shortages of water, the misuse of chemicals and pesticides (which have poisoned the water supply), the salination of productive agricultural land, and nuclear test sites, also plague the region.

The saving grace of these governments may be the oil and gas industries. Central Asia possesses huge reserves, and there is a strong desire to export for much-needed revenue, but there are problems of access. Vast distances between the fields and the potential markets in the West and the Pacific, which means high costs in terms of pumping stations and pipelines, are obstacles to rapid development. But there is even greater contention regarding the routing of the pipelines. Some progress has been made on agreeing the Baku–Tibilisi–Ceyhan route across Turkey and on the expansion of smaller existing lines with Russia. However, Moscow is eager to see oil and gas flowing through its territories so as to obtain the lucrative deals that go with it and, perhaps, the strategic leverage of controlling the flow. Iran is just as determined to assert its growing regional influence and to solve its own domestic shortfall in oil production by routing pipelines across its territory to Pakistan or the Persian Gulf ports. China is looking for oil and gas to be routed across the Tien Shan to feed its own voracious domestic consumption. The US is eager to avoid Iran and Russia if possible but sees the exploitation of these resources, and their sale on the world market, as a priority. It is to these governments and their policies that we turn in chapter Two.

Chapter 2

The Central Asian Republics before and after 1991

In the Soviet era, Communist Party membership gave one access to power, position and privilege. Since there was no political opposition, the system bred rewards for patronage rather than talent. Loyalty and industry were valued, but enterprise and innovation were not. The élites set the targets in five-year plans, urged their charges to meet them amid a fanfare of propaganda and idealism and kept a close eye on issues of security and internal order. This system, in some ways, suited Central Asia. Patronage and loyalty to the clan were deeply-rooted and historical. Where party membership and clan identity converged, one essentially had the recreation of a pre-Communist khanate. Edicts were issued, spies and informers kept the central authority abreast of the public mood, intimidation kept the people in line, and the élites maintained themselves in moderate luxury. Of course, there were periods of resistance. The Basmachi anti-Communist revolt of 1918–20 was remembered nostalgically as a period of defiance against Russia. The Soviet War in Afghanistan reawakened a dislike of Russian colonial occupation, and there was some sympathy, even from Party members, for the mujahedin. With the collapse of the Soviet Union, the élites' primary aim was to stay in power, to maintain their system of clans, corruption and coercion.

The discovery of hydrocarbons and development of the related industries has led, in some cases, to rapid economic take-off, but for many the inequality of wealth threatens social unrest. Many of the republics have responded with more coercion, which, in turn, has fostered more determined resistance. Jihadism, coinciding with an Islamic renaissance in Central Asia, is providing a platform for opposing the regimes, and in the case of Tajikistan and Afghanistan was a key element in their civil wars. Conversely, the GWOT has given some Central Asian leaders the ideological basis for greater repression. Into this fractured region, there are now the competing interests of the US, Russia and China: all are energy-hungry, and all are now participants in what some prefer to see as a new 'Great Game'. However, the republics are not passive actors in this drama, and it is to them that we now turn.

KAZAKHSTAN

Since the discovery of new fields, Kazakhstan will join the world's top ten producers of oil and gas and is likely to become an important regional power. Its growth has been astonishing as foreign investment has poured into the country. President Nursultan Nazarbayev has presided over a seismic transition from Soviet hinterland to burgeoning capitalist economy. But this change has not come without its casualties. There is a stark inequality of wealth and growing concern about the levels of financial corruption in the political élite. Environmentalists are anxious about the future of the shallow Caspian Sea as the release of heavy metals and crude threatens the flora and fauna there. Most Kazakhs are concerned with more prosaic issues: jobs, pay and housing. Nazarbayev is walking a political tightrope between the aspirations of his people and the interests of other powers who want a share of the oil and gas. Many Kazakh politicains now believe that the early deals with Russian and Western investors were unfavourable to Kazakhstan, and they want to renegotiate. There is also a growing desire to export their resources to the East, to China and Japan. But Kazakhstan is dependent on its buyers, and pressure is mounting for a legal examination of the conduct of the élites, for pipelines to be routed westwards and for the government to honour its original commitments. Underpinning these modern concerns lie historical problems, and decisions which have been taken by the Kazakh government to some extent reflect their past.

The Kazakhs emerged from a mixture of tribes that migrated across the steppes in their constant pursuit of new pastures. Persian and Mongolian empires had ebbed and flowed across the vast plains, the latter establishing a territorial entity known as the Kazakh Khanate of the Ak Horde. The silk trade led to the growth of Aulie-Ata and Turkestan as cities in the medieval period. By the sixteenth century, the Kazakhs had established a common language, cultural identity and economic system. However, the khanate fragmented into three smaller confederations based on extended families or clans. Rivalry and division weakened it and left it open to the expansionist impulse of the Russian Empire during the nineteenth century. The Russians established garrison towns and imposed the Russian language in education and the administration. But this process of Russification created a widespread resentment amongst the Kazakh people, and ideas of national consciousness began to emerge.[1] By the 1890s, as large numbers of Russian colonists arrived, a Kazakh national movement was being formed with the intention of preserving language and cultural identity. The tide of Russian settlers increased after 1906 with the completion of the Trans-Aral Railway and the encouragement of the government's Migration Department, but there was increasing competition between Kazakhs and colonists over water and land. Conscription during the Great War and the weakening of the state during that conflict fanned the flames of resentment until, in 1916, a major uprising broke out. The Revolution of 1917 offered the Kazakhs a brief period of independence, but the state was soon overrun by the Bolsheviks.

Kazakhstan was regarded by the Russian authorities as a resource to serve the interests of the Soviet Union. In the 1920s and '30s, the traditional élites were persecuted and collectivization of agriculture was imposed. As in the Ukraine, protests by Kazakhs often took the form of the destruction of their crops and livestock.[2] In one year alone, they destroyed 24,000,000 sheep and goats, 5,000,000 cattle and 3,000,000 horses to prevent them falling into the hands of the state. Before the harvest of 1930, Stalin appeared to relent on forced collectivization, but once the remaining crops had been secured, the security forces returned to the countryside to drive the Kazakhs into the *kolkhoz* (collective farms). The result was famine and widespread resistance. In 1932, the government declared that theft of state property carried the death penalty, with the result that starving people who attempted to seize food were shot. Requisitioning squads, often heavily armed, roamed the steppes in search of hoarders, just as they had done during the hungry years of the Russian Civil War. Stalin also reintroduced the idea that a small class of counter-revolutionaries, made up of wealthy peasants or 'kulaks', were deliberately trying to derail the march towards the proletarianization of the countryside. He despatched the secret police and Party activists to seek out, arrest and, if necessary, liquidate this group. When no such class was found, any Kazakh showing signs of resistance was categorized as *Kulache*. Thousands joined the other national minorities in the gulags of Siberia, many effectively being condemned to death through hard labour, cold and neglect.

Migration of non-Kazakhs into the state continued in the 1930s, but the most dramatic increase occurred during the Second World War as evacuees poured in from the west. Kazakhs were outnumbered in their own country. At the same time, thousands of them were drafted into the armed forces, the state contributing no fewer than five divisions to the war effort. There was also a significant increase in industrial activity and mining as the Soviet Union struggled to halt the German advance (there was a 40-fold increase in the years 1920–40, but the growth in the war years was exponential). New industrial cities were created, based on oil, coal and steel. Karaganda grew so quickly that it became the republic's second largest city.

Despite these dramatic shifts, the Communist apparatus, backed by efficient coercion, had put down deep roots into Kazakh society. In the 1950s, the collectivized agricultural system was firmly embedded and Nikita Khrushchev's 'Virgin Lands' scheme made a deliberate attempt to expand production accompanied by the fanfare of Soviet propaganda. The result was two extraordinary harvests followed by a collapse. The thin soils and climate could not support crops, a fact the nomads had known for centuries. The environmental damage continued with the detonation of up to fifteen nuclear weapons a year at the vast

Semipalatinsk testing site and the use of the Baikonur Cosmodrome, the launch site for the Soviet space programme. Today the industrial cities are no less oppressive. Redolent of England's dark, satanic mills of the early Industrial Revolution, the lead factories that manufacture ammunition in Chimkent, and its rubber-tyre plant, create a grey-brown haze that hovers above the streets, chimneys and furnaces. Dzhambul houses its population in Soviet-style regimented concrete blocks in eleven numbered districts. The local chemical plants on the edge of the town manufacture phosphates for fertilizer, and levels of lung disease and cancer are very high because the atmosphere is so polluted. This is not untypical. The development of the agricultural and industrial sectors was therefore played out against a background of exploitation, hubris, incompetence and environmental destruction.

By the 1980s, there was still evident dissatisfaction with Soviet rule. In December 1986, mass demonstrations were staged by young Kazakhs in Almaty to protest against Communist restrictions. Soviet troops were called in, and several demonstrators were shot and many more arrested. Nevertheless, these sentiments were not eradicated. When Mikhail Gorbachev introduced his notion of *glasnost*, Kazakhs declared their sovereignty as an independent republic within the Soviet Union as early as October 1990. After the failed coup attempt by hardliners in Moscow, Kazakhstan declared itself fully independent on 16 December 1991.

Nursultan Nazarbayev is the khan of the new Kazakhstan.[3] He came to power in 1989 as the head of the Kazakh Communist Party, but he was elected President of the republic in 1991. Despite his Communist credentials, Nazarbayev has effected far-reaching reforms to the old command economy and has taken some steps towards democracy. That said, much of Kazakhstan's spectacular growth has been dependent on generous foreign investment and the development of the oil and gas industries. Moreover, the elections held in 1999 were regarded as having failed to meet international standards. As President, Nazarbayev retains considerable power, not least with the position of commander-in-chief of the armed forces and with the power to veto legislation. The 2004 elections for the Majlis (the lower house of parliament) resulted in victory for the Otan Party, a group led by the

President himself. Most of the remaining seats were won by two other pro-government parties, one of which had been founded by Nazarbayev's daughter. The opposition won just one seat. In 2005, Nazarbayev was re-elected in a landslide victory which, according to the country's electoral commission, gave him 90 per cent of the vote. The Organisation for Security and Co-operation in Europe was not satisfied that the election had been conducted properly, but Chinese observers reported it had been 'transparent and fair'.[4] Thus while Europe criticizes, China warms to the Kazakh President.

The Kazakh economy is one of the fastest-growing in the world. Its astonishing development is due to the expansion of its oil and gas revenues.[5] The flood of foreign investment soon after independence threatened to lead to rapid inflation, but strict fiscal policies have contained the problem despite an average rise of 6.4 per cent. Kazakhstan was able to use its new wealth to repay its IMF loans seven years early, and government debts have fallen. Banking, customs and taxation are becoming more sophisticated. Grain and livestock are the mainstays of the agricultural sector, with huge areas – over 800,000 square kilometres – used for pasture and cultivation. Yet it is the extractive industries that are really generating the boom. Kazakhstan has some of the largest deposits of oil, gas, uranium and gold in the world. The oil industry alone has attracted $40 billion of foreign investments as companies look to exploit the estimated 6.1 billion tonnes of oil (2.7 billion proven reserves) and 2.5 trillion cubic metres of natural gas in the country.

Such vast sums and the actions of some Kazakh officials have led to accusations of malpractice and corruption. In 1995, it has been alleged, Lucio Noto, the CEO of Mobil, tried to buy a stake in the Kazakh oil industry by inviting Nazarbayev to the Bahamas. Nazarbayev, according to one journalist, made extravagant demands for perks, including a personal jet, four mobile television units for his daughter's media company, a large sum of cash and a tennis court for his home. While Mobil denied ever having offered such perks, it has been revealed that the company did pay money into bogus 'front' companies and that millions of dollars were not accounted for. The US Department of Justice has been investigating these allegations. In May 1996, Mobil purchased a share in the Kazakh industry for $1 billion, but half of this did not appear in the state budget. Nazarbayev blamed his Prime Minister, who subsequently fled to London, but the American Justice Department froze certain Swiss bank accounts belonging to the Nazarbayev family on suspicion that the President had embezzled the money. After initial denials, Nazarbayev admitted in 2002 that he had retained at least $1 billion in Swiss accounts in order to avoid disruption to the Kazakh economy. He feared that rampant inflation would result from such a vast injection of money. It is estimated that about a fifth of all Kazakhstan's wealth is now in Swiss accounts. The Kazakh parliament also voted in favour of the legalization of money-laundering, exempting the political élite from having to account for their wealth or pay tax on it.[6]

Kazakhstan's foreign relations reflect its position at the crossroads of Eurasia. It co-operates with Europe as a NATO 'partner for peace', but it is also a member of the Organisation of the Islamic Conference (OIC). It is a member of the Commonwealth of Independent States (CIS), but it is also a part of the Shanghai Co-operation Organisation with Russia, China, Kyrgyzstan and Uzbekistan. It is one of the founder-members of the Central Asian Eurasian Economic Community, a body established in 2000 to harmonize free trade and tariff agreements in the region. This attempt to co-operate with its neighbours, and with the interests of Russia, China and the US, has yielded results in terms of investment in the country's industries. But Kazakhstan is eager to avoid total dependence on Russia for its oil pipelines. Fearful of the high transit fees, shutdowns and bureaucratic obstructionism which have been a hallmark of the past, Kazakhs are looking to diversify their export arrangements. There is a willingness to ship a certain volume of oil across the Caspian in tankers and then to transfer it via Baku through the pipelines to the Black Sea and, eventually, through the pipeline to Ceyhan. However, Sabr Yessimibekov, the chief planner for the pipelines, believes that Kazakh interests would be better served by pumping oil to the East – that is, to China and Japan. While the Kazakhs have found working with the Chinese problematic, criticizing their bureaucratic inflexibility, work has begun on extending the pipelines and enlarging existing ones. Nevertheless, the Kazakhs regard the presence of the Americans in the region, particularly their troops in Uzbekistan and elsewhere, as a useful counterweight to Russia and China.

The key difference in US-Kazakh relations appears to be over Iran. As the shortest land route to the world's markets, not to mention the refining and port facilities of the Persian Gulf, the Kazakhs would prefer to see a pipeline extended southwards. It would be the cheapest option. Yet the Americans remain committed to their sanctions against Iran. Secretary of State Colin Powell's visit to Kazakhstan in December 2001 revealed the differences of opinion. While Powell reiterated the American position of wanting to see alternatives to the Iran route, he was flatly contradicted by Nazarbayev.[7] When President Mohammad Khatami visited just four months later, Nazarbayev agreed with the Iranian President's criticism of American global hegemony. He made no response to Khatami's assertion that the presence of American forces in the region was a 'humiliation' for Central Asia, but a Kazakh spokesman did admit that the Americans were regarded not as allies but as convenient investors and technical advisors. The Kazakh government has tried to impose fines on American companies and urges an increase in fees and prices, but the Americans have always argued that such tactics could deter future investment and make the extraction and sale of oil unprofitable – not least because of the sheer costs involved. These factors, in the long term, will hurt the Kazakh economy. What this reveals is two distinct world-views. For Kazakhs, it is a question of asserting a national independence; for the Americans, it is just a business deal. In the end, market forces will prevail.

UZBEKISTAN

Towering above the ruins at Shakhrisabz in a new square stands an enormous statue of Timur, the fourteenth-century tyrant known to the West as Tamerlane. Timur created a short-lived but extensive empire across Central Asia, his armies ranging as far to the west as Anatolia, south through Persia and eastwards towards China. Timur had overcome the Mongols, from whom he was himself descended, crushed the

Persians in the 1390s, seized northern India in 1398, taken Syria and defeated the Ottoman Turks in 1402. His expansionist appetite was only brought to an end by his death as he marched against China. It is therefore slightly disconcerting to see the Uzbek government use Timur, rather than their scholars or poets, as their national icon. His portrait hangs in Tashkent University, his effigies appear in the major cities, and, in Shakhrisabz, he stands triumphant, glowering icily towards the south.

In the nineteenth century, Russian armies clashed with and subjugated each of the Central Asian khanates in turn. Exploiting a fatal division between Bokhara, Khiva and Tashkent, they conquered each one in the years 1865–73.[8] Persia, which had been influential in the region as late as the eighteenth century, was driven south. Bokhara was turned into a protectorate and the other khanates absorbed into the Russian Empire, but local customs continued to survive, and there were episodes of armed resistance in 1898 and 1916. Even in the Soviet era, Uzbeks preferred their traditional colourful skull-caps and silk sashes to Western suits. They continued to manufacture their soft, round *lepeshka* loaves, ate their *shashlyk* and drank green tea in preference to Russian cuisine. But while most Uzbeks were eager to retain their identity, the Communist Party still became all-pervasive in the republic's social and political life. Joining and patronizing the Uzbek Communist Party were necessary to advance one's career or to avoid interference. The Soviet traditions of decision-making have not disappeared, largely because the Uzbek Communist Party morphed into the Popular Democratic Party after independence without much change of personnel. Indeed, the Uzbek leaders declared independence with great reluctance on the last day of August 1991, and they supported the abortive *coup d'état* by Communist hardliners in Moscow. Many of the political élite speak nostalgically of the Soviet days. The press is still censored, the secret police are still everywhere, and democracy is stillborn.

The executive of the Uzbek government, embodied in Islam Karimov, holds almost all power in its hands. There is no independent judiciary, the President selects his provincial governors, and referenda are staged to approve extension of his rule.[9] International observers regard the voting system as totally undemocratic, particularly since opposition groups have been excluded. Independent parties are permitted, but they cannot register for participation in elections. Amnesty International, Human Rights Watch, the US and the EU regularly express concern at violations of basic human rights. Independence was accompanied by some ethnic unrest, and 2,000,000 Russians fled the republic. The leadership encouraged the flight, passing laws to force the remainder out. Yet the groups most at risk are Uzbek religious organizations, journalists and political activists. The government nevertheless maintains that it has passed 300 laws which protect the lives of its citizens and safeguard their rights. In 2005, Karimov pledged to abolish the death penalty in 2008. However, the government's emphasis is on the 'protection' of the people, which means it can act decisively against those individuals or groups it regards as a threat to the welfare or security of the people, and thereby, the state. The shootings in Andijan in 2005 were regarded as an abuse of human rights by many in the West, but the Uzbek government insists that the incident was an anti-terrorist operation and that 'an information war has been declared against Uzbekistan.'[10] It states that accusations are made as a pretext to intervene in Uzbekistan's internal affairs. Such sentiments are an echo of Leonid Brezhnev's comments during the Cold War.

Craig Murray, the former British ambassador to Uzbekistan, was distinctly undiplomatic in his reports about Karimov's regime from the moment of his appointment. Murray submitted a string of accusations to London but also made statements to the international media.[11] He enjoyed a brief period of popularity with journalists and some Uzbeks, but the Foreign Office in Britain and the Americans were unimpressed. The Western powers had been dependent on Uzbekistan to provide bases for air missions against Afghanistan in 2001, and there was some tacit approval for Karimov's attempts to root out jihadist terrorists in the Ferghana Valley. Financial support from the US was justified on the basis that Uzbekistan was moving towards democracy and working to improve its human rights record. Murray argued that the 'War on Terror' was being used by Karimov to crush political opposition regardless of its ideology. When the Foreign Office refused to act, Murray turned to the media. He was convinced that British intelligence was turning a blind eye to torture by Uzbek secret-police and simply accepting their information. However, Murray's testimony was devalued when it transpired that he was suffering from a mental breakdown, exacerbated by an affair that ended his marriage. His outspoken remarks earned the ire of the Foreign Office, and in protest he refused to return to his duties, although there were some medical grounds for this decision too. His private life led to ridicule and his remarks about Uzbek torture, rape of detainees and extra-judicial killings were largely ignored.

Uzbekistan was one of the poorest Soviet republics, so its growth since 1991 is significant and has attracted Western interest. However, the government has been eager to avoid social unrest and to preserve the power of the political élite, and this has meant a gradualist approach to capitalism.[12] Under the Soviets, much of Uzbekistan's cultivable area was devoted to the production of cotton, and the country remains the world's fourth largest producer. Almost half the population are employed in agriculture or related industries, and some 64 per cent are classed as 'rural'. In the autumn, columns of buses deposit thousands of students from the schools and towns in the cotton fields. Like many countries in the region, Uzbekistan's population is very young – approximately 34 per cent are under the age of fourteen – so there is, in theory, a cheap supply for labour-intensive industries. But the government's reform strategy is cautious. The emphasis is on maintaining state controls, reducing imports, prioritizing imports and attempting to achieve self-sufficiency in energy. Uzbekistan has significant supplies of natural gas, coal and uranium to exploit. The government has been eager to assert that its reformist approach has been a success, even a 'model' for the region in avoiding social and political unrest. However, economists point to the postponement of structural reforms, the continued dominance of the bureaucracy and difficulties in currency conversion as major obstacles to foreign investment. Imports carry high tax duties, but they are applied in a discriminatory manner. Some charges are so high that they can be up to 150 per cent of the item value, placing them well outside the range of the Uzbek consumer.

While the Uzbek authorities maintain that they have avoided hyper-inflation, stagnation or pauperization, they can hardly claim the success that Kazakhstan has enjoyed. Inflation has risen steadily since 2004. The International Crisis Group has also pointed to the widespread problem of corruption throughout the country. While there is considerable interest in the low prices for exports such as gold, cotton and gas, the Group is concerned that 'revenues from these commodities are distributed among a very small circle of the ruling elite, with little or no benefit for the population at large.'[13] The Uzbek political élite appears to be hostile to the emergence of an independent private sector that it cannot control. Like China, it is eager to create the conditions for economic growth, but not at the expense of the political status quo.

Uzbekistan has aspirations for regional leadership, and it has the largest army in Central Asia to support its ambitions. With 650,000 men, it is gradually shedding its Soviet structure in favour of light formations. Its equipment is old and outdated, and there is a lack of specialized training, but the government is eager to develop the army's mobility and to expand its Special Forces elements. Given the sort of threat the country faces, namely terrorism and insurgency, the changes required are pressing. After 2001, foreign assistance, particularly from the US, took the form of advisors and finance, although support had been growing since 1998. It is estimated that, in 2004, Washington gave Uzbekistan $500,000,000 in aid, of which a quarter was devoted to military spending. Karimov approved the establishment of an American air base at Karshi-Khanabad which was used in the operations against Afghanistan, but after American criticism of the Andijan shootings in 2005, the Uzbek government demanded that the Americans withdraw. The EU, another strong critic of Andijan, banned arms sales to Uzbekistan that same year. Subsequently, Karimov turned back to Russia, concluding a mutual-defence pact. However, American–Uzbek co-operation may not be at an end. There has been some speculation that Uzbekistan may still be processing terrorist suspects for the West and that American intelligence or covert forces may be working in the Ferghana Valley against jihadists there.

Uzbekistan continues to co-operate against terrorism with regional and international partners, not least because of its own security concerns. As a member of the Shanghai Co-operation Organisation, it hosts the Regional Anti-Terror Structure (RATS). It has provided 'peace-keeping' troops to Tajikistan, after participating in the Civil War, and co-operates with the CIS states despite having left their collective security body in 1999. Uzbekistan has also been a coalition partner against the Taliban in Afghanistan and against Iraq. Since the spat with the Western powers over Andijan, however, Karimov has moved closer to Russia and China, but the common link of counter-terrorism is likely to ensure that relations will not be severed with regional or international partners.

TAJIKISTAN

Modern Tajikistan does not resemble its previous historical extent. The cities of Samarkand and Bokhara were the cultural centres of the Tajiks, and the khanate of Bokhara remained the state to which Tajiks owed their allegiance throughout the nineteenth century. In the Pamirs and other areas remote from the city-state, loyalties were less clear cut, and there were disputes with the Afghans and Chinese over territorial borders. This contest was further complicated by the Great-Game rivalry of Britain and Russia. Both powers regarded the Pamirs as strategically important and were eager to exclude the other from the region. The nomadic herders of the Pamirs made the establishment of territorial claims based on the occupation and allegiance of the people very difficult, not least because they tended to avoid paying tax or paid whichever authority sought to make its presence felt. Nevertheless, despite some skirmishes between the Afghans, Russians and Chinese in the early 1890s, imperial Russia gained jurisdiction over the majority of Tajiks in 1895, with just a small proportion left inside Afghanistan.

The collapse of tsarism in 1917 meant a brief period of independence, but the Tajiks were forced into an asymmetrical guerrilla war by the Bolsheviks. The advance of the Communists was met with fierce resistance at various points, including Transcapia (Turkmenistan) and Tashkent, but nowhere was the fighting more intense than in the

Pamirs. The mountains gave the Basmachis an ideal location for defence, but the Communists resorted to the destruction of villages and mosques, and to tough tactics against the civilian population. Eventually, after four years of continuous fighting, the sheer weight of numbers and dwindling Basmachi resources forced them to capitulate.

Initially, the Communists maintained the territorial link between Uzbek and Tajik territories, but, in 1929, Tajikistan was hived off and the populations divided. Tajikistan was left as a remote backwater of the Soviet Union and hardly developed at all. Nevertheless, by the late 1970s, Islam was proving to be the nucleus of anti-Soviet feeling, if not a self-conscious national identity. When the USSR collapsed, the Tajiks eagerly declared their independence. The lack of 'national' unity meant that the country almost immediately descended into civil war. Political factions, underpinned by clan identities, vied for power. Emomali Rahmonov emerged as the national leader, but it was not until 1997, after the death of an estimated 60,000 people, that he and the opposition parties signed a ceasefire. The war drove out the vast majority of ethnic Russians who had settled in the republic, but the Russian government, the Uzbeks, the Afghans and (allegedly) the Iranians all tried to influence the civil war. In 1999, in 2005 and again in 2006, Tajikistan held democratic elections, which were won by Rahmonov, but international observers were dissatisfied with the outcome.[14] Although Tajikistan is the only Central Asian republic to permit opposition parties to engage the government (a point the government *had* to concede because of the civil war), few have much faith in the survival of democratic politics. Islamism provided an element of unity during the Soviet years and was deepened by the civil war, so advocates of Sharia law and other Islamist measures have enjoyed growing support. Nevertheless, clan loyalties, and the desire to central-ize and maintain power, appear to take precedence, but this makes the chances of further civil conflict in the future more likely.

As well as internal divisions, Tajikistan has many obstacles to its economic development and therefore its military potential. Half of the country stands above 3,000 metres, and it is entirely landlocked. Three islands of Tajik territory lie inside Uzbekistan or Kyrgyzstan and so present problems in communication and access. The relative poverty of Tajikistan before independence was exacerbated by the civil war, and the country is largely dependent on foreign financial assistance. Rehabilitation programmes have been paid for by foreign donors in an attempt to get former fighters back into employment. In 2000 and 2001, international support was needed to feed the population because drought had brought about a famine. The country is dependent on its exports of cotton and aluminium for its revenue, but there was substantial growth after the war in the years 2000–2004. Since then, economic performance has deteriorated.

KYRGYSTAN

Kyrgyzstan appeared to hold out a hope for democracy after independence, but this seems to be wilting under the pressure for centralization. There has been widespread disillusionment with two leaders, Askar Akayev and Kurmanbek Bakiev, who, ironically, both enjoyed landslide electoral victories. However, they failed to deliver expected improvements, are thought to have been corrupt and turned to coercion as an instrument of policy.

The Kyrgyz emerged as a separate people over many centuries, and most believe that their Mongol and Kipchak ancestors were driven south into the mountainous areas of present-day Kyrgyzstan from central Russia by the Mongol invasions in the 1200s.[15] The Kyrgyz were ruled by a succession of dynasties until the nineteenth century, when the Russian Empire began to conquer Central Asia. The Khanate of Kokand held jurisdiction of the south until it too was incorporated into the Tsar's dominions in 1876. Only the Pamirs provided a refuge, and it was from here that resistance was sustained for many years. Some Kyrgyz were displaced into Afghanistan, and this complicated the establishment of borders in the Pamirs in the 1890s. The last significant migration took place in 1916, when Russian reprisals against the Central Asian revolt drove many Kyrgyz into western China. Despite the chaos, Communist rule was established over 'Kara-Kirgyz' in 1919, although a Kyrgyz socialist republic was created by Stalin in 1936.

The Kyrgyz appeared to have accepted Soviet rule but were the first to discard it when Moscow's grip weakened. The Soviets introduced a number of changes, not least a standardized version of the Kyrgyz language and improvements in literacy. But many cultural traditions survived, and these were important in fostering and preserving a sense of national identity. On the surface, Gorbachev's glasnost appeared to have had little impact. There were some press freedoms, and, although an organized political opposition was not permitted, self-conscious Kyrgyz groups did emerge to deal with, among other things, housing shortages. In 1990, a Kyrgyzstan Democratic Movement (KDM) had been formed, and it enjoyed the support of most of the Kyrgyz parliament. That summer the sense of national identity was tested in an ethnic clash with Uzbeks in Osh, a Kyrgyz city but one dominated by Uzbeks. The violence was so bad that a state of emergency was declared and a curfew imposed. It took two months to restore order. The Kyrgyz continued to press ahead in their own direction. In October 1990, Akayev, a liberal and President of the Kyrgyz Academy of Sciences, was elected President, and, in January 1991, he appointed a number of young reform-minded politicians.[16] Changing the name of the capital from Frunze, the name of a Red Army hero, to Bishkek, its pre-Revolutionary title, and the replacement of Russian with the native tongue as the official language marked the culmination of the assertion of Kyrgyz national identity.

However, from an economic point of view, the Kyrgyz were more pragmatic. In a referendum of March 1991, 88.7 per cent of the population voted in favour of a proposal to retain the USSR as a renewed federation, from which the CIS was later conceived. The reason for this sentiment was that the Kyrgyz economy was to a large extent dependent on its old Soviet hinterland. Nevertheless, the determination to assert national independence was reinforced by an attempted coup d'état in August 1991. When the Moscow hardliners tried to seize power, there was a parallel attempt to depose Akayev. But the coup collapsed. Akayev led the entire government and secretariat in a mass resignation from the Communist Party and announced the country's full independence. Standing for election in October of that year, he won a landslide victory.

But Akayev found it impossible to sustain the level of support he had enjoyed in 1991. There were nationwide protests after five people, demonstrating against arbitrary arrests of opposition spokesmen, were shot dead by police in March 2002. Akayev appeared to respond to the national mood by announcing a constitutional-reform process that would be staged in public in consultation with various government bodies. In fact, the referendum of 2003 that confirmed the government's proposals was widely criticized. The amendments to the constitution gave the President greater powers. Suspicions were confirmed when elections were staged for a new, smaller and single legislature. They were regarded as 'rigged' in favour of the President's men. In March 2005, there was a wave of protests that caused Akayev to flee the country. After this 'Tulip Revolution', a new government was established by opposition leaders under the presidency of Kurmanbek Bakiev.[17]

Despite another landslide election victory to confirm Bakiev's mandate in 2005, public support declined rapidly. The chief problem is the government's wrangling over the constitution when most Kyrgyz want to see an end to widespread corruption. Various factions are eager to assert their power in government and there have been accusations that some have links to organized crime. Four members of parliament have been assassinated since 2005, apparently because of these criminal associations. Yet Kyrgyzstan is also divided over the privatization of state businesses, the growth or limitation of democracy, ethnic relations and jihadist terrorism spilling over from the Tajik border to the south.

However, underpinning all its other concerns is an anxiety about the economy. Despite some reserves of natural gas, coal and gold, much of the country's wealth was generated by the sale of agricultural produce, and traditionally it was dependent upon the USSR as an outlet for its resources and the source of its imports. On independence, Kyrgystan received the financial support of the IMF, the World Bank and the Asian Development Bank. The government reduced its expenditures, ended subsidies and introduced VAT as part of its conversion to a market economy. However, this did not assist the state farms and industries that faced closure because of the loss of the Soviet export markets. With about half the population engaged in agriculture and much of industry based on agricultural processing, the effects were severe. Unregulated, small-scale trade has always been important – bazaars and roadside stalls were a common sight in the republic – but this has increased by necessity. While many consumer items are in short supply, there is generally an abundance of food. The great hope for the country is that it can exploit its mountainous terrain to provide hydroelectric energy and export its surplus.

TURKMENISTAN

Much of Turkmenistan is desert. The harsh, unforgiving Kara-Kum has been a natural barrier between the Central Asian steppes and the civilizations of the south for centuries. In the summer months, the temperatures are so extreme that one can literally fry an egg on the roof of a car. In this environment, control of the water supply has been critical, and there have been generations of conflicts over the oases of the region. Silk traders' caravans and nomads had relied on them, and the Mongols' destruction of the caravanserai at Merv (Mary) in the thirteenth century disrupted a critical nodal point in that commercial system. In the fourteenth century, nomadic Tartars known to their rivals as Turkmen (or Turkomans) began to settle the area. Control of water and the limited grazing was, once again, the source of almost constant warfare. The Turkmen, who were accomplished horsemen, often raided the pastoral peoples of northern Afghanistan, Bokhara and Persia and established a system of slavery. By the nineteenth century, Russians had been added to their quotas. Slaves and carpets were sold to the urban centres of Central Asia in exchange for a variety of manufactured goods. In turn, this system was also destroyed. Russian imperial armies fought the Tekke Turkomans, the leading branch of the clans, between 1879 and 1881. Their light cavalry was ideal for desert skirmishing, but, at Geok Tepe, a vast earthen fortress, they were no match for breach-loaders and artillery. Edward O'Donovan, a journalist, witnessed the final defeat of the Tekkes as an independent people. Hundreds of civilians fled across the desert as Geok Tepe fell, but there was no quarter from the imperial cavalry and their freebooting allies: it is estimated that 20,000 were slaughtered.[18]

In 1918, at the height of revolutionary unrest in Russia, it appeared that the Turkmen might assert their independence successfully. A

British contingent had deployed to protect Baku from the Turks and a British-Indian detachment marched into 'Trans-Caspia', as it was then known, to prevent the Bolsheviks selling vital cotton supplies to the Germans. An anti-Communist alliance emerged and established the Centro-Caspian Dictatorship, but a tiny force of 400 men under Col. Denis Knolly assisted in driving off the Bolsheviks at Dushak, Kushk and Merv.[19] Already overextended by the Great War, the British government had no intention of maintaining its presence in the region and the military forces withdrew. However, it was not until 1920 that the Communists succeeded in taking the lands of the Turkmen.

Under Soviet rule, Turkmenistan became a socialist republic in 1924 but remained an impoverished backwater. In 1948, an earthquake (the fourth in recent history after 1893, 1898 and 1929) destroyed much of Ashkabad, the capital. Measuring 9 on the Richter Scale, it killed 110,000 and left the city looking like a war zone. The Soviets initiated a total reconstruction in the dreary concrete Soviet style. Other Russian engineering proved more positive. The Qaraqum Canal, completed in the 1960s, extends 1,100 kilometres across the country, linking all the southern urban areas in one fertile ribbon. In addition, the 1968 discovery of abundant reservoirs of natural gas has given the country a viable future. But the most important legacy of the Soviet era has been in politics. The rigid party system has overlaid an equally powerful clan network, and the Tekkes are the dominant group in public life. The stranglehold of the Communist Party has never been broken, and, despite a change in titles and a curious personality cult surrounding the former head of state, the old dispensation has survived.

Until recently, visitors to Turkmenistan were immediately struck by the idiosyncrasies of the 'leader cult'. President Saparmurat Niyazov, the *Turkmenbashi* (leader of the Turkmen) who died in December 2006, evoked a tribal approach to politics as much as an old-style Communist obsession with 'personality'.[20] A statue of him, made of gold, revolved on its dais so as to be constantly facing the sun. His sunny countenance appeared everywhere, from banknotes to bottles of vodka. He was the most frequent feature of television and radio. He had written two books and these were compulsory subjects of study at all schools. One, entitled *Ruhnama*, he told his readership, would make one more intelligent, would ensure that one recognized the divine and would mean access to heaven if one read it three times. Days of the week were named after members of Niyazov's family, and many institutions were given his mother's name. All watches and clocks had to sport his face on their dials, and the national anthem was created by his own hand. After heart surgery in 1997, Niyazov banned smoking across the country to 'set an example'. His personal preferences tended to dictate other aspects of social policy. He declared a ban on beards and long hair for men. He banned opera, ballet and the playing of recorded music on television, at public events and at all weddings. It was as if the entire population of 5,000,000 Turkmen were Niyazov's own extended family, or perhaps his own property.

While many foreign commentators have commented on the quirky nature of Niyazov's government, the reality was a lot less cheering. No political opposition was permitted. All power was concentrated in the hands of the *Turkmenbashi*. No criticism of the leader or his family was tolerated. No one, for example, was allowed to mention that Niyazov was very short (barely 1.5 metres) and that he wore a wig. Religious groups were carefully monitored and were supposed to 'register' through several layers of bureaucracy. Many groups probably operated underground as they did in the Soviet era, but it was impossible to be sure of numbers or political feelings of the population. The media are still in the pocket of the regime, and there is no freedom of assembly.

In November 2002, there was a dramatic protest in the form of an assassination attempt against Niyazov. Gunman fired on his car, but there were no casualties. Niyazov blamed opposition members in exile for hiring mercenaries, but opponents overseas claimed that he himself had staged the event in order to crack down on groups inside the country. Forty-six Turkmen were arrested and convicted for the plot, including the former Prime Minister, Boris Shikhmuradov. They all got life sentences. Niyazov also lost no time in using the media to promote his own glory in the incident. His paternalism and leadership qualities apparently knew no bounds. In the 2004 parliamentary elections, all the candidates were approved by him personally. And yet, in April 2005, he surprised everyone by announcing that there would be contested presidential elections in 2009. Legions of sycophants begged him to renounce this decision, but he only agreed to review the situation nearer the date. It may all have been part of his manipulation of politics or the salving of his enormous ego, of course. By appearing to be modest, he may have hoped for waves of popular backing.

The founder of the Turkmen of the World Foundation died of heart failure on 21 December 2006. A caretaker regime was led by the head of the Majlis, Avazgeldy Atayov, but he was dismissed after allegations of criminal activity. Under the Turkmenistan constitution, the acting President cannot stand for election, and elections have to be held within two months of the death of the *Turkmenbashi*. Gurbanguli Berdymukhamedov, the former Health Minister was elected President on 11 February 2007, in a process condemened by international observers. Although a favourite amongst the political élite, he has been responsible for presiding over one of the region's worst health systems. He implemented Niyazov's order that all hospitals outside the capital were to be closed, cutting 15,000 doctors' jobs in order that the military could take over. The facilities and organization of the system were already bad. The life expectancy of a man in Turkmenistan is only 56. Colleagues of Berdymukhamedov could use this reptutation to topple him, especially if they fear a purge will be implemented. However, of the presidential candidates fielded, all but one was approved by the ruling élite. The only exception is that put forward by exiles in Turkey.

What may determine the future of Turkmenistan is the economy. The country has been unable to sell its natural gas in the quantities it would like because of disputes between the littoral states over the resources of the Caspian and the lack of pipelines out of the country. Russia refused to purchase Turkmen gas in 1994, and debts in the republics that were former Soviet customers caused a fall in production and a deficit in the state budget. Foreign investors have tried to make deals with the country, but the instability of policy caused by the personality of Niyazov has made long-term projection difficult.[21] Substantial debts and wasteful spending on grandiose projects have also been deterrents. There appears to be a lack of regulation in state funds, some of which are held in offshore accounts. Ashkabad has had significant renovation, but the provision of basic services outside the capital has been neglected. Despite promises of free water, gas and electricity to every home, interruptions to supply and shortages are frequent. Many Turkmen live in poverty when their leaders and their apparatchik entourage live in excessive luxury.

AFGHANISTAN

After twenty years of war, Afghanistan was a land of ruins. From the jagged remains of public buildings in Kabul, their battered pillars looking like mouldering teeth sprouting iron rods from their decayed crowns, to the exploded stone trunks of the 2,000-year-old Buddhist statues of Bamian, the devastated landscape mirrored the nature of the broken state. In the 1970s, the Soviets carried fire and sword through the land in a hopeless attempt first to save the socialist state, then to crush insurgents wherever they appeared. The Soviets eventually withdrew in the hope that their approved candidate could maintain authority. But civil power disappeared during the civil war of 1989-96, leaving the country in the hands of warlord factions. Neighbouring states sought to influence the outcome of the fighting – Iran and Pakistan in particular – and it was the Pakistanis who enjoyed the greatest success when they sponsored Pushtun fighters as their protégés.

Many of these young men were drawn from the refugee camps, but the Pakistanis could rely on a sizeable number of indigenous supporters too. These religious students, the *Talib'an*, had been schooled in the radical ideology of Pakistan's madrassahs. They were disciplined and indifferent to death, and they brought with them an austere political and social order.[22] Using the arms and mobility provided by Islamabad, they defeated each faction in turn but failed to break the united forces of the 'Northern Alliance'. In areas they occupied, they imposed their ideas with brutality and terror. Osama bin Laden described the Taliban's regime as the closest approximation to a true Islamic state. He and his fellow 'Arab-Afghan' veterans of the Soviet war were given support to establish training facilities, and Al-Qaeda, which had been founded in 1989, regarded Afghanistan as the springboard for the establishment of a new Islamist order across the Muslim world.

The Afghans were regarded as a troublesome tribal people in antiquity, prone to raiding caravans, descending onto neighbouring pastoral peoples and occasionally forming dynasties which sacked Delhi or marched on Persia. Babur, the Central Asian founder of the Mughal dynasty in the sixteenth century, regarded the locals as disagreeable but the climate as excellent. He used the Afghan mountain valleys, particularly Kabul and Ghazni, as his base for operations against rival Central Asian khans, but raids into India proved more lucrative, and he eventually settled on the plains of the subcontinent. It was not until the eighteenth century that a lasting independent dynasty was established in Kabul under the Durranis. That said, Afghanistan was barely a united country even in the nineteenth century. Outlying provinces regarded Kabuli edicts with suspicion and contempt. The knot of mountains and valleys in the east and centre of the country and the absence of modern communications made it very difficult to establish any centralized authority. This makes the achievements of Abdur Rahman, the ruler from 1881 to 1901, even more remarkable. He set up the first rudimentary bureaucracy, delimited the borders of his state, reorganized the army and imposed a tough, authoritarian order. However, clan loyalties remained important, and there were several rebellions against his repressive rule.[23]

Afghan rulers also had to contend with considerable foreign interference. Both Russia and Britain took a keen interest in Afghan affairs, since the kingdom stood astride strategically important mountains adjacent to their imperial possessions. Britain was the guarantor of Afghan territorial integrity but had de facto control of Afghan foreign policy. On two occasions, in 1838–42 and 1878–81, Britain briefly occupied Afghanistan. Both invasions were concluded relatively swiftly; both faced major uprisings once resistance had become more organized. These rebellions were punctuated by military setbacks for thinly extended formations, punitive retribution, a loss of political will to continue the occupation, and consequent withdrawal. In 1919, Afghanistan went on the offensive when its ruler, Amanullah, wrongly calculated that Britain was weak after the First World War. His forces, which included large numbers of Pushtun volunteers on the British side of the border, were defeated by air power and combined arms operations perfected by fighting in Europe and the Middle East. Nevertheless, anxious to reach a favourable settlement, the British government abrogated responsibility for Afghan foreign affairs and the country celebrated a new independence.

Amanullah initiated a dramatic period of modernization.[24] He signed commercial deals with European powers, founded new schools and promulgated a new constitution with rights for Afghans built in. He built a new parliament building, encouraged women to go unveiled and obliged officials to wear Western dress. He introduced new civil and criminal codes, and banned child marriage. He also built new railways and roads to improve the country's infrastructure. The parallels are striking with Amanullah's contemporary Kemal Ataturk in Turkey, and Turkish advisors were indeed prominent at court. Amanullah went on to introduce a new solar calendar, abolished slavery and forced labour, reorganized the system of taxation and launched anti-corruption campaigns. He introduced a new livestock census, tried to introduce the metric system, brought in a new currency and opened the first national bank. He pressed for the introduction of identity cards, prohibited the exaction of blood money and abolished subsidies to tribal chiefs. It was a whirlwind of change.

In foreign affairs, initially Amanullah was eager to see the restoration of territories which had been lost to the Russians in the nineteenth century, particularly in the Pamirs. But these were abandoned in favour of a treaty of friendship with the Soviet Union in May 1921. Afghanistan received financial support and military technology, the most valuable acquisition being Russian aircraft and pilots. The growing Soviet influence alarmed the British, and they imposed restrictions on the transit of Afghan goods through India. Amanullah worsened relations by hosting radical Indian nationalists.

Although his reforms had little impact on much of the rural population, the intention of his measures certainly alienated them, as well as the religious teachers and the old élites. The army grew angry when its pay was reduced, and new recruiting patterns were introduced which took powers away from tribal leaders. When Amanullah was advised to 'retire' the older officers who seemed opposed to reforms, an anti-Turkish faction began to develop in the army. In 1928, a revolt by

Shinwari tribesmen in Jellalabad initiated the collapse. Royal troops deserted. As the tribesmen advanced on Kabul from the east, a second column of Tajik-Afghans advanced from the north. Amanullah made a token effort to retain the capital but fled to Italy. He had failed because he had tried to move too quickly, with insufficient security, to a modernized state. His closeness to the Soviets was less important than the general Westernizing trend of his reforms. Curiously, the Pathans in British India believed the British had deliberately influenced the mullahs to get rid of Amanullah, but this was largely because they did not wish to think ill of a man who had assisted them against the British in 1919. Habibullah Kalakani, Amanullah's successor, was soon deposed and then murdered. Nadir Shah took power with the help of the Wazirs, a Pathan group, from the North-West Frontier Province, but he was assassinated in 1933 and succeeded by Zahir Shah, a moderate monarch who was only deposed in 1973.

American and Soviet interest in Afghanistan developed during the Cold War. Both sent aid and advisors and assisted in large-scale engineering projects. The Soviets were particularly keen to foster Marxist ideology in students and government officials, and they benefited from a dispute between Afghanistan and Pakistan in 1961. The Pakistanis believed that the Afghans were deliberately trying to encourage a secessionist 'Pushtunistan' movement, but the confrontation between the two countries meant that Afghanistan was forced to turn to the Soviets as an outlet for its goods and a source of imports. The result was that Afghanistan moved inexorably into the Soviet sphere of influence. Khrushchev visited Afghanistan in 1955, reinforcing the offer of military and financial aid. A brief experiment with democracy between 1953 and 1963 failed, although it did lead to the flourishing of two rival Marxist organizations, Parcham and Khalq. It also inspired Mohammed Daoud Khan, the former Prime Minister, to make a bid for power via *inquilab* (revolution). Using Parcham supporters, he seized control of the state in a coup. The Soviet Union believed that this was a move in their favour and began to make more demands as their aid increased, but Daoud resisted. The death of a Parcham member panicked the Afghan Marxists into thinking that he was about to purge them. In the Saur Revolution of 27 April 1978, Daoud was murdered, hundreds were arrested, and the rival Khalqi faction, under Nur Mohammad Taraki, established a dictatorship.

It was opposition to this new and apparently pro-Soviet dictatorship, and utter chaos in the country, that encouraged the Soviet Union to invade Afghanistan in 1979.[25] As lawlessness grew, Soviet leaders feared that, in light of the radicalism of the Iranian Revolution, Islamist unrest might affect the southern Soviet republics. This was not the onward march of socialism but an attempt to restore order on the periphery of the Soviet sphere of influence. It was supposed to be another Hungary or Czechoslovakia, but Moscow miscalculated. The fact was that the Marxist parties in Afghanistan had already alienated the population. Hafizullah Amin, a Khalqi, introduced state terror to re-establish order, murdering his rivals (including colleagues like Taraki) and potential opposition. Resistance grew, and Afghanistan was in a state of anarchy, if not civil war. In December 1979 Soviet forces therefore swept in, establishing control of urban areas and setting up a new government under Barbak Karmal. Despite his mission to reunify the socialist factions, modernize the army, popularize the regime and carry out economic development, the fact was that Karmal, like Karzai in 2001, was seen as a puppet of foreign forces.

The Soviet occupation was badly managed and the resistance determined, ruthless and widespread. Pushtun volunteers were involved from the beginning, but the Soviets were generally frustrated by the fact that their enemies were indistinguishable from the civilians. Their tactics were clumsy and counter-productive, with land clearances, indiscriminate bombing and atrocities. Arab volunteers were attracted to the conflict, although many were viewed with suspicion because their tactics were, at times, suicidal, and they seemed haughty about their interpretation of Islam. America became involved in the supply of arms and money (some $2 billion in total), channelled through their Pakistani allies. However, the Pakistan Inter-Services Intelligence (ISI) agency had been increasingly radicalized after Gen. Muhammad Zia-ul-Haq's Islamization policy was introduced in 1977. The ISI tended to push funds and arms towards their favoured factions of the mujahedin resistance, even if, as in the case of Gulbuddin Hekmatyr, these warlord leaders were ineffective fighters.

The Soviets were unable to impose any order on their Afghan protégés. Parcham and Khalqi factions continued to bicker and intrigue against each other but also commit ever more sickening atrocities to coerce and terrorize people into submission. The KHAD secret police were particularly notorious. Afghan troops sometimes deserted and occasionally murdered their Russian officers; some defected to the resistance. Sickness and exhaustion increased throughout the Soviet army, and the number of 'zinkies' (corpses sent home in zinc-lined coffins) rose steadily. Karmal endeavoured to popularize the regime with a new, more 'Islamic' constitution, and he tried to draw on a dislike of Pushtun-Pakistanis. But he failed to attract any significant backing. Gorbachev, who came to power in the Soviet Union with his own agenda of improved relations with the West and the reinvigoration of the economy, 'retired' Karmal. His replacement, Mohammad Najibullah, tried to establish control of communications by creating local militias and paying large subsidies to their commanders; this is what ushered in the era of warlordism. Soviet forces, who still operated with exclusive control in the south and east, switched their tactics to the command of roads and urban areas, launching major operations against the mujahedin if they appeared in force. Najibullah continued to rely on coercion and buying support, but Gorbachev could see that it was time to leave. Equipping the regime with its arms, the Soviets fought their way out.

With thousands of Afghan dead and many more wounded or traumatized by the war, there was little prospect for peace because so many factions were armed and schooled in coercion and violence rather than the politics of concession and compromise. After failed attempts to overthrow Najibullah in a coup and in open battle, the resistance seemed no more effective than the government. Only after the defections of his paid accomplices did Najibullah resign. The result was chaotic. There were battles for the capital fought by at least five major groups between 1993 and 1995. There were massacres of Sikhs, Hindus and Shia Hazaras. Warlords taxed and seized anything of value, then paid for their followers' loyalties in a new baronial order. Afghanistan had returned to the state it had been in the eighteenth century, except that the weapons were far more lethal. Kabul was reduced to ruins, and, into the maelstrom, Pakistan hurled its new force, the Taliban.

The Taliban claimed they were brought to power by the Afghan people, who were sick of corruption and warlord violence, but this is a myth. Armed, equipped and financed by Pakistan (a country looking for 'strategic depth' in its confrontation with India and Afghanistan), they were merely another fighting faction with more capability than their rivals. They only managed to take control of the capital because of the divisions among their opponents. They tried to seize Mazar-i-Sharif in 1995 but were driven out by forces loyal to Gen. Rashid Dostum, the Uzbek-Afghan commander of the north-west. When they eventually overran the city, they massacred hundreds and ordered that the survivors could not move the bodies for days. When the Taliban encountered resistance from the Shia of the Hazarajat, they murdered and destroyed property with impunity; once in power, they continued their reign of terror. They imposed their own interpretation of Sharia law, insisting that men wear beards and women remain completely covered. They banned music, kite-flying and televisions. They established a network of informers and summarily executed transgressors of their laws. Afghans described the Taliban's random brutality, beatings and public executions with just one word: *wahdat* (terror). If their state enjoyed so much popular support, as they claimed, then it is curious that they required such coercion to maintain it. They had inherited fifteen years of a tradition in which violence was the primary means for the state to establish and exercise its authority.

Nevertheless, the Taliban were never secure in their power, and the United Front opposition provided the US-led Coalition with a useful ground-force element in the overthrow of Mullah Omar's regime in 2001. Operations, backed by overwhelming American air power, were swift. With Kabul taken, the US forces concentrated on hunting down the leadership of Al-Qaeda, establishing the Guantanamo facility in Cuba to house some of their prisoners. These operations drew them close to Pakistan as thousands of Taliban fled eastwards across the frontier.[26]

In their wake, the Coalition has begun the immense task of political and civil reconstruction. The financial cost is enormous. Thousands of bridges, culverts and tunnels were destroyed. An estimated 10,000,000 mines are strewn across the country. Infrastructure and communications were in ruins. Ninety per cent of roads and irrigation systems were damaged; eighty per cent of homes and orchards were destroyed. Many farmers had already turned to poppy cultivation to exploit the lucrative trade in opium, a system the Taliban had supervised. The recovery of the north and east was well underway by 2006, but in the south and east, the Taliban appeared determined to continue the resistance, and suicide bombs were detonated in the capital. The Coalition, made up of NATO countries, has sought to extend the remit of the Kabul government over the south by training and deploying elements of the new Afghan National Army (ANA). The hard 'crust' of the operations has, however, fallen to the NATO troops, particularly the British and the Canadians. In an effort to demonstrate their jurisdiction but also to draw the Taliban into battle (where air power and heavy weapons can be brought to bear), the British army established 'platoon houses'. These consisted of small detachments (under 30) in strong positions. As expected, they were subjected to attacks, although many privately admit that the intensity and determination of the resistance was a surprise. The political unpopularity of the 'War on Terror' in Europe, which to many seemed to have evolved into the extension of America's global influence rather than an effort to eradicate terrorism, led to refusals to send more reinforcements to assist in the Afghan operations. This cast doubts on the future of the NATO alliance.

Politically, Afghanistan is a limited democracy. Hamed Karzai, a Pushtun from Kandahar, was elected President with some haste in the first Loya Jirga, or general assembly, in 2004. Women play a part in politics and have been encouraged to vote, although its also true that in rural areas remote from Kabul, they are still regarded as the property of their menfolk. Since a formal taxation system had collapsed, the government's main source of revenue has been through customs and the $2–3 billion it has received in aid. In fact, only 15 per cent of donor money reaches the government; most is spent by the aid agencies and donor countries themselves.(The Afghan budget for 2004 was $550 million.) The reason for this is not simply donor logistics but widespread corruption in the Afghan administration. The revaluation of the currency in 2002 has been a boost to investors, as has the clause that they will not be taxed for the first four to seven years. Agriculture is recovering, and an influx of returning Afghans has brought back a range of skills and entrepreneurship. However, apart from the physical damage, one of the biggest obstacles for any market-led recovery is the sheer poverty of the population. There is still too little food (not helped by a long running drought in the south), clothing, medical care and housing. Infant malnutrition stands at 50 per cent; infant mortality at a shocking 150 per 1,000. Life expectancy is between 41 and 43 years, the lowest in the region. In Ghor Province, the Catholic Agency for Overseas Development (CAFOD) estimates that 5,000 died of starvation in the winter of 2005. The news went unreported because the world's attention was at that time focused on the consequences of a dramatic earthquake in northern Pakistan.

For Afghan democracy to flourish, there needs to be a sustained period of peace, growth and stability. In 2005, there was much talk of a new 'Marshall Plan' for the region. However, it is a question of priorities when it comes to spending. The US spent $17 billion on its military operations in Afghanistan. The Afghan government estimates that it needs $10–15 billion over ten years for reconstruction. But such statistics do not expose the sheer complexity of the situation, which is quite unlike that in Europe or Japan in the period 1945–9. Schools can be built, but there need to be training for teachers and continuing incentives for young people to attend. About half of all primary-school-age children are getting some form of education, but half of these 'drop out' because of the need to find work on public work schemes or privately in order to feed themselves. Hundreds have ended up mending roads. Problems remain, but there is a good chance that Afghanistan will make a recovery. The country needs time, a spirit of reconciliation, physical security and money. It needs reconstruction and good governance, a reduction in corruption, better law enforcement and more widespread education. Faced with endemic feuding, extortion, intimidation, a corrupting drugs trade, terrorism, warlordism and external pressures, it is easy to be pessimistic. But the pessimists perhaps underestimate the Afghans.

Chapter 3

Islam and Islamism

Under the Soviets, there were campaigns designed to eradicate Islam from Central Asia.[1] By the 1930s, there were fewer than a hundred mosques still operating and no madrassahs. To win hearts and minds to the socialist cause, the Soviets introduced education for all and a health-care programme. They industrialized the towns, mechanized agriculture and expanded irrigation. Having brought all the Central Asian states into one polity, communications were improved and there was an increase in the internal trade of goods. Raw materials poured north into the Soviet heartland, while thousands of Russians were resettled to manage and administrate the reforms and new industry. The aim was clear: wean the Central Asians from 'reactionary' Islam and convert them into urbanized proletarians. The Basmachi revolt and other Middle Eastern resistance had indicated that Islam was a mobilizing force, capable of unifying people against Soviet rule. Any unrest might provide an opening for foreign intervention, as had occurred during the Russian Civil War. As the Cold War developed, this became a more pressing concern. Eager to prevent a radical version of Islam from emerging, the Soviets subsequently created a closely regulated 'official' Islam. State-approved mullahs and registered mosques were established. Muslim holy days were marked, and there were invitations to Middle Eastern religious leaders to discuss how Communism and Islam might be compatible (an experiment attempted at Baku in 1920 with little success). Islam came under one final onslaught in the mid-1980s under Gorbachev, and accused once again, of being an anti-modern influence. For the Central Asian republics' leaders, Islam continued to be a potentially radical force, capable of mounting mass protests and overthrowing the authorities – as had happened in Iran in 1979 and Afghanistan in the 1980s.

The fact that Islam had gone underground in the Soviet era has assisted the more radical Islamist groups since the 1990s in their opposition to the Central Asian governments. Devout Central Asians had continued various religious practices in secret,[2] and Soviet officials, with clan connections to those involved in Sufi activities, ignored what was going on or participated themselves. This collusion reinforced a sense of difference from an all-pervasive Russian influence and was also reflected in the systems of patronage that survived throughout the Soviet era. Clan loyalties ensured that, regardless of Party membership, certain groups could dominate the echelons of local power, be that in administration, in the running of local collective farms or in industry.

In the 1980s, religious beliefs, clannishness and national identity were transformed. In Moscow, Gorbachev's policy of restructuring and candour was interpreted as an opportunity to express new identities and aspirations. While he did not approve of Islam, he was unable to prevent the spread of feelings of nationalist and Islamic distinctiveness.[3] Yet perestroika also coincided with the closing stages of the bitter Soviet War in Afghanistan. Many returning Soviet soldiers had expressed sympathy for the courageous and determined resistance of the Afghan mujahedin. A few Muslim soldiers had defected and joined the fighters, and here they came across the austere, intolerant Salafest Wahhabi doctrine of the Arab volunteers. Some young men, inspired by the idea of defying the Soviets, headed for Pakistan to study. The form of Islamic teaching they were exposed to did not resemble the Sufi or moderate Sunni traditions of Central Asia: it was the radical Deobandi ideology, which advocated a new world order, created, if necessary, by a jihad. These two ideologies might not have taken root so easily, however, had it not been for the conduct of the wars in Afghanistan and, later, Chechnya. The widespread destruction of property, the deaths of thousands of civilians, the exodus of 5,000,000 refugees and stories of atrocities and torture began to radicalize Central

Asia. Returning soldiers and those who had fought for the mujahedin had been steeped in a particularly ruthless experience. Young Afghans, who then endured a twelve-year civil war, had no other skills than those connected with conflict. In short, a whole generation had been mobilized, radicalized and militarized.

Crucially, young men from Central Asia and Afghanistan made contact with and learned from other Muslims from no less than 43 countries. It is estimated that as many as 100,000 men from around the world fought in the Soviet–Afghan War; tens of thousands attended Pakistani madrassah complexes, often travelling up into the North-west Frontier Province for guerrilla training. Central Asians were often given free accommodation and instruction. Not only did they hear from Palestinians and Arabs about alleged oppression by Israelis and Arab oligarchies; they were indoctrinated with the Deobandi philosophy. Deobandism had emerged in the nineteenth century in British India, inspired by anti-colonial and anti-Western resistance. A strict Sunni sect, the Deobandis disapproved of Shi'ism and of any form of liberation of women. In the 1960s, radicals were advocating a modern form of jihad and resistance to Western modernism, and, noting the mobilizing of the Iranians in their 1979 revolution, the Deobandis began to advocate the formation of a mass movement that would build into an irresistible jihad.[4] With the Soviet withdrawal from Afghanistan in 1989, the Deobandis were convinced that it was they, by force of will and divine providence, who had achieved victory. They failed to acknowledge the financial and military support of the US. Nor were they prepared to admit that their radical philosophy had to be imposed by force on the people of Afghanistan, using the backing of Pakistan, with the consequence that Afghans were condemned to years of terror, poverty and ruin. To the Deobandis, all that mattered was the waging of jihad and the radical purification of the faith.

The Deobandis found common cause with the Saudi Salafest Wahhabists in the interpretations of Islam. Salafi Wahhabis are bitterly opposed to the 'heresy' of Shi'ism and Sufism in South-west Asia.[5] In their world-view, women are virtually invisible, while men are expected to conduct themselves soberly and with dignity, since maintaining prestige is a critical element to their society. It is interesting to note that the Saudi regime aligned itself with Wahhabi Islam from the outset and is compelled to act in accordance with the wishes of a very conservative ulema. Osama bin Laden, although a Saudi, has family roots in Hadramawt in Yemen, and it is here that the most austere forms of Wahhabism still exist. Women, for example, are largely confined to large accommodation complexes and rarely appear in public. In a sense, it is curious that such conservative figures could embrace such a populist, radical version of Islam, but the answer lies in a wounded sense of pride, envy for the mobilization of Iranians and Afghans, and a desire to assert their religion and culture – which they believe to be the only true way of life – over the successful and powerful modernists of the West and East Asia. Salafis are angry at the Arab regimes for failing to adhere to the strictest forms of the faith, for failing to defeat heretical sects and for tolerating the presence of Westerners (and Israelis) in the 'land of the holy places'.

However, Deobandism and Wahhabism have not been accepted by all Central Asians. The Tajik Islamic opposition, for example, drew their inspiration from the resistance of Ahmad Shah Masoud, the Tajik-Afghan who fought the Soviets and then the Taliban. Masoud embodied a moderate version of Islam and Tajik national identity.[6] The IRP was founded in 1991 with the aim of spreading Islamic belief, promoting a spiritual revival and assisting with the economic independence of Tajikistan. In contrast to the Taliban and other radicals, it favoured democracy rather than an Islamic state. It openly supported popular opposition to the government during housing riots, and provided food and blankets to protestors, which led to the toppling of the government of President Nabiev in September of the same year. When the civil war broke out, the IRP formed guerrilla bands in the mountains, and they eventually helped form the post-war coalition government. The IRP was less successful elsewhere. In Kyrgyzstan, it only managed to recruit from the Uzbek population in the rural south. In Uzbekistan, it was undermined by more radical movements, such as Tauba, Islam Lashkarlary and Adolat, and suffered a loss of momentum when its leader, Abdullah Utaev, went missing in 1992; it is alleged that he was murdered by the Uzbek secret service. In Kazakhstan, the IRP was dominated by non-Kazakhs – which hampered its appeal – and it failed to get established at all in Turkmenistan. Millions more are deterred by the violence of Deobandi and Wahhabi Jihadists, and today there is little support for such haughty, alien beliefs. Some Central Asian governments, particularly Karimov's in Uzbekistan, have chosen to label all opponents of the regime as Wahhabi terrorists. This generalization may help to explain why an idealistic but largely peaceful new movement known as Hizb ut-Tahrir, also imported from South-west Asia, is taking root in Central Asia.

HIZB UT-TAHRIR AND THE ISLAMISTS

Hizb ut-Tahrir is a popular and growing movement in Central Asia. Paradoxically, it does directly address the concerns of the people, such as the growing inequality of wealth, unemployment and a lack of political rights. Its aims are anachronistic, even atavistic. Yet it is the very 'other-worldly' and idealistic nature of Hizb ut-Tahrir that perhaps explains its appeal.

Hizb ut-Tahrir wants to see the establishment of a single, unified caliphate across Central Asia, from Xinjiang Province to the Caucasus. Ultimately they wish to see the entire Muslim world united as one *umma* without national borders. They long for the reconstruction of the *Khilafat-i Rashida*, the empire that lasted from 632 to 661, shortly after the life of the Prophet. This period is held in special reverence because it appeared to be a more pure, spiritual age when Islam had not been sullied by sectarian division or modern influences. To achieve a multi-ethnic single polity, Hizb ut-Tahrir's followers believe that creating a mass movement will eventually overwhelm one of the regimes of Central Asia or the Middle East. Having established one unified state, they argue, others will inevitably follow. Sheikh Abdul Qadeem Zallum, a prominent leader of Hizb ut-Tahrir, states his aim as 'transform[ing] Muslim lands and this has to be done by re-establishing the Khilafah'.[7] Hizb ut-Tahrir feel that the Prophet Mohammed provided a blueprint for overthrowing regimes in that, first, he spread his message secretly; second, the revelation was espoused openly; and third, he launched a jihad. Hizb ut-Tahrir argue, rather inaccurately, that the Prophet also faced propaganda and foreign sanctions, and that his followers suffered torture, just as Hizb ut-Tahrir's members do in the early 21st century.

Hizb ut-Tahrir do not just suffer from a selective and historicist misunderstanding of the early career of Muhammad; they conceal a far more sinister plan. The organization was founded in 1953 by Sheikh Taqiuddin an-Nabhani Filastyni, a Palestinian who had graduated from Al-Azhar University in Cairo before becoming a school teacher and then a judge.[8] He was forced to flee Palestine soon after the creation of the State of Israel and established the movement in Jordan. In his writings, he described a Muslim world divided and unable to conceive of any other form of political system than 'depraved' democratic nation-states. An-Nabhani was convinced that nationalism was a barrier to Muslim unity and strength. He was the first to argue that, by following the life of the Prophet, a strategy could be developed for overcoming the differences of the Muslim world. This in itself was wholly idealistic since Muslims were divided on sectarian and ethnic grounds (not to mention between classes and cultures) as much as by 'Western' notions of national identity. What was more disturbing, perhaps, was the celebration of the period of Arab expansion. Although a thrilling time for the advocates of Hizb ut-Tahrir, the empire was achieved by a process of war, conquest and, in many cases, forced conversion. Thousands of 'unbelievers' were slaughtered. And if the *Khilafat-i Rashida* was the model to emulate, the fact that it only survived for 30 years would surely suggest that there was something inherently weak about it.

The movement believes that enlisting massive numbers of supporters will help to avoid violence, but it conceals its ultimate objectives. By sheer weight of numbers, its members argue, it will be able to overwhelm regimes. Certainly, the Uzbek authorities take this threat seriously enough to arrest and intimidate members of Hizb ut-Tahrir, but it difficult to see, in light of the government's determination to break up opposition groups and maintain its exclusive hold on power, how a series of mass protests can succeed. There seems to be a similar utopianism when it comes to the form of the caliphate the movement desires. It would a politically centralized empire, governed by one man and advised by a religious council, or *shura*. The Caliph would rule as a dictator, controlling the army, the administration, the economy and foreign policy.[9] Despite claims that the movement would embrace the 'inherent diversity of Islam' and that they support *ijtihad* (reform), it is difficult to believe that, in practice, it would really allow 'wrong' interpretations – that is, ones it did not approve.[10] A single language, Arabic, would be imposed. Women would be restricted in their life and activities. Strict interpretations of Sharia law would be used. The Minister of Defence, or Amir of Jihad, would pursue just one objective: the preparation of the people of the empire for a global jihad against the non-Muslim world. All men, from the age of fifteen, would be conscripted and obliged to serve. The war would not be concluded until the world had been converted to Islam or those who resisted had been killed. Thus the world would enter a new dark age in which a handful of male theocrats and oligarchs would preside over a global war, the subjugation of women and non-Muslims, and, if necessary, the extermination of those who resisted – whose numbers could potentially run into the millions.

These ideas sound exactly like those espoused by Salafest Wahhabis, although they too often stop short of describing the final encounter with the non-Muslim world. There seem to be differences only in method. Hizb ut-Tahrir was once aligned to the Wahhabis but disagreed with the notion of guerrilla wars being ignited in separate nation-states and with the formation of a jihadist 'army' too early. Hizb ut-Tahrir instead called for the creation of a mass movement and the peaceful introduction of Sharia by the consent of a believing public. But in fact there is more common ground in their methodology. Both movements share their common roots in the Muslim Brotherhood, or *Ikhwan ul-Musilmeen*. In the 1930s, this Egyptian movement advocated a struggle against colonialism but wanted to see, first, a seizure of power and, second, the creation of modern Muslim states. This made the Brotherhood distinct from the anti-colonial rebellions and resistance of the nineteenth century, when, essentially, the fight had been to preserve existing polities. Different groups have tended to interpret the original ideas of the Brotherhood in their own way. Some chose to establish resistance organizations using terrorist tactics, such as Islamic Jihad in Egypt and Palestine. Others believed that modern, and therefore

Western-style, institutions were to be rejected altogether. But the revolutionary method was generally accepted.

Movements like Al-Qaeda use the language of revolution alongside a selective reading of Islamic texts and the use of modern communications technology and weapon systems (including those developed in the West), to justify the creation of an idealized and distinctly anti-modern version of the Muslim past; a past, incidentally, that never existed. There is a reverent respect for the memory of the Ottoman Empire since this is seen as a close approximation of these movements' ideal state. The Ottomans established a dominion in the fourteenth century based on the Muslim kingdoms of South-west Asia. They made their capital at Constantinople after it was taken from the Christian Byzantines in 1453, and, under Mehmed II, they advanced into south-eastern Europe. Vienna was besieged on two occasions. They established control of Egypt and the entire North African coast, overran the Caucasus and waged war on the Persians. The Ottoman Empire appeared to be wealthy and powerful, driving back Europeans and heretical sects alike.

However, Hizb ut-Tahrir seems less willing to acknowledge the failures of the Ottoman system, seeking only to blame Western colonialism for its demise. The fact is that such an extensive empire could not be ruled efficiently from the centre, so provincial governors were appointed. The sheer wealth of the empire encouraged corruption, there were episodes of fratricide whenever a Caliph grew old, and, by the nineteenth century, provincial governors had begun to assert their autonomy. Non-Muslims were tolerated but treated as second-class citizens. Herded into communities, the *rai'yah* (shepherded people) were regarded effectively as the property of the Sultan. They could not ride horses or carry weapons, and they were barred from the army, civil service or positions of authority. In western and eastern Africa, Arab traders ran an extensive system of slavery which lasted until the late nineteenth century, when Africa fell into European hands. Perhaps the turning point in the Ottoman relationship with the West was in 1699, when the Austrians began to take back control of the Balkans, a process that was completed in 1913. This was in part due to the take-off of the West as it generated new commercial wealth, underwent extensive internal reforms and achieved scientific advances. By contrast, the Ottomans were a dead, stifling hand on the Muslim world. Their conservatism brought to an end an era of Muslim scientific scholarship and condemned the empire to stagnation. Hizb ut-Tahrir seems eager to re-establish such a system, although they seem less willing to tolerate non-Muslims within their empire. For all their criticism of Western colonialism and secular dictatorship, they seem to wish to embrace the idea of imperialism and dictatorship on their own terms.

Perhaps the most absurd misinterpretation of history favoured by Hizb ut-Tahrir is their belief that Ataturk, the architect of Turkish modernism, was little more than a puppet of the West and its Jewish allies. The demise of the Ottoman Empire was, they argue, brought about in part by the conquests of the Western Allies in the closing stages of the First World War, but the final destruction of the Islamic state was carried out by Ataturk in the 1920s. They fail to mention that a modernist movement, the Young Turks, had already begun to change the Ottoman regime from within, before the First World War, in 1908. Nor do they mention that Ataturk, far from being a puppet of the West, went to war with Greece in 1919–22 over the territory of Smyrna and was prepared to fight the British on the Dardenelles in the famous Chanak Incident (1923) as part of his assertion of national independence. Ataturk carried out extensive reforms and abolished the old Ottoman systems of administration, emancipated women, introduced national education and established a Turkish national identity. It is these measures which Hizb ut-Tahrir so deride.

The organization is virulently anti-Zionist to the point of anti-Semitism, belying its Middle Eastern roots. Karimov of Uzbekistan is described as a handmaiden of the Zionist world conspiracy and is accused of maintaining a front for Israel. Hizb ut-Tahrir wants to see the removal of all Jews from Central Asia, even though their ethnic cleansing would uproot a portion of Central Asian society that has been in the region for 2,000 years. To Hizb ut-Tahrir they simply 'do not belong here'.[11] A similar fate awaits the Shias and Sufis. Traditionally, Central Asian Islam has always been tolerant of different practices, but these foreign, strident beliefs represent a wave of Islamist radicalism that is sweeping across the Muslim world. In Indonesia and Malaysia, whose forms of Islam have also been historically tolerant, a similar process of radicalization is taking place. A more interconnected world, particularly in communications, has meant that many young Muslims are exposed to conflicts and injustices that were once distant and unknown. Now they are immediate and apparently 'local'. The obligations of Islam and strong traditions of solidarity mean that it is impossible to remain a spectator to disputes such as the Israeli–Palestinian conflict, the Chechen Wars or the battles over Lebanon.

Hizb ut-Tahrir is banned in most Muslim countries, and, in another paradox, it has therefore sought sanctuary in Europe. The multicultural, tolerant and cosmopolitan cities of the West have provided the sort of environment the movement lacks in its own homelands. It uses cities like London and universities across the UK to recruit, raise funds and spread its message.[12] It is a well-organized group that has a strong appeal for young male Muslims.

However, in Central Asia, Hizb ut-Tahrir is thriving in a more clandestine fashion. Its leaders' identities and locations are kept secret. Activists operate in seven-man cells, each one led by a cell chief. Only the chief knows the identity of the next layer of the hierarchy. The leader sets out the tasks of the group members, usually the formation of new *daira* (cells) as study groups and the distribution of propaganda. Such tight security is essential: Uzbek security police have been able to penetrate several cells by posing as recruits, although they have found it more difficult to identify and arrest the leaders. However, Hizb ut-Tahrir does not rely on word-of-mouth contacts alone. They like to use the *shabnama* (night chronicle), a newsletter pushed through letterboxes at night by activists. Posters are also put up at night. Hizb ut-Tahrir now also makes extensive use of modern communications technologies to spread their message. Videos, CDs, printing and photocopying facilities and email are all used.

The movement has had to learn how to win over the public after a faltering start. Hizb ut-Tahrir did not appear in Uzbekistan until 1995, when a Jordanian calling himself Salah'uddin recruited two Uzbeks in Tashkent and began distributing Arabic leaflets in the city's underground. Few could read the texts, but translations were soon available and new cells were established in the capital, then in Ferghana, and eventually in Kyrgyzstan and Tajikistan. Hundreds have been arrested for belonging to the organization, but Hizb ut-Tahrir estimates its membership to be in the tens of thousands. Others put the figure closer to just 7,000.[13]

The communications equipment and initial funding for the movement, like its ideology, is not indigenous to Central Asia but imported. The close approximation to the ideas and aspirations of the Salafest Wahhabis is no coincidence. They reject the idea of the modern state, and the ideas of democracy, socialism and capitalism. They disapprove of many entertainments and cultural activities (such as music, dancing and even kite-flying). They claim that they do not deny women an education, but it seems they have a very limited view of the form this education should take – largely preparation for serving men. Olivier Roy noted that Hizb ut-Tahrir have a strong faith in Sharia law as the means to solve all their social ills.[14] Like the Taliban and Al-Qaeda, there is really only one policy objective after the waging of jihad, and that is the imposition of Sharia.[15] They do not, in fact, need to overthrow the state, since they aim to transform the state from within. By winning over the mass of the population to their way of thinking, they believe the regimes will collapse and offer no further resistance. They are somewhat arrogant in their beliefs, since they state that all other Islamist movements will eventually be proved wrong. Such notions are based on a misreading of the Koran, a claim that the Prophet predicted that there would eventually be seventy-three Islamic movements, only one of which would be right. The Koran *actually* states there should be a group that 'invites to the good, orders what is right and forbids what is evil – and they are those who are successful' and makes reference to the idea that, since not all are believers, only a few will be favoured.[16] There is no mention of any number, and the passage refers to the need to be guided to do what is right and good, as that is the true measure of a person's success.

REACTIONS TO HIZB UT-TAHRIR

Hizb ut-Tahrir is a well-organized movement and has been successful in distributing literature throughout Central Asia, but it draws its strength from urban, more educated elements of society. Students, teachers, urban workers and men in their twenties are well represented, as records of their arrests indicate. Hizb ut-Tahrir has less support from rural populations, where the more radical IMU and IRP enjoy some sympathy. Nevertheless, it is unclear how much backing Hizb ut-Tahrir has from personnel within the administration, army, intelligence services and police. Officially, of course, it is an illegal organization, but Ahmed Rashid suggested there may be some who favour the movement.[17]

In 1998, following the Law on Freedom of Conscience and Religious Organisations, the government of Uzbekistan launched a crackdown on all Islamist suspects. It was declared illegal to preach Islam. All mosques and imams had to be registered. Women were arrested for wearing the hijab, and thousands of men with beards were questioned. Men travelling to Pakistan, or who had more than one wife, were also subject to interrogation. Many were arrested. Even fathers whose sons were suspected to be members of Hizb ut-Tahrir or other Islamist organizations were arrested. The following year, fifty-five death sentences were awarded and fifteen executions took place; some of those convicted were members of Hizb ut-Tahrir. The movement stated, in wildly exaggerated figures, that 100,000 members were imprisoned. The American Human Rights Report and the Independent Human Rights Organisation of Uzbekistan estimated that the figure was nearer 5,000.[18] But prisoner numbers increased so dramatically that a new incarceration unit was established at Jaslik in the autonomous region of Karakalpakstan. It is overcrowded and has polluted water which infects the inmates with hepatitis. Prisoners are made to work on forced-labour projects and cannot pray or read the Koran. There have been accusations of torture and estimates of around 50 extrajudicial deaths. The Uzbek authorities regard the imprisonment of more than 5,000 members of Hizb ut-Tahrir, and a further 1,600 members of the insurgent IMT and their Wahhabi allies, as a success. What is of concern to human-rights organizations is the high number of apparently innocent practising Muslims and civil rights activists who are imprisoned, as well as the general conditions and treatment of all political prisoners.

The Uzbek government encourages the use of informers, the *Mahalla*, to assist in the policing of the state.[19] In 2000, it was estimated that there were 10,700 suspected 'enemies of the state' in the country.

Yet, as other historical examples show, denunciations and informing on neighbours or strangers has a dynamic of its own. In the end, it does not matter how many actual enemies of the state there are: what happens is that people believe that informers are everywhere and society becomes obsessively self-regulating and self-policing. No one dares to speak out or criticize; almost everyone is eager to conform. If suspects are arrested, the human rights organizations believe, beatings and torture are common. In some cases, beatings are carried out to extract confessions. There have been allegations that electric shocks are administered, and victims are almost suffocated. Some have died during these sessions. The police are not above planting weapons, drugs, ammunition or inflammatory literature in order to make an arrest, get a conviction or sometimes just to extract a bribe. These tactics are not unknown in other Central Asian states when dealing with religious organizations or democratic activists. In Azerbaijan, for example, democratic-opposition members were arrested, beaten up, intimidated and kept under surveillance during the election period of October 2003.

The centre of Hizb ut-Tahrir's activities in Uzbekistan, other than in the capital, has been the Ferghana Valley, and this is also the focus of the movement's efforts in Kyrgyzstan. Trials of Hizb ut-Tahrir suspects have revealed the same range of activities: the distribution of propaganda texts, video and audio tapes and posters. The accused are men aged between 18 and 25; many were trained in Afghanistan alongside the IMT and the Taliban. Trials and Hizb ut-Tahrir literature have revealed their disgust with Christians in Kyrgyzstan, by which they mean hatred for ethnic Russians. They want to see churches demolished and the government punished for pandering to the immigrant Russian population, who make up 17 per cent of the country's people. They fail to realize that the economic consequences of ejecting the Russians in one go could be severe, as Tajikistan discovered in the civil war of 1992–6. Christian worship has increased in the north of the country, adding to the bitter annoyance of Hizb ut-Tahrir and thus fuelling ethnic tensions. In fact, there is already a deep-seated antagonism between the ethnic Uzbek population of southern Kyrgyzstan and the Kyrgyz themselves. A quarter of the population in the southern province, but as many as 40 per cent in the city of Osh, are Uzbek. Hizb ut-Tahrir fails to acknowledge this obvious division because it does not fit into their world-view. They continue to espouse their utopianism while the majority are concerned with government corruption, poverty and a lack of progress in solving the economic problems of the country. Yet it is the esoteric values of Hizb ut-Tahrir that are, in themselves, appealing. The people of Central Asia are likely to listen to a movement that offers even a vision of a brighter future while their actual prospects remain so grim. Young men especially look to a movement that offers them some empowerment, status and a higher cause.

In Kazakhstan, Hizb ut-Tahrir leaflets appeared for the first time in the largest city, Almaty, in July 2001, prompting concerns that radicalism would spread in the country. Similar anxieties were voiced by the Tajik government when Hizb ut-Tahrir started to appear in the northern provinces. President Rahmonov has appealed to the more moderate IRP to condemn the radicals. However, the IRP has noted that Hizb ut-Tahrir doesn't just appeal to disgruntled members of its own organization who are dissatisfied with the peace settlement after the civil war; it has also found strong support among a new generation of young men. Children of the civil war period, they look to Hizb ut-Tahrir to give them an untainted introduction to Islam. Perhaps, unsurprisingly, some of these radical idealists have drifted into the ranks of the insurgent IMT.

HIZB UT-TAHRIR AND INSURGENCY

One persistent question that has emerged in Western governments and intelligence agencies is whether Hizb ut-Tahrir is a terrorist organization. It denies any links with violent groups and argues that it has not been involved in kidnapping, bombings or insurgency training in camps. It states it has always advocated peaceful change. However, ideologically, it has much in common with organizations like the Salafest Wahhabis and the IMT. It does not espouse jihad in the way that Al-Qaeda does, but it envisages the same ultimate objective.[20] It is therefore a question of ends and means. Hizb ut-Tahrir is, in many ways, the acceptable face of an intolerant political idea.

Members of Hizb ut-Tahrir were co-located with the IMT in Afghanistan during the Taliban years, and they co-operated at every level.[21] Drawn from the same countries and even the same clans, links perhaps inevitably developed. The Kyrgyz authorities state that Hizb ut-Tahrir literature was found on the bodies of IMT fighters killed near the border, and they believe that Hizb ut-Tahrir members received military training in the same camps. The movement was sympathetic to its Taliban hosts. Here, after all, was the first state to fall to its ideology and the first to impose the sort of measures Hizb ut-Tahrir favoured: restrictions of women in public life; the imposition of a rough Sharia law; and the banding together of Afghans, Chechens, Arabs and other Central Asians in a common cause, albeit an exclusively radical and Sunni one. Hizb ut-Tahrir would also have approved of the fact that Sufis and Shias were persecuted. Nevertheless, they made a distinction from the sort of lifestyle the Taliban imposed. Where the Taliban favoured a life of rural austerity and preparation for the next life, Hizb ut-Tahrir wanted a more comfortable life on earth, the creation of a version of heaven on earth prior to the life hereafter.

The closeness of Hizb ut-Tahrir to the extremists is further revealed in their views on Osama bin Laden. Like many Muslims around the world, there is a degree of sympathy for a man who, forgoing his millions, stood up to the West and embraced a life of piety and sacrifice. One leading Uzbek member of Hizb ut-Tahrir stated, 'We have no special relationship with bin Laden, but he supports all Islamic movements in Central Asia and he is very famous here for doing so.'[22] Kyrgyz and Uzbek leaders argue that Hizb ut-Tahrir members met Osama bin Laden in September 2000 in Kabul, where, no doubt, he gave his blessing to their mission. Many of the rank and file of Islamist groups, in common with Islamists around the world, are prepared to believe any conspiracy theory against the West and are always prepared to give Osama bin Laden the benefit of the doubt. Some still convince themselves, in spite of all the contrary evidence, that somehow the US States orchestrated the attacks of 9/11 on themselves so as to launch a global war against Islam. Osama bin Laden was, so the theory goes, entirely innocent of the crime. Yet they are all prepared to admit that Al-Qaeda is essentially an ideology of resistance to the West and to apostate rulers which bin Laden and his confederates advocate and often fund or support. Inspired by his example and teachings, jihadists are prepared to carry out the most foul atrocities. Certain in their conviction that Allah approves of their 'defensive' measures, they kill and are killed in greater numbers.[23] And yet, despite years of war, terrorism and 'martyr-dom', the Islamists and their jihadist commandos are not one step nearer their goal of a united califate.

While advocating the 'peaceful jihad' of conversion and persuasion, members of Hizb ut-Tahrir are not above threatening violence. In fact, their role in supporting the insurgents of Central Asia is revealed in the following short statement. An Uzbek leader of the movement noted, 'ultimately, there will be a war because the repression by the Central Asian regimes is so severe and we have to prepare for that. If the IMU suddenly appears in the Ferghana Valley, HT activists will not sit idly by and allow the security forces to kill them.'[24] The IMT insur-gents are dependent upon local support to be able to move, as Mao Zedong once styled it, 'like fish through water'. It is likely that Hizb ut-Tahrir supply the IMU, harbour them in safe houses and provide them with information. They also appear to embrace provocation. The same Hizb ut-Tahrir leader pointed out that intervention by Russian troops if there was a crisis in the governance of Uzbekistan (perhaps caused by the assassination or overthrow of Karimov) would play into the Islamists' hands, as it would 'expose everybody, force polarisation and the war will begin'.[25] This appears to be an argument in favour of civil war, a final settling of accounts that would result in an Islamist victory not unlike the Taliban's in Afghanistan in 1995–6. The consequences of an Islamist takeover would mean ethnic cleansing on a vast scale. But, like the Taliban, Hizb ut-Tahrir appears to be inept when it comes to economic matters, condemning the people of the region to worsening poverty and a perpetuation of war.

Rashid argued that legalizing Hizb ut-Tahrir might go a long way to solving the problem.[26] It would force the movement to advocate actual economic and reform policies rather than vague promises. It might give them a stake in the future of the country and would therefore avoid a civil war. Yet, after 2001, the Uzbeks suppressed this movement and others even more ruthlessly. Members of Hizb ut-Tahrir tried in

October 2001 were accused of being allies of Al-Qaeda as well as belonging to an illegal party. They received sentences of between nine and twelve years. Such convictions were designed to attract American support against a common enemy. Rashid believes that it is the regimes that need to change if there is to be less radicalism in Central Asia, but it is difficult to see what an incentive might be: faced with insurgency, terrorism and radical ideologues, do they really have any choice but to fight on? Reforms might look like a capitulation to extremism and an encouragement to push harder against a weakening regime. The Central Asian governments must hope that the radicals will lose momentum and fail to attract mass support.

It is more likely that economic performance holds the key to change in Central Asia. A fairer distribution of wealth, an abundant food, water and energy supply and a reduction in the severest security measures might swing the public mood away from the Islamists. At present, there is disillusionment, if not despair. Support for idealists reflects the degree of stress and hopelessness felt by the population. Hizb ut-Tahrir itself is nevertheless doomed to failure. It will be unable to overcome the class, ethnic, clan and national divisions of the people of the region. It will be unable to implement its cherished caliphate or to fulfil the promises it holds out to so many young men and women. As a result, it is likely, as is already happening on a small scale, that some of these will join insurgent bands and fight the regimes. Already there is an established base of support for the extreme ideas of Salafest Wahhabi Islam, sympathy for the Taliban and admiration for Al-Qaeda. It was precisely this breakdown of toleration and faith in radicalism that brought about the bloodiest conflict in modern Central Asian history: the Tajik Civil War.

Chapter 4

The Tajik Civil War and the Islamic Renaissance Party

The Pamirs, rather like the Himalayas, are described as the Roof of the World. Nine-tenths of Tajikistan is mountainous, with half of it more than 3,000 metres high. There are 10,000 square kilometres of glaciers. Cascading from these are icy rivers, some of which drain into lakes like Karakul (formed 10,000 years ago when a huge meteorite struck the earth) before rushing down into Uzbekistan and western China. Most of the Tajik population live in the western fringes near the capital, Dushanbe, with intensively farmed fields, cotton plantations and hydroelectric schemes competing for space. The eastern half of the country is vast and more remote. It is easy to appreciate why smugglers and guerrilla bands were able to 'disappear' in this great wilderness. But remote mountain communities developed strong clan identities over many centuries, and it was these that fuelled a bitter and ulti-mately futile war.

The Tajik Civil War of 1992–6 went largely unreported in the Western world despite the fact that it left an estimated 40,000 dead. Preoccupied with events in the Middle East, with the break-up of the Soviet Union and with international terrorism, the West had more pressing issues to confront. Yet, the war was a conflict with immense significance for Central Asia, and, subsequently, the West as well. The war's origins stretched back far beyond 1992 and the independence of Tajikistan; it was a manifestation of a complex ethnic struggle for power, territory and resources characterized by clan warfare and contests for control of certain regions. The capital itself changed hands several times, and there were massacres in some of the outlying districts. There were many external interventions, by Uzbeks and Kyrgyz, from neighbouring Afghanistan, by jihadists across the Muslim world and, most decisively, by the Russians. Re-establishing peace was a protracted affair but ultimately successful, and a unique coalition of Islamic and secular, formerly Communist parties was created. The survival of that coalition is not guaranteed, and the precarious state of the Tajik economy has given rise to a great deal of instability.

THE ORIGINS OF THE WAR

Tajikistan did not enjoy the same sort of national homogeneity as other Central Asian republics. Stalin's division of the borders and ethnic groups of Turkestan in 1929, particularly the dismemberment of the Ferghana Valley, was designed to weaken each of the Central Asian peoples. As a consequence, Tajiks lost their spiritual centres of Bokhara and Samarkand, and significant numbers found themselves to be minorities in other republics. In the new Tajikistan Soviet Republic, thousands of Uzbeks made up a portion of the population, perhaps upwards of 23 per cent, while Russians dominated the administration and services. Stalin's purges of 1927–8 and 1930–1 decimated the Tajik élites.[1] By the end of the Soviet era, some 40 per cent of the population were non-Tajiks. Furthermore, a significant minority of ethnic Tajiks was resident in Afghanistan but cut off from the Soviet Union. Nevertheless, geography played its part too. The pockets and ribbons of settlement, hemmed in by the Pamirs, forced their communities to look inward. The result was that there was little sense of national identity; clannishness was far more common. Soviet policies tended to reinforce this phenomenon of a scattered, divided society. Collectivized agriculture (accompanied by considerable coercion) broke up some of the traditional valley loyalties. Despite this, Tajiks still looked to their geographical and clan identities as the alternative to Sovietization. The net effect was that, when a conflict began after independence, the country fractured quickly, and clan identities often determined which warlords were supported. It also led to bitter episodes of ethnic cleansing and feuding. However, some unity was actually restored following the intervention of Uzbekistan, which provided a common enemy.

Perestroika created a wave of new expectations in Tajikistan, which had become one of the poorest and most neglected states of the Soviet Union. The Communist Party of Tajikistan (CPT) was alert to these new aspirations and took the initiative to win greater public support. It established a cultural foundation to preserve a unique Tajik heritage, renamed Leninabad Province as Khujand and permitted the media to express national concerns. In 1989, it passed a language law that asserted Tajik over Russian as the official state tongue.[2] It even petitioned Moscow (in vain) to restore Samarkand and Bokhara to Tajikistan. The public were nevertheless suspicious of this old guard changing its policies simply to win popular support. The language law was considered a concession to a growing opposition movement. Even in the late 1980s, opposition groups had begun to emerge, and perestroika gave them the opportunity to express themselves more publicly and stridently. There were calls for full independence from the Soviet Union. However, all these developments tended to be driven by urban activists, particularly in Dushanbe. Both the opposition and the government seemed to ignore the rural population, which was thought to be ill-educated, conservative and even Islamist.[3] That did not stop either of them from enlisting rural support once the civil war had broken out.

The breakdown of order can be traced to the housing riots of 1990. As fighting raged in Karabakh and Afghanistan, there were fears that thousands of refugees would flee to the overcrowded capital. But the wave of demonstrations, sit-ins and other protests was really indicative of a deep-seated discontent with the Communists. Conscious of their unpopularity and of a worsening crisis, the CPT chose a succession of leaders before settling for the ageing Rakhmon Nabiev as President in September 1991. Suspicious about his election, thousands turned up to protest in Azadi Square, refusing to leave until new elections were promised and articulating a series of grievances. The government was forced to hold new presidential elections that November. Nabiev won by a narrow margin, again leading to accusations that the vote had been rigged. There was widespread support for the leading opposition candidate, Davlat Khudonazarov, who polled 34 per cent of the vote, not least because he represented an alliance of nationalists, democrats and Islamists. Although the Islamists argued for the creation of an Islamic state, what united them with the democrats and nationalists was a strong desire to defeat the Communists. By March 1992, dissatisfaction with the government had reached such a pitch that demonstrations turned violent. The response was swift and bloody: many were killed, but the result was that order collapsed completely. There were assassinations, gun battles and kidnappings on a daily basis. Opposition groups began to form guerrilla units and establish bases in the valleys but also looked to the ethnic Tajik Afghans for weapons and logistical support. On the other side, the Nabiev regime armed militias to augment their armed forces.[4]

Full-scale fighting broke out in May 1992 with Russia backing the old Communist élite against the opposition factions. Alongside the nationalists, democrats and Islamists stood the clans of Garm and Gorno-Badakshan, who were eager to bring centralized tyranny to an end and create greater autonomy for themselves. Local identities thus surfaced as a new layer of complexity in the civil war. While some were certainly motivated by ideological agendas, others saw the conflict as a more pragmatic struggle for power between regions and clans at a local level. Qazi Akbar Turajonzoda, the leader of Tajikistan's 'official Islam' and a government-approved figure, defected to the opposition and promptly fled to Iran, from where, at least initially, he continued to lend moral support to the Islamist cause. He was subsequently expelled from the IRP for criticizing its centralizing tendencies, arguing instead for a grass-roots and evolutionary, rather than revolutionary, organization. Other groups and individuals pursued their own agendas during the war. The Pamiris declared Gorno-Badakhshan an autonomous republic in April 1992. The Kulabis and Khujandis, while pro-government, nevertheless threatened to secede from the country unless the President prosecuted the war against the opposition more vigorously.

The opposition gradually pressed the government forces back into the capital, forcing Nabiev to resign in September 1992. However, the triumph was short-lived because of the intervention of Russian and Uzbek troops.[5]

They soon drove the opposition out of the capital. Following a coup attempt by Communists from Kulyab, the pro-government factions and their foreign backers established a new government under the leadership of Emomali Rahmonov, a man who only really represented the clans of the Kulob and Kulyab regions but who nevertheless enjoyed more backing than Nabiev's regime (which drew its support from Leninabad-Khujand Province).[6] Predictably, Rahmonov gave all government posts to his clan allies from Kulyab, ending any chances of a compromise peace that year. Opposition groups, which had boycotted the 1994 'elections', accused the government of fraud and intimidation. Meanwhile 200,000 ethnic Russians tried desperately to get out of the country, and thousands of internally displaced persons (IDPs) poured into the capital to escape the indiscriminate violence of the countryside.

The most intense phase of the war now unfolded with Kulyabi militias battling the opposition groups. Backed by Russian and Uzbek matériel, including aircraft and troops, the militias defeated the Pamiris, Garmis and IRP bands. The IRP and other opposition insurgents made hit-and-run attacks on militias and government forces, retreating periodically into the mountains of Karategrin, Tavildara, Kurgan Tyube and across the border into Afghanistan. However, the conflict was so embittered by this stage that the militias acted with great brutality towards their opponents: villages were razed, minorities driven out or murdered en masse, opposition leaders were executed, and 80,000 fled into northern Afghanistan. The atrocities were particularly severe at Qurgonteppe, just 80 kilometres south of the capital, because this was a stronghold of the IRP and their Garmi hosts.[7]

Confronted with this ethnic cleansing of fellow Tajiks, Ahmad Shah Masoud, the Afghan leader of the moderate Jamiat-i Islami movement, turned his attention to supporting the opposition. Backed by Masoud, what emerged was the United Tajik Opposition (UTO), which kept the resistance in the south alive from their bases in Taloqan and Kunduz. The membership was diverse: the Democratic Party of Tajikistan, Lali Badakshan (the Pamiris party), the Rastokhez Popular Front (an intellectual democratic group) and the IRP. Secular Tajiks sought support in Moscow while IRP men lobbied Saudi Arabia, Pakistan and Iran for backing. Meanwhile, more radical Islamist elements maintained their own insurgency. Backed by Wahhabi and Deobandi groups in Afghanistan, the IMT and other factions attacked Tajik government forces, and suspected collaborators, without restraint. There was some local co-operation between UTO and IMT, but the leaders of both factions distanced themselves from this. In Afghanistan, radical Wahhabi Islamists were actually fighting Masoud's men, so the links were always tenuous.

By 1996, the UTO and the Wahhabi radical groups were engaging Russian troops and Tajik government forces all over the country, including the capital. The civil war had reduced the state to a ruin. Over 1,000,000 refugees and IDPs had fled their homes and were dependent on aid agencies to stay alive. The economy had collapsed. Roads, bridges, communications and services were wrecked. An estimated 60,000 were dead – as many as the total death toll of the Sri Lankan civil war. Yet the conflict had raised barely any interest beyond Central Asia, a fact partly explained by its inaccessibility and dangerous nature for journalists – an unprecedented number were killed in the fighting. The government was dependent on Russia to maintain its authority, but it could find no military solution to the protracted guerrilla warfare of the UTP. Equally, the UTO was not strong enough to overwhelm the government.

RUSSIAN AND UZBEK INTERVENTION

The presence of large numbers of Russians and Uzbeks in Tajikistan always made some sort of intervention likely, and the fact that Russian military units had been stationed on the old Soviet frontier made an aggressive solution possible. Russians had been dominant in the political and economic administration of the country, and the Law on Language passed by the Tajik government in 1989 appeared to represent a deliberate attempt to oust Russian influence. Islam Karimov, who was determined to assert Uzbekistan's independence and replace Russian hegemony in the region, was also eager to crush any Islamist forces and prevent Tajikistan from becoming a base for opposition groups which might threaten his regime.[8]

When the civil war broke out, the former Soviet 201st Motor Rifle Division was officially neutral, but government and insurgent groups either purchased or confiscated weapons and equipment. The Russians moved to have the unit placed under the control of the Russian Federation in 1992, and it remained so until 1996, thus providing the Tajik government with an exclusive use of aircraft, armour, transport, weapons and ammunition. Detachments of the 201st took part in actions against insurgents in Dushanbe and Qurghonteppa as they threw the opposition forces back in 1992, but stood idle when government militias cracked down on civilians sympathetic to the opposition in the aftermath of that campaign. However, this alignment meant that the division was attacked by insurgents, and it responded by launching its own operations against rural strongholds. In mid-1993, a joint CIS peacekeeping force was created, bringing more Russian units, Uzbek forces and token battalions from Kazakhstan and Kyrgyzstan (although the latter were subsequently withdrawn) into Tajikistan. The 201st retained its formidable missile and artillery assets with 185 guns and 180 M-72 main battle tanks. Russian border guards, numbering 16,500, were mainly deployed in the south, effectively putting Tajikistan's territorial integrity, as well as its security, into Russian hands.

There are parallels with the conflict in Chechnya, as we shall see. Russian operations in Tajikistan drew less international attention but were contemporary. The motives for intervention, particularly the desire to restore order and reassert influence, were clear. An internal putsch failed to secure power satisfactorily in both cases, and the Russians quickly committed themselves to a military intervention so as to secure control and establish an 'approved' government. Yet, both conflicts degenerated into insurgencies and atrocities which drove the Russian army into more aggressive reprisals. Insurgents in Tajikistan made reference to the Chechen struggle to legitimize their own campaign, and it was no coincidence that Chechen fighters eventually found their way into the conflicts in Afghanistan and Central Asia. At times, the Russian army appeared to be acting almost independently of Moscow. The threats against the civilian population of Grozny may have contrasted with Russian commanders' willingness to negotiate with the UTP at a local level, but there was a common theme: the desire to fulfil their own interpretation of their mission's objectives. Lieut.-Gen. Chechulin, the Russian commander of border guards on the

Tajik–Afghan frontier, for example, believed that negotiated settlements between the Tajik factions were not necessarily binding on his troops.[9] This could be taken to mean that he only acknowledged orders from Moscow, but some felt this echoed sentiments expressed by Russian commanders near the closing stages of the First Chechen War which seemed to be defiant of Moscow's direction. However, the links established by Evgeni Primakov, Director of the Russian Intelligence Service, with the UTO were not part of any elaborate conspiracy but an attempt to construct an avenue for negotiations with the leaders of the opposition. It was these preliminary contacts that led directly to peace talks from 1994.[10]

Russian influence also took political and diplomatic forms. In January 1993, the Minister of Defence was a Russian colonel (and later major-general) Aleksandr Shishlyannikov, and the high command of the Tajik armed forces was dominated by Russians. The year before, Russia had admitted Tajikistan to the rouble zone and taken over its ruined economy. In return, Tajikistan had forfeited its entire gold and currency reserves, as well as substantial amounts of industrial plants, factories and other infrastructure. The introduction of the new currency in 1995, on Moscow's prompting, did nothing to end this dependency. Rahmonov was conscious that he needed Russian backing to stay in power, and there is no doubt that he was a useful tool against the opposition. There was some speculation that Russia was eager to prevent another 'Afghanistan' debacle. By arming and backing its protégé, it could avoid being ensnared in a long-term insurgency but could strike back into Afghanistan should the need arise.

This thinking probably informed Moscow's refusal to accept Uzbek proposals. The Uzbeks had initially supported Nabiev and the Khujandis, a neo-Communist faction closest to the Uzbek border.[11] However, the fall of Nabiev meant that Russia had pushed for the leadership of Rahmonov and the Kulobi clan, and backed their candidate when Uzbek-inspired Khujandis had tried to overthrow Rahmonov and seize power in December 1993. President Karimov tried to get Russia to support Abdul Rashid Dostum, the Uzbek-Afghan warlord who operated in north-western Afghanistan against the Wahhabi and Deobandi jihadists (but who also provided support to Uzbek-Tajiks in the Tajik Civil War). Moscow refused. Rahmonov also began to oust Uzbek-Tajiks from positions of authority in favour of his own men. Karimov could not afford to challenge the Russian policy directly, because it was obvious that Russian military strength was needed to keep Tajikistan from falling into the hands of the UTO. Instead he chose to try to win Russian favour and influence the overall policy as an ally. He gathered the support of the Kyrgyz and Kazakh governments to call for Russian forces to be designated as UN peacekeepers. He stressed that the enemy was a common foe for Russia and all Central Asian republics, labelling all the opposition as 'Fundamentalists'. He also proposed the establishment of joint military bases to secure the country. Karimov's anxieties about the 30,000 Russian troops near Uzbekistan's eastern border were revealed by statements to the international press about Russian neo-imperialism. He was critical of the other republics that contemplated or enacted dual citizenship for Russians in Central Asia, knowing this would mean Moscow's interference in their internal affairs.

The extent of Karimov's concerns led to a change of policy in 1995. He began to make overtures to the Tajik opposition via his Khujandi allies, presumably to create a new coalition against Rahmonov and the Kulyabis. At the same time, he approached Presidents Nazarbaev and Akaev in April of that year to discuss a joint peace plan for Tajikistan. His success appeared to indicate that Russian direction was not required in Central Asia, and that Uzbekistan was providing regional leadership. To put pressure on Moscow, Karimov threatened to withdraw Uzbek, Kyrgyz and Kazakh peacekeepers and then cut railway lines into Tajikistan to hamper the delivery of Russian fuel and goods. But Russia's relationship with Rahmonov gave Moscow the upper hand, and there is some evidence to suggest that Russia has been playing its own diplomatic game.

While the line in Moscow throughout the 1990s was to condemn the excesses of Islamic fundamentalism and the banditry in Tajikistan, there may have been a realization that jihadist terrorism against the Central Asian states kept them dependent on Russia's goodwill and assistance. Ahmed Rashid suggested that there was Russian military assistance to the insurgent IMU in the form of transport aircraft out of

Tajikistan to safety in Afghanistan.[12] This could have been Moscow's clandestine attempt to remove the terrorist threat from Central Asia, but Rashid suspects that Russia is playing a double game. However, it may not be as it appears at all. Moscow has no desire to assist the IMU, which has close links to Chechen fighters. Moreover, since 1995 the 'Russian' border-guard units have been staffed mainly by Tajiks – 12,500 out of the original 16,500 are non-Russians. The fact that they use Russian military aircraft, transport, arms and equipment may have given rise to the confusion. The point is that Moscow's priority was to establish and maintain Rahmonov's 'approved' regime in power and throughout the peace negotiations of the 1990s. In this endeavour, the Russians did not offer concessions to their opponents. Rather, they pressed for every concession they could get from the opposition.

RE-ESTABLISHING PEACE

The turning point in the war came in 1996 with the victory of the Taliban in central and southern Afghanistan. Sayed Abdullah Nuri, the leader of the Tajik IRP, and the government of Rahmonov shared the same concern, that a weakened Tajikistan would offer little resistance to the onslaught of the extremist Taliban. The UN provided the framework for negotiation, but it took several rounds of talks in Moscow, Teheran, Islamabad and Khos Deh in Afghanistan before a peace deal could be agreed. The UN deployed a Mission of Observers to Tajikistan (UNMOT) from as early as January 1993 that helped to secure a ceasefire in 1994.[13]

Each of the participants had their own motives for re-establishing peace. Rahmonov calculated that his dependence on Russia and Uzbekistan for security ultimately weakened his position as leader of the country, and that he was unable to govern with such a narrow base of support. The IRP believed that Russia and Uzbekistan were eager to destroy them, so a *rapprochement* with the government would strengthen their position in Tajikistan and provide a base for agitation against the Central Asian leaders. The Russians and Iranians saw a need to support Masoud as the best hope of victory against the Taliban, and they now urged compromise, while Uzbekistan believed that the best means to protect the Uzbek population inside Tajikistan was to bring the civil war to an end and concentrate their efforts against the radical Islamists threatening their own domestic security. Masoud hoped for Russian, and perhaps even Iranian, military supplies to prosecute the war against the Taliban. Peace was thus re-established by the willingness of the belligerents to compromise, anxiety about a new external threat, the encouragement of external players and the hopelessness of continuing the struggle.

The terms of the peace were eventually accepted. There was a general amnesty for all fighters and exchanges of prisoners. The IRP guerrillas were incorporated into the regular armed forces with success, although there were some exceptions. Tajik refugees were encouraged to return. The IRP was legalized, and there were elections in February 2000. Crucially, a coalition government was formed that included Islamists as well as democrats, nationalists and government factions. Despite accusations of vote-rigging and malpractice, the coalition government was returned with a narrow majority. Surprisingly perhaps, the IRP performed badly, winning less than 10 per cent of the vote. Nevertheless, it was highly significant that the IRP did not resume the war; they accepted the result and went into democratic opposition.

There were, of course, some who wished to continue the fighting. The Khujandis, led by Abdumalik Abdullajanov, the former Prime Minister, believed they might lose power with a compromise peace. Col. Makhmud Khudoyberdiev, an Uzbek-Tajik officer, led an attempt to seize control of Khujand in November 1998. Having taken the provincial capital and the airport, he fortified the single mountain pass that connects the region to the capital further south. The government forces launched a counterattack and, after four days of intense fighting, overran the province, but there were 700 casualties, of whom half were civilians. There were other incidents. In 1999 there was a spate of bombings, assassinations and kidnappings in the capital. Two opposition groups fired on each other, killing five people. In the countryside, government troops fought several skirmishes with splinter groups of the IRP.[14]

The greatest threat to peace was the lack of an economic 'dividend'. Unemployment was widespread, and reconstruction of agriculture and industry was slow because of a lack of domestic revenue or international aid. The UN, which kept dialogue alive between the factions, requested $34,000,000 for reconstruction from the international community, but in 2000 received only $15,000,000.[15] In 2001, the situation was worse. Estimating a need for £85,000,000, it got only a quarter of that sum. The result was that there were shortages of food, water and power. A drought in the period 2000–2005 crippled agricultural production and kept over a million Tajiks dependent on aid from the UN's World Food Programme. Young men who had learned the business of war and who faced unemployment were tempted to emigrate, join organized crime groups, engage in drug-smuggling or seek out rebel bands in the mountains.

The presence of the Taliban did not assist the peace in Tajikistan. Seizing control of central-northern Afghanistan in 1998, they threatened to cross the frontier and wage war on the Tajik government. But they also used Tajikistan as a conduit for their burgeoning drugs revenue, and impoverished Tajiks were all too ready to join the trade. According to Tajik government sources in May 2000, ten times the volume of heroin had arrived in the country compared with 1999.[16] Drug money led to bribery and corruption throughout Tajikistan and fuelled security problems. Drug gangs fought pitched battles with government forces, and the insecurity further delayed economic reform and reconstruction. The government therefore turned to Masoud to fight the Taliban on its behalf, supplying him with arms and equipment. However, this did not prevent his headquarters at Taloqan falling to the Taliban in September 2000, and so a redoubling of effort was required: the Russian Defence Minister, Igor Sergeyev, the Iranian Foreign Minister, Kamal Kharrazi, and President Rahmonov pledged their support to Masoud at Dushanbe in October of that year, and, as a result, the Taliban were checked at Badakhshan. Yet Tajikistan remained in a critical condition, and commentators felt its fate might yet be decided by extremists from outside but also from within.

THE ISLAMIC RENAISSANCE PARTY AND ISLAMISM

Unlike the imported beliefs of the Wahhabis and Deobandis in movements like Hizb ut-Tahrir and the IMU, the IRP was a home-grown faction. It achieved a rare union of 'official Islam' and more radical, underground movements, and was inspired by the anti-Communist resistance of the mujahedin in Afghanistan and by the opportunities presented by the fall of the Soviet Union in 1991. The underground Islamic movement had been led by Mullah Mohammed Rustamov Hindustani in the 1970s; it was he who had introduced ideas from Islamist movements in the Middle East and Pakistan to the Ferghana Valley. He was eventually arrested and died in 1989 in captivity, but one of his protégés, Abdullah Saidov, kept up the momentum of a clandestine movement. Under his *nom de guerre*, Nuri, Saidov formed a group called Nahzar-i Islami (Islamic Knowledge) to spread Islamic training in Tajikistan. As early as 1987, he led a public demonstration in support of the mujahedin at Panj, close to the Afghan border. He was arrested but released the following year, and immediately resumed his work of spreading Islamic literature and organizing his movement, later renamed the IRP.[17]

The IRP was not purely a political and educational pressure group, and it was not long before it developed a military branch in emulation of the Afghan mujahedin. The leader of this wing was another of Hindustani's followers, Muhammad Sharif Himatzoda. He had been raised from peasant stock, trained as a mechanic and joined the mujahedin, establishing contact with the extremist Hekmatyr and the leader of the Jamiat-i Islami of Pakistan. Himatzoda soon established a reputation for ruthlessness and brutality to rival that of the most dedicated Deobandi-inspired fighters.

The IRP had been conceived as a movement in 1990 at Astrakhan by Muslim intellectuals who wanted to see the extension of Sharia law across Russia and the whole Soviet Union. Nevertheless, it was decided to set up independent branches in each of the Soviet republics. While the Russian branch campaigned openly, the Central Asian republics, including the government of Tajikistan, banned the IRP. However, Nuri and Himatzoda convened an illegal gathering in 1991 and agreed to establish an underground newspaper, promote independence and spread Islam. Publicly they claimed to want to establish a democratic state, but some suspected this was window-dressing and that what they really wanted was the introduction of Sharia law and the establishment of an Islamic state. During the 1990 disturbances, the IRP called for the closure of shops that sold pork and alcohol, and demanded that more mosques be opened.

During the civil war, the IRP clearly saw itself as another group of holy warriors doing battle with infidels and their apostate allies. However, the war was not regarded as a jihad by the majority of the country. Instead, it was a power struggle complicated by clans who wanted to establish hegemony over small regions. The IRP could control areas where its warlords could command a personal following, but it lacked a national presence. As with the Afghan mujahedin, the absence of a common enemy created splits, factions and open conflict. The movement was fatally weakened by its lack of unity. Turajonzoda, the 'Official Islam' leader who had joined the IRP, was expelled in 1998 when he accepted the post of Prime Minister from President Rahmonov. In February 2000, IRP hardliners tried to assassinate him in Dushanbe; they opposed his moderate line. The IRP insisted that only one party could implement an Islamic state. Even Nuri was accused by some of being too conciliatory towards the Rahmonov government.

The most obvious divisions came with the plan to incorporate former IRP insurgents into the Tajik armed forces. Several IRP commanders and their followers refused, and some aligned themselves with more extreme groups like the IMT. Namangani, the leader of the IMT, had been a fighter for the IRP during the civil war, but he refused to accept the compromise peace and established a base, in defiance of the Tajik authorities, in the Tavildara Valley. From there he made terrorist raids into Kyrgyzstan and Uzbekistan between 1999 and 2001. Rahmonov tried to deny that terrorists were operating from within Tajikistan, but he secretly ordered former comrades of Namangani to dissuade him from raiding other states. The IRP was divided over the issue, but the leaders complied, and, on three occasions, Namangani and many of his fighters were persuaded to withdraw to Afghanistan. Other IRP gangs refused to join the regime they had spent so long fighting. They remained in the mountains, raiding, ambushing, kidnapping, murdering and robbing to maintain their war effort. The warlord Rakhmon Sanginov constantly raided villages to the north of the capital until the summer of 2001. Cornered by Tajik regulars, he and 45 of his men were killed in a month-long campaign.[18]

Himatzoda and Nuri led the rump of the IRP in peaceful opposition to the government. Nuri was supported by a new generation of IRP men who believed that jihad was not the only way to secure an Islamised Tajik state. Himatzoda also embraced the idea of creating a consensus by incorporating opposition groups in a democratic process. The trappings of Islamism appeared to drop away with this change of heart; Himatzoda trimmed his beard and adopted Western dress. However, some IRP men in government, such as Mirzo Ziyoyev, while rejecting the methods of extremists like the IMU, nevertheless still sympathized with their struggle. They found it hard to abandon the emotional ties they had established as fellow-fighters in the civil war, and their contacts remained alive. However, the IRP was generally opposed to Hizb ut-Tahrir, which had begun to gather support after the civil war. The IRP regarded Hizb ut-Tahrir as a rival organization competing for the same supporters. By associating with a government that was unable to deliver change, they risked losing their followers to a new movement untainted by the war or the regime. But their rivalry was more important than accusations of collaboration. The IRP therefore supported the Rahmonov regime in banning Hizb ut-Tahrir.

The continuing conflict in Afghanistan, with Masoud's Tajik-Afghans fighting on against the Taliban, and the ongoing insurgency in Tajikistan against irreconcilable jihadists (some of whom, like the IMU, had effectively established jurisdiction over remote parts of the country and enjoyed the support of local people who were eager to acquire their money and sell their meagre surplus), not to mention continued corruption, drug-trafficking and lawlessness, made the future look very bleak indeed. Yet Western interest in Tajikistan grew as there was a greater awareness of the international threat posed by jihadists like the affiliates of Al-Qaeda. In the summer of 2001, the US, the EU and Japan pledged $430,000,000 in loans and financial support, doubling the offer of the previous year.[19] Just as important as the donor money was the growing realization across Central Asia that jihadists had little to offer except violence and economic collapse. The civil wars in Afghanistan and Tajikistan convinced many that such extremism was counter productive. The love affair with the mujahedin was perhaps coming to an end.

This feeling helps to explain why support for the IRP declined significantly even in their previous heartlands. Operation Enduring

Freedom, the American-led operation against the Taliban in 2001, smashed the hardliners' ability to supply the jihadists still in Tajikistan. Many of the IMU were killed, and the movement scattered. Inside Tajikistan, mullahs were unable to command public attention as they had done at the height of the civil war. Attendance at mosques and madrassahs declined, and there was something of a re-secularization of public life. Unlike Afghanistan under the Taliban, support for Masoud meant that Pakistani and Saudi funds to develop a radical madrassah culture never materialized. The Tajik government was determined to exclude these foreign influences and banned external funding of religious seminaries as early as 1993. Young people are more eager to get jobs, earn a living and enjoy themselves than ponder the spiritual world, and, as ever, the fate of the family and the clan was uppermost in their minds.

Today, as in Afghanistan, young people feel a desire to put the civil war behind them. The consequences of the war are still to be seen everywhere, and Islamists are, to some extent, blamed for it. However, the government is at risk if it fails to deliver on expected improvements and may face protests, as has occurred in Kyrgyzstan. Moreover, the resurgence of Taliban operations in Afghanistan and the regrouping of the IMT threatens a return to terrorism and destabilization. One can only hope that the pace of reconstruction and the spirit of reconciliation will prevail over the recidivism of state officials and the violent atavism of the jihadists. In 2006, Rahmonov was re-elected.[20] Despite crippling power shortages and accusations of irregularities in the conduct of the election, the Tajiks chose not to re-ignite the civil war. That must surely be an encouraging sign.

Chapter 5

The Afghan Civil War and the Taliban

The collapse of authority in Afghanistan in 1979, the Soviet invasion to restore order, the bloody and protracted civil war and the Taliban regime of the 1990s have left the country with profound and distressing legacies. Yet the consequences not only affected Central Asia; they led ultimately to the formation of Al-Qaeda, a global jihadist movement, and the spectacular terrorist attack of 9/11. Western military intervention later that year, and a long-running insurgency against Coalition forces since, illustrate that the political landscape of the region is still strongly contested. Reconstruction is delayed by the continued fighting, and corruption flourishes in the impoverished economic climate. The costs of conflict and reconstruction are considerable – the Afghan government estimates that it needs $10–15 billion over ten years, while the US spends many billions more on its military campaign to hunt down Al-Qaeda and its associates.[1] But, as Western authorities repeatedly point out, the price of failing to rebuild Afghanistan, like Iraq, may be even greater. A resurgent Taliban, a reinvigorated Al-Qaeda and a perceived victory over the world's strongest Coalition could herald a new, revived era of global terrorism.

The Saur Revolution of 27 April 1978 began the process of collapse in Afghanistan that led directly to Soviet intervention. Daud Mohammad Khan had, as Prime Minister, seized power in a bloodless coup in 1953 but resigned ten years later over the 'Pushtunistan' dispute with Pakistan. The Pushtuns, ethnically akin to the Afghans and only separated from the jurisdiction of Kabul by a border drawn up by the British in the nineteenth century, sought to carve out a new homeland for themselves at the expense of Pakistan's territorial integrity. Daud, himself a Pushtun, had favoured the idea of a separatist movement but was keen to exploit a nationalist-ethnic issue in order to popularize his position at home. The Pakistan government also found it useful to criticize Afghanistan for 'encouraging' the separatists for its own domestic ends. But the result was far-reaching. The severance of relations between Pakistan and Afghanistan meant that Afghanistan was forced firmly into the arms of the Soviet Union as an outlet for its goods and therefore its customs revenue. It is alleged that the USSR in fact dumped a good deal of the Afghan goods they purchased, suggesting what they valued were the contact and influence over a state on their sensitive southern border. With Pakistan and Iran in the American sphere, Afghanistan provided the Soviets with a useful buffer in the region.[2]

For years, Afghanistan was courted by both the US and the Soviet Union in their Cold War rivalry, but by the 1960s the number of Russian advisors was increasing. The Afghan Marxist party, the People's Democratic Party of Afghanistan (PDPA), although divided into two rival factions, Parcham and Khalq, gained support in urban areas, particularly among students and intellectuals. The brief experiment with a limited democracy between 1963 and 1973 merely encouraged the growth of these radical factions, which, in turn, alienated the religious conservatives. The more traditionalist elements of society were also offended by the influx of Westerners on the 'hippy trail', the growth of narco-corruption and the rise of 'foreign' influences. Much of Afghanistan would have been recognizable to Babur of the sixteenth century, but it was the unchanging nature of religion, agricultural life and tribal culture that now seemed under threat from 'modernity'. Nepotism in government, declining state revenue and resentment at Soviet influence brought matters to a head. Daud seized power for a second time in 1973 in what he called a 'revolution', a title designed to appease his Soviet neighbours. The Russians responded: financial aid increased to $1.25 billion by 1979, and in 1977 Brezhnev appeared to give the Soviet seal of approval in a state visit.[3]

In fact, Daud was an unreliable ally. He wore his Communist credentials lightly and would have preferred to make Afghanistan a non-aligned nation. He resented Brezhnev's demands and the influx of yet more Soviet advisors. Indeed, his subsequent moves to bring the dispute with Pakistan to an end were in direct conflict with Soviet policy. Moreover, the death of an official of Parcham, the faction that ostensibly supported him, soon generated fears of a purge of the entire PDPA. Given Daud's true allegiances, this fear had some grounds. The result was that Khalqi and Parcham, led respectively by Barbak Karmal and Mohammed Noor Taraki, launched a coup d'état against Daud. In the mêlée, he was murdered. In the aftermath, thousands of 'bourgeoisie' were arrested.

The Khalqis, who emerged as the dominant faction, could command no consensus. They issued decrees but imposed them with coercion. They demanded land reform and called for women's equality, outraging rural, conservative opinion. Opposition was met with brutality and murder. The infamous Pul-i-Charki prison began to take political prisoners and torture them. On 17 March 1979, Khalqi officials and their Soviet advisors were attacked by a mob chanting Muslim slogans.[4] As anxiety about an Islamist movement destabilizing the southern USSR grew in Moscow, Hafizullah Amin took over as Prime Minister. His method of restoring order was to impose yet more terror and coercion. He executed his rivals, including Taraki. He sent his secret police to suppress, arrest or murder all opposition. Villages which supported the embryonic resistance were razed and the inhabitants butchered.[5] An attempt by insurgents to seize the centre of Kabul was betrayed and the fighters were massacred.

Afghanistan had descended into civil war. But with Iran in turmoil in 1979 and the West deploying medium-range nuclear missiles in

Europe, Moscow felt it had to act to restore order and influence. With Hungary (1956) and the Prague Spring (1968) in mind, the Soviet Union launched an air-mobile *coup de main* on Kabul. Amin was caught and killed by the KGB. A motor rifle division thrust southwards. Within days, the Soviets controlled the main corridors of communication and the urban centres, and had installed their approved candidate, Barbak Karmal, in power. Like Karzai in 2001, Karmal's role was to reunify the political parties, modernize the army, popularize the regime, extend the government's remit and carry out economic development. However, the presence of foreign troops did not endear him to the broad mass of the Afghan people. The USSR's intervention was seen as another form of coercion. This is a precedent that Karzai and the Coalition forces will want to avoid.

THE MUJAHEDIN RESISTANCE AND THEIR INFLUENCE

The Soviet troops made little attempt to win the hearts and minds of the Afghan population. Since the resistance dressed in civilian clothes and attacks against Soviet forces normally took the form of ambushes, the troops often assumed that all Afghans opposed them. A culture of bullying within the Soviet forces also encouraged a similar attitude of punishment towards Afghan civilians. Soviet tactical doctrine, designed for the European theatre, dictated that thrusting along narrow axes, securing lines of communication and destroying utterly any location of resistance by combined armour-infantry-air assault was the method for fighting a conventional operation.[6] The only other experience the Soviets could draw upon was the example of Hungary or Czechoslovakia. In these cases, Soviet forces had moved directly to the main urban centres, and, largely by their presence alone, or with the support of secret police and Special Forces, they had quelled popular protests. Resistance in Afghanistan left the Soviets in a quandary. They had initially treated the campaign as one of quelling civil unrest, but, while the actual situation had moved on, the fighting had not made the transition to a European-type, conventional conflict. The Soviet army had little experience or training in a protracted counter-insurgency role. This explains their techniques of 'clearance', in which they sought to control certain areas by destroying property and fighters in their path and driving out the population.[7]

The Soviets faced several problems in trying to crush the insurgency. They found it impossible to close the eastern border with Pakistan, across which trickled the arms, ammunition and personnel to sustain the resistance. Detachments of Special Forces did eliminate certain groups of fighters, but their own units could be isolated and destroyed at times. The general configuration of the ground – with a complex of mountains, valleys and caves – provided the mujahedin with a large arena for guerrilla operations and plenty of places to conceal themselves. In contrast to the fluid, lightly equipped resistance, many Soviet troops were pinned to the defence of roads, settlements and communications. In fact a third were tied up in this way. In addition, the scorched-earth policy and somewhat indiscriminate use of mines made the civilian population sympathetic to the resistance.[8] In a notorious and cynical example, the Soviets found that their 'butterfly'-shaped anti-personnel mines were easily avoided by the mujahedin, so allegedly a decision was made to apply Disney characters to them in the expectation that Afghan children would try to pick them up. That said, the mujahedin themselves used children to lay mines.[9] Even the Afghan army, which was supposed to be supporting the Soviets, was plagued by desertions, defections, informers, ghost pay rolling and even murders of Russian officers. The Soviet army was also deprived of vital intelligence. Since the resistance rarely used radios, the Soviets needed human intelligence, but the infamous KhAD was only able to provide a limited amount of information.

The mujahedin made up a highly motivated movement with generally good morale. They combined a set of nationalist principles with religious devotion and personal values of honour and courage. Afghan fighters prided themselves on their toughness. They travelled light – a weapon, a blanket or scarf, ammunition and a minimal amount of food. Where the civilian population could not house them, they slept rough. They preferred to fight using hit-and-run tactics, and were far from suicidal, although they were just as capable of pressing home an attack as regular soldiers. For some, death was in the hands of Allah and would mean access to Paradise, but this tended to be an attitude more acceptable to the Arab volunteers. Some Arab fighters who joined the conflict did favour a self-sacrificial and reckless approach to combat, but even they preferred a heroic death. Few wanted to risk crossing minefields, which might result in mutilation; a 'clean' death would mean their body would enter Paradise intact. It was for the same reason that the mujahedin refused the CIA's suggestion to covertly put explosives into Soviet fuel tanks: it did not fit with their preference for masculine, heroic battle albeit in a hit-and-run setting.

The mujahedin knew their own territory and they felt compelled to fight, but the war gave certain individuals a new and important status as fighters. There was some encouragement in the fact that outsiders, especially Arabs, had come to fight on their behalf. Significantly, the status of the mullahs – the religious leaders in rural areas – was elevated. These men provided the ideological justification for the fighting and sustained the resistance psychologically. Nevertheless, the resistance would have struggled without the influx of foreign money and weaponry. The Americans allocated $2 billion to the mujahedin, dwarfing the contribution of the Arab states.[10] They also provided weapons, often purchased from developing countries to avoid being traced back to the US. Critically, the Americans donated Stinger SAMs to bring down Soviet aircraft. The effect of these weapons has been some-what exaggerated, but they did alter the Soviets' ability to deploy air assets and use air mobile units at will.

In histories of the war, many have tended to overlook the weak-nesses of the resistance. Their foreign donors had their own agendas which did not always coincide with the mujahedin's plans. Saudi Arabia, for example, saw the war as an opportunity to contain the Shias in Iran by setting up a Sunni, pro-Wahhabi regime in Kabul. The US was keen to support the resistance as a part of the Cold War effort to undermine the Soviet Union, but the Americans effectively abandoned Afghanistan in the early 1990s once the Cold War had come to an end. Iran supported Shia resistance groups as a means to forestall Soviet influence in the Gulf region. Pakistan saw an opportunity to bring the Pushtunistan proposal to an end, by aligning itself with the Pushtuns against the Soviets. Under Gen. Zia-ul-Haq, the armed forces were

'Islamicized' as part of a policy of gaining popular support across Pakistan; the conflict in Afghanistan provided the perfect backdrop against which to advocate a 'holy war'. These conflicting interests fuelled the underlying divisive and clannish nature of the country.

Although an inspiration to many Muslims in Central Asia, particularly those who resented Soviet rule, the mujahedin were not a homogenous organization but a patchwork of competing factions. Individual leaders, who formed coteries of fighters in varying numbers, were effectively rivals and sometimes represented distinct ethnic groups: Gailani, Mojadidi, Mohammedi and Khalis were Islamists; Hekmatryr was the protégé of Pakistan; Rabbani and Sayyat were pro-Saudi; and the Behesti, Mazari, Akbari and Mohseni were Shia factions (until Iran insisted on the formation of a united Hezb-e Wahdat in 1990); while Ahmad Shah Masoud, Maulawi Haggai and Ismail Khan were more 'secular' warlords. The fighters were often ill-disciplined and disorganized, and lacked co-ordination in their operations. They were better at raiding and when operating at night, but their fire discipline was bad: at times, large quantities of ammunition were expended to no effect.[11]

However, the Afghan Communist government was no better, and the brutality of Karmal's regime was unbridled. KHAD continued to carry out its duties of counter-insurgency, surveillance and intelligence-gathering with considerable violence. The effect of this was to encourage subsequent regimes which lacked popular consensus, including that of Najibullah and the Taliban, to resort to the same repressive techniques. Karmal's attempts to popularize the regime failed. He tried to make it appear more 'Islamic', called for a war of liberation against Pushtuns and restyled the PDPA as the 'National Fatherland Front'. The Soviet army launched more offensives. But there was no lessening of the resistance. In the mid-1980s, Gorbachev could see that the war could not be won using the old techniques. Describing Afghanistan as a 'bleeding wound', he 'retired' Karmal and began to explore ways of 'Afghanizing' the war effort.[12]

The Soviets chose Dr Najibullah, a Parcham member of the PDPA, to improve the situation. He created militias to take over control of road and urban-area protection. These militias were paid subsidies, which created a legacy of increased warlordism. After the Soviet withdrawal, some militias clashed in their attempt to control their fiefdoms, fuelling the slide to civil war. Moreover, despite some larger Soviet offensives in 1986 and 1987, the mujahedin grew bolder: there were major attacks on Kabul, Qalat and Kunduz. The latter had an ominous outcome, however. The mujahedin acted in a heavy-handed way towards the civilian population, costing them their previous popularity. They were in danger of being seen as ruthless brigands, no better than the Najibullah regime itself. Najibullah resorted to buying support and abandoned his attempts to reunite the PDPA. He continued the policy of coercion and ignored the Soviet Union's calls to initiate one of reconciliation.

Following UN shuttle talks, the Soviets had an agreement under which they could leave Afghanistan with a fig-leaf of prestige, but the country they left was in ruins. Violence did not lessen, keeping away reconstruction agencies and the 5,000,000 refugees who had fled across the borders. Cash and munitions kept the war going: Moscow continued to fund and arm Najibullah, who authorized the printing of more money and became dependent on the militias and their warlord leaders, especially those drawn from the minorities. Following an attempted coup by Gen. Tenai in March 1990, it was clear that the army was unreliable, and Najibullah lost no time in carrying out a purge. When the Soviet Union collapsed shortly afterwards, many assumed that the Najibullah regime would disappear, but, surprisingly it survived for a further two years. The reason for this was the weakness of the resistance. Mujahedin factions were divided against each other. Arab volunteers, who massacred prisoners as a matter of course, alienated many Afghans and deterred defections from the Afghan national army. Hekmatyr, Pakistan's chosen warlord, murdered no less than thirty mujahedin leaders and switched sides, joining Najibullah in an attempt to gain political power. In his own volte face, Najibullah tried to recruit Pushtuns into the government, but the fall of Mazar-i-Sharif to Gen. Dostum, on whom he had previously depended to control the north, spelled the end to his ministry. As the various factions converged on the capital, there was a brief period of hope for a compromise. It did not last, and, by February 1993, Afghanistan was in the full grip of a bleak, wintry civil war.

The civil war led to the collapse of any unified authority that could have prevented the rise of the Taliban, and this was the direct result of Pakistan's interventions. As Russian involvement came to an end, the Afghans lost their common enemy. Pakistan and Iran were the only two external players left trying to influence the chaotic division of the country. However, Hekmatyr was initially excluded from the Afghan negotiations for a new government. His response was to launch rocket attacks on the city. Mohammad Rabbani, then heading the interim government, decided to offer Hekmatyr a government post, but this failed and instead his militia clashed with the fighters who belonged to the Shura-i-Nazar (Council of the North), a coalition of groups who had fought the Soviets. As a result, the capital was wracked with factional fighting. In the north of the city were the fighters of Masoud, the defender of the Panjshir Valley and popular 'Lion of the North'. In the centre was the Jumbesh-e Meli Islami, the faction of Gen. Dostum. To the west were the Hezb-e Wahdat Shia fighters of Mazari and also the rival Ittehad-e Islami, the Saudi-backed Sunnis. Outside of the city was Hekmatyr. In 1993, Wahdat attacked Ittehad while Hekmatyr launched an offensive against Masoud's men. Masoud and Ittehad then united to fight Wahdat, and Dostum joined them, thus creating the 'United Front'. There were massacres of civilians, and it is estimated that as many as 10,000 were killed. Looting and rape were widespread. Sectarianism, which had always been a feature of the conflict, worsened with a particularly notorious massacre of Shias at Afshar in February 1993.[13]

In 1995, there was a brief interlude of peace when Ittehad and Masoud's Shura-i-Nazar gained control of the city, but another force now entered the conflict. It was ironic that, just as there was a possibility of order being restored, Pakistan's new faction deepened the war. The *Talib'an*, Pushtuns recruited from the refugee camps and religious schools of tribal north-west Pakistan, were armed and supplied by Islamabad.[14] They took on the divided warlords in the south, driving them out of Kandahar. Hekmatyr, now out of favour with Pakistan, finally accepted a government post as Prime Minister, but the withdrawal of his men from the outskirts of Kabul occurred at just the moment when the Taliban were preparing for a major offensive. They had briefly allied themselves to the Shia Wahdat, but this unholy alliance was brought to an abrupt end by a skirmish outside the city. The Taliban seized and executed the Wahdat leader Mazari. Gen. Dostum had pulled out of Kabul to reinforce his control of the north-west, which left the forces of Masoud to face the Taliban onslaught. Backed by Pakistan's weaponry, fuel, aircraft, funds, intelligence and abundant supplies, Masoud knew that his men might well be trapped in the capital. He therefore withdrew to conduct a campaign from the Afghan-Tajik heartland of the north-east.

Pakistan lost control of its Taliban partners in the 1990s. Islamabad had hoped that they would provide Pakistan with strategic depth, a secure hinterland and, potentially, oil resources from the north of the country (and perhaps from post-Soviet Central Asia too) to aid in concluding the Kashmir question with India.[15] In 1999, the Pakistan government used a similar technique of equipping and arming irregular forces (namely the Kashmiri Separatists), backed with the expertise of Special Forces, to initiate the Kargil offensive. The campaign was unsuccessful, but the protracted insurgency in Kashmir that followed was difficult for the Indian army to suppress. In fact, the logic of the policy of arming and equipping radical Islamist forces should have been obvious to the Pakistanis; they would, when sufficiently secure, pursue their own agenda.

The Taliban attracted many foreign idealists and religious dogmatists. It was a movement of militant and militarist thinkers and a magnet for many who felt angry at the world order, not least the weak position of the Muslim world compared with the West. Mullah Omar, its leader, stage-managed the idea that Afghanistan was the model Islamic state. He claimed that since Allah's power was not divisible, there could be no democracy in Afghanistan. The Taliban idealized the past and claimed that they had been the ones to drive out the Soviets. Osama bin Laden, who had been compelled to abandon his base in Sudan, found support in Afghanistan. Memories of his construction of hostelries for foreign fighters, and funding of their families, during the Soviet occupation were refreshed. He reciprocated the hospitality of the

Taliban by praising their efforts, but he was focused on more distant objectives. He saw the Taliban's regime as a platform for the training of legions of mujahedin who would fight the 'Jews and Crusaders' who controlled the Middle East. Like the leader of the Egyptian Islamic Jihad, Ayman al-Zawahiri, bin Laden was particularly eager to recruit men who would engage in covert operations against the West. He wanted to harness the idealism of the Taliban and take it beyond Afghanistan into a global jihad against all unbelievers. If the mujahedin had defeated the Soviet Union, he reasoned, why not the US too?[16]

Continuing armed resistance and their own ideological doctrines convinced the Taliban that Afghan society needed security and protection. In 1996, Masoud was still defiant in the north-east with the Hazaras in the central-western region and Dostum in Mazar. In a major offensive against Mazar, the Taliban revealed their ruthlessness. They had persuaded the faction of Malik Pahlavan to abandon Dostum's command and join them, thus giving them control of the city. However, fighting broke out between Pahlavan's men and the Taliban soon after, and there were massacres on both sides. As the Taliban reeled from the city and rallied to re-enter it, Dostum's forces arrived and drove them back. In 1998, the Taliban made a third attempt to seize the city, and they succeeded. In three days of killing, they and their Arab allies (led by Mullah Abdul Manan Niazi) slaughtered hundreds. In the Mazar hospital, 30 patients were killed in their beds. There were grotesque episodes of torture: some victims were asphyxiated or boiled alive in the sun by being locked inside metal containers. The Taliban ordered that the corpses were to be left in the streets – no one was permitted to bury them as a mark of shame. Eyewitnesses reported seeing dogs feeding on the carrion flesh. The Taliban were just as furious in their assault on Bamian in 1998, massacring the inhabitants. At Yakaolong, 300 people were killed when they were herded into a mosque which had rockets fired into it. Elsewhere, the Taliban engaged in ethnic cleansing, and razed crops and villages.[17]

The Taliban's fear of uprisings and resistance led to fierce repression. Afghans often refer to the Taliban years with one word: *wahshat* (terror). The religious police, the AMNAM, banned the private ownership of televisions and radios and claimed to want Afghanistan to be 'weapons free' (except, of course, for their own). Moderate Afghans who opposed them were assassinated. There were public executions for dissent. The Taliban also tried to ensure compliance by imposing cultural and social disciplines. There was to be no music, dancing or drumming which might encourage impure thoughts. There was to be no visual representation of living beings, which resulted in the vandalizing of the Kabul Museum, the Bamian Buddhas and other structures. Women were denied employment, which led to the deaths of some war widows through starvation. Stoning was introduced for women accused of adultery. Women had to remain entirely covered in public. In May 2001, all non-Muslims had to wear a yellow patch, a chilling echo of Nazi practices in Europe.

The Taliban exhibited a gross naïveté when it came to international opinion. Mullah Omar refused to negotiate with the UN and, suspicious of all foreigners, took an arrogant and high handed view of NGOs who wanted to assist with reconstruction. The Taliban approached the international oil companies about the routing of pipelines from Central Asia and the country's oil reserves, but they began their discussions with the demand that the companies pay the entire costs of reconstruction. If they won no friends in these situations, they positively enraged the world community by hosting the hijackers of Indian Airlines flight 814 in 1999. But their greatest error was allowing bin Laden to establish his training camps for his global jihad. From its nerve centre in Afghanistan, Al-Qaeda carried out co-ordinated attacks in Kenya and Tanzania in the vicinity of American embassies. These attacks were designed to cause mass casualties – the new signature of the movement. The Americans responded with cruise-missile attacks into Afghanistan which killed some of the fighters in their bases. The Taliban knew that the US had a 'global reach', but they remained defiant and refused to hand over bin Laden and his associates despite American calls to do so.

The decision to harbour bin Laden was not an easy one since relations were somewhat strained. Al-Qaeda was much an ideology as a movement. It represented the aspiration to create a unified Muslim world, purged of its modern Western impurities, corruption and immorality. It was territorial, in that it aimed to recreate the Arab empire of the eighth century. It was a total war mentality too. In 1998, bin Laden issued a *fatwa* that argued that the killing of Western civilians was entirely justified and should be considered the duty of every Muslim. This world-view was intolerant of sectarianism in the Islamic world, since there would be no room for the Shia, Sufi and other branches of the faith. It was also an ideology that implied extermination, grandiose dreams of empire and a single caliphate. And it was an expression of how powerless Al-Qaeda really was. It simply lacked the capacity to mobilize the fractured Muslim world, and its dreams of empire concealed a sense of humiliation and that Islam was weak in comparison with the modern, wealthy and militarily powerful West. Some of the Taliban resented bin Laden's *fatwas* and Arab hubris, although it is also true that some embraced the global idealism of Al-Qaeda. Mullah Omar felt that, according to the tribal tradition of *Pakhtunwali*, he had to be seen to offer hospitality to a former fighter of the Soviet war. He was also eager to continue the stream of funding the Saudi had brought with him and his alliance against Masoud's resistance in the north. Indeed, Al-Qaeda carried out a suicide bombing and killed Masoud on 9 September 2001. And two days later, they attacked New York and Washington, killing 2,893 in the cities and a further 233 on United Airlines flight 93. It was the world's worst terrorist atrocity and was bound to evoke a military response from the US.[18]

The Global War on Terror appeared to be a vague expression of military objectives, and it was unclear just how America's overwhelming military power would be deployed against terrorist organizations which tended to be concealed within civilian populations. But it coincided with American concerns about rogue states, the sponsorship of terrorism and the transfer of WMD. It was also clear that the Americans would make some force adjustments in light of the new threat. There was an immediate stepping up of intelligence-gathering operations, for example. In the case of Afghanistan, it also seemed clear that the US could launch air strikes and perhaps use ground operations to neutralize Al-Qaeda's training camps and its command-and-control structures. Yet there was also a political dimension to achieving these objectives. President George W. Bush put it bluntly to Gen. Pervez Musharaf, the Pakistani head of state: Musharaf would have to terminate his support of the Taliban or face American financial and perhaps even military action. The Pakistan President complied. Uzbekistan, eager to gain American approval, also opened up its air space to the Americans.

With a fleet in the Indian Ocean, stealth bombers making long-range missions from the US and Europe, and Special Forces on the ground co-operating with the Northern Alliance of anti-Taliban fighters, the result was inevitable. The Taliban withered under the air bombardment. Twelve thousand bombs were dropped and 6,700 guided munitions were used. AC-130 gun-ships strafed Taliban positions, and cruise missiles destroyed the training camps and infrastructure. The operations were so swift that the media struggled to keep up. They accepted Taliban offers to film wounded Afghans in hospital to achieve some sort of journalistic 'balance', but the air assault represented the most accurately targeted one in history. Never before had military forces possessed such a capacity to discover and destroy their enemies so precisely. Attack helicopters could hover great distances from the target zone and pinpoint individual fighters, both day and night and in variable weather conditions. The only opportunity the Taliban got to retaliate was in a prisoner revolt in Mazar. It was a hopeless and point-less act of resistance that concluded with the fall of Kunduz on 26 November 2001, a very one-sided campaign.

THE KARZAI GOVERNMENT

The immediate questions at the end of the conflict on 9 December 2001 were: What sort of government would Afghanistan have? How would the country be reconstructed? At the Bonn Conference on 3 December, six neighbouring states, Russia and the US agreed that Afghanistan should have a multi-ethnic, freely elected government. This was an encouraging start, showing that the self-interest of foreign states had perhaps, finally, been put aside. The problem was that the Taliban and some of the warlords, including Dostum, were not involved in the negotiations. An interim administration was, nevertheless, accepted. Entitled the 'Emergency Loya Jirga', it was led by the moderate Pushtun Hamid Karzai.[19] Karzai commands no party of his own and has aroused some suspicion because he is favoured by the United States. However, he is a member of the influential Popolzai clan and embodies the widespread feelings of disaffection with the Taliban and the protracted wars. Initially a supporter of the Taliban, his father's murder turned Karzai against the Pushtun movement. In 2001 he was eager to establish a more permanent political authority. He, his foreign partners and the Loya Jirga quickly moved to establish a currency, a supreme court, UN support for refugee repatriation and reconstruction, and a human-rights commission. Afghanistan also obtained the International Security and Assistance Force (ISAF) under the command of the British Maj.-Gen. John McColl. This group, while initially small, provided a vital deterrent to warlords who might be tempted, as in 1993, to sweep into the capital.

Afghanistan's needs are simply overwhelming.[20] In short, it requires money, trust between factions, the subsuming of the militias (with a strength of 45,000) into the armed forces and an expansion of civil power in the form of the police. The country depends on donor money for reconstruction, but it needs to maintain a sustained growth of 9 per cent per annum to become a viable economy. It faces some big challenges. Its army and police are barely trained, and individual personnel can be bribed. Much of the cash available is generated by drugs money. Opium production currently generates $2.3 billion a year, and, in some parts of the country, it has been more lucrative than other types of farming. Although ostensibly a democracy, only 1.5 million of the potential 10 million voters were registered in 2004, and there was some disquiet that government and opposition candidates had not been prosecuted for their alleged war crimes. The track record of the warlords has also caused concern, and their loyalty to the regime is very much in doubt. When Jawed Ludin, the Chief of Staff of the Afghan National Army, announced that he was considering arming the militias to augment the small police and state military forces in June 2006, there was anger and fear in southern Afghanistan.[21] Habibullah Jan, a former militia commander who had become an MP for Kandahar, predicted that this would create a lawless group of 'thieves and looters' just as it had done under the Soviets. International observers were also concerned that it would strengthen the warlords at the expense of the central government. In fact, the government has found it very difficult to prevent the formation of private armies. There has been a danger that these militias simply regard the enemy as the foreign forces in their midst and not the Taliban. This was evident when protests erupted in Kabul in May 2006 following a road-traffic accident involving American forces. Suicide attacks took place in the capital in June, although the victims were Kabuli civilians. As corruption flourishes among government officials and their security forces, the Taliban's argument that they aim to root this out as well as driving out the foreigners gains greater currency.

Afghanistan's security situation is just one of several concerns. The physical infrastructure is in ruins, and the country needs to build modern public-sector institutions which allow market-led development. In the north, there were encouraging signs in 2004–6. Agriculture is recovering, despite the problem of landmines. The return of many of the 5,000,000 refugees has brought in much-needed manpower. Westernized Afghans have also injected new vigour into the economy. However, while Afghanistan has received £2–3 billion in aid since 2001, only 15 per cent of the donor money has been allocated to the government, undermining its legitimacy.[22] There have been rumours of waste, particularly in large reconstruction projects. A great deal of money allocated to Afghanistan is actually absorbed by the presence of aid agencies like the UN. But the project is vast. In 2001, almost all the roads, bridges and much of the domestic housing needed repair. With virtually no organized taxation, the government relies on customs revenues to generate a surplus income, but the people have little in the way of food, clothing, medical care and sometimes even accommodation. Infant malnutrition stands at 50 per cent. Infant mortality stands at 150 per 1,000. Life expectancy is 41 to 43 years. In education there is a lack of schools and trained teachers, but pupils drop out in order to earn money, often in public-works schemes like road-mending, just to stay alive. Armed groups use extortion to maintain their influence, and brigandage is common in rural areas.

David Tarr of the University of California has identified a model of nation-building needs for Afghanistan,[23] suggesting that it needs the '6M': manpower, money, machinery, materials, markets and management. He has added to this the 'LE and FP', Law Enforcement and Free Press, continuing with PIS (Physical and Ideological Security), PLC (Political Legitimacy and Consensus), GGDA (Good Governance, Democracy and Accountability), I&I (Infrastructure and Incentives) and, finally, PS (Popular Support). Yet Afghanistan needs more than this. It needs a sustained period without foreign intervention and an ideology of reconciliation, which will take time to evolve. The survival of Afghan democracy will depend on economic growth and stability.

The Americans encouraged other NATO partners to assist in the security of the country in 2006. However, the reluctance or refusal of some European states to participate has caused doubt about the future of the alliance and some concern to Karzai's government.[24] Even the troops that were deployed were often restricted in their operations by their governments. Spanish troops in Herat, for example, rarely left their compounds. German troops refused to permit other national forces to use their helicopters. Each nation has a different interpretation of what a provincial reconstruction team can do, resulting in uneven development. In the south, British forces were not given permission to tackle the opium fields, since this, they were told, was the remit of the Afghan government. Extending the authority of the government though has been a tough assignment, not helped by the rifts between Afghanistan and Pakistan.[25] The Taliban have put up some stiff resistance. A Royal Fusiliers battalion was engaged in almost a hundred days of continuous combat. Small detachments of the Parachute Regiment were forced to fight for days as the Taliban enveloped their positions, although the so-called 'platoon houses' tactics were deliberately designed to draw their insurgent opponents into killing zones. The civilian casualties that have resulted from the fighting, and the snatching of suspected Taliban leaders, have caused anger among Afghans. When properties are destroyed and people killed, it is hard to appreciate that the West has come to carry out reconstruction.

Despite the continuing insurgency by the Taliban in the south, the religious zealots have little that is constructive to offer Afghanistan. Their brutality, like that of the pro-Soviet regimes before them, was counter-productive. The Taliban practised the very crimes they claim they had come to stop. Their idealism blinded them to the realities of the situation. Security and protection of 'Islamic culture' (as they interpreted it) at the expense of human rights and free expression condemned the country to stagnation. They failed to see that the values of civil liberty were not Western 'evils' but universal ones, essential to any society. The Taliban feared difference and they feared change, which are the principles of modernity. They denied global linkages in terms of ideas and economics, and this explains their desire to avoid negotiation and dialogue. Their 'do or die' philosophy is evidence of their weakness. Like the authoritarian regimes of the twentieth century, they demanded of their followers a self-sacrificial, total-war mentality to make up for their evident material deficiencies. The fantasy realm of fighting for a greater Muslim empire and doing battle with the overbearing West gives them the prestige they lack in the real world. Al-Qaeda and the Taliban share this delusion, and ultimately, they will share the same fate.

Chapter 6

The Islamic Movement of Uzbekistan/Turkestan and Regional Insurgency

The most notorious terrorist organization of Cental Asia is the Islamic Movement of Uzbekistan (IMU), known since 2001 as the Islamic Movement of Turkestan (IMT). It is a deeply ideological group, steeped in the theories and techniques of jihadism, and could be regarded as the Taliban of the Pamirs. It is characterized by its anti-democratic vitriol and its equally splenetic condemnation of the Uzbek government. Its cadres are young, violent and strongly influenced by Salafest Wahhabi doctrine. In three campaigns it waged between 1999 and 2001 against Uzbekistan and Kyrgyzstan, it earned a reputation for ruthlessness and brutality. Police officers who were kidnapped were beheaded; the Movement's sub-units were virtually wiped out in pitched battles with the security forces; if forced to withdraw, they would shoot their own wounded rather than let them fall into the hands of their enemies; even those among their own ranks who tried to take advantage of an Uzbek government amnesty were executed. It is estimated that they and their allies control 70 per cent of the regional drugs trade to fund their organizations. Despite their violent history, however, they have suffered major setbacks. Although they once had bases in Tajikistan and Afghanistan, they were scattered by Operation Enduring Freedom in 2001. Their 'alumni' have since tried to regroup, making suicide-bomb attacks in Uzbekistan and issuing new threats, but they have failed to achieve any of their objectives.[1]

In September 1998, Tohir Abdoulalilovitch Yuldeshev and Juma Namangani (whose real name was Jumaboi Ahmadzhanovitch Khojaev) announced the formation of the IMU in the Taliban-dominated city of Kabul. Concurrently, the IMU was aligned with the International Islamic Front (IIF) of Osama bin Laden. Eager to acquire nuclear material and expert knowledge from disaffected residents of the former Soviet Union, bin Laden welcomed the IMU as another element in his Salafest Wahhabi Al-Qaeda foundation, which is what the IIF was sometimes called. The IMU leaders, for their part, were conscious that they needed the manpower, expertise and, crucially, the funds that Al-Qaeda and the Taliban could provide if they were stand any chance of fulfilling their ambitious goals. Yuldeshev outlined the aims of the IMU as the creation of an Islamic state by means of a violent overthrow of the secular governments of Central Asia, particularly Uzbekistan.

An examination of the original text of the IMU's 1998 declaration yields some interesting details which might otherwise be overlooked. The Islamist agenda, as one would expect, is a key aspect: 'We declared a Jihad in order to create a religious system, a religious government. We want to create a sharia system.'[2] However, Yuldeshev referred to the inequalities of power as much as transgressions against the faith in his claim that the IMU was 'Fighting against oppression within our country, against bribery, against the inequities – and also the freeing of our Muslim brothers from prison . . .We consider it our obligation to avenge [those that have died in prison] and nobody can take this right away from us.' Much like their hosts the Taliban, the IMU sought to establish political and religious justifications for their attempts to seize power, but it was surprising to find an inherent criticism of other jihadist movements. Yuldeshev argued, 'We want the model of Islam which has remained from the Prophet, not like the Islam in Afghanistan or Iran or Pakistan or Saudi Arabia – these models are nothing like the Islamic model.' These remarks hint at a long-standing tension between the Wahhabism of bin Laden and the interpretation of the IMU leaders and, moreover, reflect a common set of fault lines that divides all jihadists. Yuldeshev believed that 'Before we build an

Islamic state we primarily want to get out from under oppression. We are therefore now shedding blood, and the creation of an Islamic state will be the next problem . . . We don't need foreign contacts because our roots are deep and are located in our homeland.' The 'deep roots' are a reference to the anti-Communist Basmachi resistance of the 1920s; Yuldeshev clearly believed that Karimov's regime was merely an extension of the old Communist order. The comment about foreign contacts is, however, a curious one, particularly when foreign volunteers (as opposed to Central Asians) have been a prominent feature of the movement. The remark may have been intended for an Uzbek audience, to assert the purity of the cause and not deter nationalists, but it may also have been intended to warn other jihadists like Al-Qaeda not to try and direct the organization (a point that had created some irritation between 'Afghan'-Arabs and mujahedin in the 1980s). On one point, though, there was no doubt at all. Negotiation or compromise was not to be considered. Yuldeshev bellowed, 'We do not repent our declaration of Jihad against the Uzbek government. *Inshallah*, we will carry out this Jihad to its conclusion.'

The uncompromising attitude of the IMU can be traced back to the months immediately after Uzbeksitan's independence. Yuldeshev, a fiery mullah, had led a protest delegation at Namangan in the Ferghana Valley in December 1991 against the town's mayor.[3] The dispute centred on the mayor's refusal to grant permission to build a new mosque, fearing the radical purpose to which Yuldeshev and his followers would put it. Yuldeshev and others stormed the local Communist Party of Uzbekistan (CPU) offices and occupied them. Unsure of the intentions of this apparent fringe group, the government took no action. This only emboldened Yuldeshev further. Having already acquired funding from Saudi Arabia and gathered some 5,000 activists about him, he imposed strict prayer regimes on local people.[4] He insisted that women give up their traditional colourful scarves and embroidered clothing in favour of white burqas. Vigilantes enforced these rules and carried out night patrols to combat crime. Shopkeepers were also subject to spot-checks to keep prices stable. New madrassahs were opened, each propagating Yuldeshev's radical brand of Salafest Wahhabi Islam. In Namangan, his mosque was adorned with a slogan expropriated from his former Communist masters but which also pointed to his desire to create a new caliphate across Central Asia. It read simply: 'Long Live the Islamic State'.

Yuldeshev had issued a challenge to the Uzbek government as early as the spring of 1991, calling upon Karimov to introduce Sharia law across the country. Arrogantly, Yuldeshev assumed that as the Soviet Union was tottering to its final collapse, it would inevitably take with it all the Communist regimes of Central Asia. He therefore called upon Karimov to debate the future in Namangan from what he believed was a position of strength. This belief explains why he split from the IRP: he was critical of its decision to work with the government and to participate in parliamentary elections. Yuldeshev argued that what was needed was an Islamic revolution, which, like the Iranian model, would enjoy overwhelming popular support. Forming his own revolutionary party, Adolat (Justice), he deliberately set up to rival the IRP and undermine its support. Building mosques and madrassahs across the Ferghana Valley with foreign funds, 'official Islam' and IRP spokesmen were unable to stem the growth of this Saudi brand of radicalism. Other radical groups also flourished, including Hizb-i-Islami (Party of Islam), Islam Lashkarlary (Fighters for Islam) and Tauba (Repentence). Karimov initially tried to conciliate and agreed to meet with Yuldeshev at Namangan in April 1991, but the public meeting degenerated into a heated argument, largely because it was impossible for Karimov to fulfil the militants' demands without dismantling the state. However, Karimov, who had to handle the more pressing matter of transition from the Soviet Union, did not act against the radicals until the storming of the CPU headquarters that December. Four months later, the crackdown began with a handful of arrests, but Yuldeshev and several of his followers did not wait for the full force of the state to fall upon them: they fled across the border to Tajikistan.

THE IMU LEADERSHIP AND CAMPAIGNS IN THE '90S

Yuldeshev used his credentials as an imam to embark on an odyssey of fund-raising and networking in order to fund a military campaign and overthrow the Karimov regime. After a brief period studying at an IRP-run madrassah in Tajikistan in 1992, he was forced to move on again by the outbreak of the civil war. Like many IRP leaders, he sought refuge in Afghanistan and assisted in leafleting, but he soon realized that he would have to establish more extensive networks of support if he was ever going to realize his aim of seizing power in Tashkent. He travelled to Pakistan, Saudi Arabia, Iran, the United Arab Emirates and Turkey, picking up information about the ideology and methods of Islamist groups. Perhaps the most important organization he made contact with, however, was Pakistan's ISI. They gave him funds and allowed him to establish a base at Peshawar, the city that stands as the gateway of the lawless North-West Frontier Province. Between 1995 and 1998, Yuldeshev was able to make contact with a variety of jihadist groups. The Jamiat-i-Ulema Islami, the organization that provided funds for the Taliban, also raised cash for Yuldeshev and helped move his follow-ers into Pakistan's radical madrassahs. Critically, the Arab-Afghans, who were allies of the Taliban, provided him with an introduction to bin Laden.[5] Uzbek volunteers were also able to train in terrorist tactics in Afghan or at frontier bases through their madrassah contacts. These international contacts helped Yuldeshev build even wider networks.

Although unconfirmed, it is likely that Yuldeshev received funds from Islamist 'charities' and front organizations, some of which concealed official intelligence services. Uzbeks exiled to Saudi Arabia in the 1920s, many of whom had become Wahhabis, may have been an obvious point of initial contact, but Saudi businessmen also chan-nelled funds into Yuldeshev's organization, and there may have been contacts with the chief of Saudi intelligence, Prince Turki al-Faisal. A more certain aspect of his odyssey is that Yuldeshev travelled to Chechnya during the first war; from there he advocated a militant-spir-itual and armed Islamic revolution in Uzbekistan. This platform was carefully chosen. Apparently speaking from the heart of the Islamic struggle against infidels, he was aiming not just to broadcast the anguish of fellow Muslims but to establish himself as the leading spokesman of the wider Central Asian cause. His audience was clearly the one that lay across the Caspian to the east, but some Chechens would later join the IMU and fight in the hills of Kyrgyzstan and

Uzbekistan to assist their former friend and ally. This sort of linkage was also evident in Yuldeshev's visits to Turkey. Here he made contact with Islamists and argued that a pan-Turkic caliphate in Central Asia would directly assist a similar grouping in Turkey itself. Meanwhile, funds were secretly carried into Uzbekistan to help establish sleeper cells which would provide crucial support to a future insurgency.

The other important exile from Uzbekistan in 1992 was Juma Namangani, the former Soviet paratrooper and Afghanistan veteran who had undergone a radical 're-conversion' to Islam after fighting the muja-hedin.[6] Namangani had been involved in the storming of the CPU offices in his hometown and, like Yuldeshev, was on the run because of Karimov's crackdown. He had arrived in Kurgan Tyube, a southern province of Tajikistan, with a following of 30 militant Uzbeks and a handful of Arabs who had been funding Adolat, Yuldeshev's radical party. Gradually more Uzbeks joined Namangani's group, as well as foreign volunteers who had grown disillusioned with the Afghan Civil War. Arab fighters saw in Namangani's movement a chance to project the international jihad beyond the squalid and desultory struggles in Afghanistan. His expertise in Soviet army weaponry, explosives, tactics and drills made him particularly valuable, but it was his desire for action that was attractive to a growing body of militant men. The IRP made use of his experience and skills in the Tajik Civil War, directing him to the Tavildara Valley as a base of operations in 1993. IRP men also joined his band, and, although he twice lost Tavildara, his personal daring and successful ambushes against Tajik government forces in Gorno-Badakhshan and the Karategin Valley earned him a glowing reputation. Namangani directed one critical action at the Haboribot Pass and gained the respect and grati-tude of the entire IRP, a fact that was later to protect him from the wrath of the Uzbek and Kyrgyz authorities. The Tajik Minister of Emergencies, Mirzo Ziyoyev, was once the IRP's chief of staff and therefore Namangani's commander. Namangani called him 'brother' and Ziyoyev acted a key negotiator with the IMU in the late 1990s, producing bitter criticism from Karimov. Given these close contacts, Karimov believed the Tajik govern-ment was colluding with the jihadist terrorists.

Nevertheless, Namangani was something of a liability to the IRP even during the civil war, and the sincerity of his jihadist credentials

seemed to be in doubt. His former comrades described his understanding of Islam as rudimentary. It was not religion that directed his
actions but a desire to take risks and effect immediate changes. While
understanding the importance of strict discipline to overcome the
stress of combat, Namangani was nevertheless sometimes given to
insubordination and tended to act with rashness rather than think
through any careful strategy. His military experience in Afghanistan
had schooled him in the art of guerrilla warfare, but it is likely that the
jihadists simply offered him a sense of purpose, a 'mission', which
made those skills valued. Moheyuddin Kabir, the principal advisor to
the IRP's leadership in the civil-war period, noted that Namangani was
'easily influenced by those around him . . . shaped by his own military
and political experiences rather than Islamic ideology', and that his
hatred of the Uzbek government 'is what motivates him above all'.[7]

Namangani refused to accept the compromise peace in Tajikistan
in 1997 and became an embittered outlaw rather than a 'heroic leader'
of a jihadist movement. Ziyoyev had to persuade him to end the
fighting after long negotiations, but even when the renegade leader
agreed, he retained his base in the Tavildara Valley with a small
entourage of Uzbeks and foreign fighters. This bandit-in-waiting
eventually established himself in Hoit near the Kyrgyz border with a
community of 40 Uzbeks and Arabs, as well as his Tajik wife and
daughter. With a dismal performance in farming, he turned to running a haulage business between Dushanbe and Garm. The most
lucrative cargo was heroin; Namangani had few qualms about shipping narcotics in order to feed his followers, who were growing in
number. Essentially, his reputation meant that disillusioned former
fighters drifted to his headquarters, as did a large number of Uzbek
radicals who were the targets of Karimov's regime. Eventually, by
1999, there were 200 men at Hoit, drawn from Uzbekistan, Tajikistan,
Chechnya and the Middle East, some with their families. They urged
Namangani to lead an international force against the Central Asian
regimes. However, the most critical influences came from two events
in 1997. The first was the fact that the Taliban had taken power in
Afghanistan. The second was the arrival of Namangani's former
leader, Tohir Yuldeshev.

Yuldeshev and Namangani were, in many ways, no further forward in achieving their goals than they had been in that fateful attack on the CPU offices in 1991, but they resolved to change the situation. Although Namangani had been well equipped and had commanded a large force in the Tajik Civil War, he had lost his manpower and much of his firepower. He and Yuldeshev had lost their erstwhile allies, the IRP, to a government of national reconciliation which featured large numbers of former Communists. The remaining base at Tavildara could be closed under the new Tajik government's pressure. However, both men knew that the Taliban were likely to be sympathetic to their cause and that Yuldeshev's networks provided them with an opportunity.

However, there had been some development in Uzbekistan itself. Yuldeshev had ordered a variety of vicious atrocities against Uzbek security personnel, resulting in a government crackdown. Eager to snuff out the violence before it gathered momentum, Karimov's regime condemned the indoctrination of Islamists, made a number of arrests and passed the Law on Freedom of Conscience and Religious Organisations (1998), which demanded registration of mosques and their ulema.[8] Family members of Yuldeshev and Namangani were forced to denounce them as terrorists, and Namangani's mother was subjected to public humiliation until she cursed him. The government and police had threatened those who defied the regime, and there had been accusations of arbitrary arrest, intimidation and even torture of suspects. The Uzbek government's methods were undoubtedly strict, but this was precisely because it felt so threatened. Karimov had been enraged by terrorist attempts to assassinate him and by the gruesome murder of loyal government employees. The effect of this crackdown, of course, had been the alienation of many young Muslim men. Corruption, relative inequalities in wealth and high unemployment added to their anger or despair. Yuldeshev and Namangani, having provoked a stronger reaction from the Uzbek government, now saw their chance to capitalize upon growing internal unrest.

The two leaders decided to move to Afghanistan as a base of operations against the Uzbek government. This was, given Yuldeshev's meetings with the Taliban that year, a natural step. Already the Taliban were offering their newly-won state as a haven for other terrorist organizations, including Al-Qaeda, which had been forced to leave Sudan in 1996. Yuldeshev's brand of Sunni extremism complemented the Salafest Wahhabi and Deobandi ideologies. The Taliban regarded the IMU as an ally against Karimov because the Uzbek leader had already announced his implacable opposition to the Kabul regime. Moreover, bin Laden was eager to develop Yuldeshev's Adolat as a branch of his own organization. Consequently, Yuldeshev and Namangani announced the creation of the IMU in 1998 in Kabul, committed to the destruction of the government in Tashkent.[9]

The results of the new training facilities afforded to the IMU in Afghanistan were soon apparent: a wave of car bombings across the Uzbek capital in February 1999. Thirteen were killed and 128 injured. In Kyrgyzstan in May of the same year, a similar plot was uncovered before it could be initiated. On 2 April, a shoot-out with an alleged jihadist gang outside Tashkent left eight of the militants dead. Initially, Karimov was convinced that secular political opponents had orchestrated the attacks, particularly members of the Erk and Birlik parties. However, among the 2,000 suspects arrested, there were many Islamists, and it was not long before the Uzbek government regarded the IMU as responsible. Karimov believed that a coalition of his foreign rivals had supported the atrocities, including Pakistan, Turkey and Tajikistan. In particular he referred to the Taliban and Chechen jihadists in the IMU's support network. The lack of specific focus probably indicated just how little the Uzbek government knew about the attackers, although Uzbekistan's intelligence services were not devoid of information. The government appeared to be concerned that militants and democrats might forge an alliance and take control of the Ferghana Valley, as in Tajikistan. As always, conspiracy theorists and cynics argued that the Uzbek security services were probably behind the attacks themselves, creating an opportunity for a crackdown against opposition groups.[10] In fact, Karimov did not need the bloody murder of so many to rationalize such a policy. There is plenty of evidence to show that he was genuinely furious about the attacks since they undermined the tough, impregnable image he liked to project. Similar ideas that renegade members of his clan, or those who aimed to separate the Ferghana Valley from Uzbekistan were behind the attacks lack any substantiating evidence.

Karimov's first response was a diplomatic offensive, but this was only partially successful. He tried to undermine the IMU by deliberately appealing to the Taliban. However, at a meeting in Kandahar in June, Mullah Omar refused to negotiate unless Uzbekistan recognized the legitimacy of the Taliban government. Typically, the Taliban engaged in deception, denying they were assisting the IMU and refusing to extradite any of their members. Relations with Turkey were just as fruitless. The Turks, incensed by accusations that they had assisted the IMU, broke off diplomatic relations. This did not deter the Uzbek courts from convicting 22 men of terrorism, accusing them of receiving support from Afghanistan, Turkey, Pakistan and Chechen trainers. Karimov also exerted pressure on Tajikistan. He accused Rahmonov's government of harbouring the IMU; it is true that the terrorists were operating from a base in the Tavildara Valley. However, Rahmonov's authority was hardly accepted in some of the more remote parts of the country, and the government had to rely on former IRP comrades to persuade the IMU to evacuate to Afghanistan. Nevertheless, Uzbekistan's diplomatic efforts to neutralize the IMU did not prevent a terrorist offensive against Kyrgyzstan in the late summer of 1999. It was clear that tougher measures were needed.[11]

Namangani cultivated his image as an Islamist freedom fighter by actually avoiding media coverage, but his campaign was reliant on the myth rather than the reality of his power. Despite an offensive of kidnapping and murder in southern Kyrgyzstan, and a declaration of jihad against Uzbekistan in August 1999, he avoided the limelight. He let his reputation flourish instead. Like bin Laden, it was the clandestine nature of the man that spread his appeal and allowed rumours to develop. The real, as opposed to the mythologized, Namangani, was able to combine his experience of organizing and fighting an insurgent campaign with this growing reputation to mobilize an increasing number of men. Some were styled 'sleepers', with instructions to assist the IMU fighters when needed. While this appears to have been a clever strategy to enlist the local population, it could also be seen as evidence of the IMU's relative weakness. Namangani was unable to command mass support despite the relative unpopularity of the Karimov regime. He was unable to arm all of his potential fighters and so relied on unarmed cells to assist his cause. This weakness was confirmed by his reliance on external support to maintain his cause. The Taliban provided the bases and weaponry. Osama bin Laden, Islamist front organizations, Pakistani madrassahs and Saudi benefactors provided the crucial funding. Drug-trafficking, over which the Taliban asserted their control, also provided substantial financial backing. Moreover, the campaign of 1999, far from unseating the Uzbek or Kyrgyz governments, was a token gesture of futile violence. The killings achieved nothing. They did not advance the cause of jihad or the caliphate at all. Like terrorism the world over, such tactics confirm its lack of mass support and military power or, to put it more simply, the utter weakness of the movement.

JIHADIST OPERATIONS IN KYRGYZSTAN AND NARCO-TERRORISM

Despite his links with the Taliban, Namangani's forward base of operations was still the Sanguor Training Camp in the Tavildara Valley.[12] This narrow gorge provided ample cover against air strikes and could be protected from a series of defiles. As it was close to the Afghan border, funds and some logistics could be brought in, but food supplies were also procured from the local Tajik population. It was not that they were necessarily sympathetic to the cause, but they needed the revenue from selling their produce. That said, Namangani cultivated his reputation among local Tajiks, marrying a Tajik woman who had been widowed during the civil war. This achieved the dual purpose of cementing Uzbek–Tajik links for the IMU and marking Namangani out as a pious Muslim: it is especially blessed to marry, and therefore support, a woman who has been widowed in a jihad. Namangani also extended his contacts to create a network of sympathizers into the north of Tajikistan. To improve relations with the authorities, he promised not to interfere in Tajikistan's politics, arguing that he was only opposed to the Uzbek and Kyrgyz governments. Although he appeared to be conciliatory, this was a necessary tactical judgement since he feared the Tajik government might move against him. In the event, it was not entirely successful, particularly as the Rahmonov regime came under increasing pressure to deal with Namangani, deporting him in the winter of 1999–2000 and again in 2000–2001.

In preparation for Namangani's first campaign, the IMU ordered its 'sleepers' to return to Uzbekistan in the spring of 1999 and began the deployment of truckloads of ammunition and supplies through Tajikistan. Near the border, this matériel was transferred to mules and horses to make the crossing of the mountains. The route the insurgents followed took them into the Uzbek exclave of Sukh and the Tajik exclave of Vorukh inside Kyrgyz territory. These two zones acted as staging posts, since – regardless of their sovereignty – they are both populated largely by Tajiks supportive of the IMU. Vorukh had once been a Basmachi stronghold, and its mullahs were strongly in favour of a jihad. From a strategic point of view, the zones' proximity to the Ferghana Valley made them very useful, and since both lay inside Kyrgyzstan, it was difficult for the Uzbeks to operate against them. In 2001, the Uzbek and Kyrgyz governments were close to concluding a settlement that would create a land corridor for Uzbekistan in return for territory elsewhere, but news of the proposal was criticized by the Kyrgyz public and the plan was abandoned. In fact, the Kyrgyz authorities also had their doubts about the scheme since they feared that territorial adjustments might encourage separatism. Their anxieties had some justification. Looking southwards into Tajikistan, with its autonomous regions and recent memories of clan-based civil war, the Kyrgyz had no wish to replicate that situation.

The first IMU operations took the Kyrgyz government by surprise. On 9 August 1999, a group of twenty-one men took four officials captive and demanded a ransom, with free passage to Afghanistan. Without the assets or experience of counter-terrorism, the Kyrgyz government capitulated and allegedly paid the kidnappers $50,000. Two weeks later, IMU kidnappers seized twenty hostages including a general and four Japanese.[13] This time the Kyrgyz army was deployed to locate the kidnappers in Batken Province. There were skirmishes with IMU units, which drove the kidnappers back towards the mountainous border. Some of the hostages were released, and, with the assistance of Japanese intelligence officers, there were some negotiations. These revealed the

IMU's thinking. The kidnappers demanded another ransom and the release of several thousand Uzbeks held in Karimov's prisons. But they did not have it all their own way. The Kyrgyz army located and engaged the IMU detachments. As a major offensive got under way to sweep them southwards back into Tajikistan, negotiators managed to persuade the the IMU to release the Japanese captives and several more Kyrgyz.

The Uzbeks also participated in the counterattack. Uzbek aircraft made strafing runs into Tajikistan as far south as Garm and Tavildara, resulting in civilian casualties. Further air raids in southern Kyrgyzstan, in Batken and Osh, led to the deaths of twelve Kyrgyz farmers. These attacks suggest that the Uzbeks wished to tackle the IMU at a distance to prevent further bomb attacks against their capital. They also reveal the eagerness of the Uzbek government to project their power beyond their own borders.[14] However, although the deaths of Tajik and Kyrgyz civilians suggested a disproportionate response, it is now clear that, in some cases, impoverished Kyrgyz and Tajik herders joined the IMU for cash. In Batken, unemployment stood at between 60 and 90 per cent. Agriculture ruined by salination, shortages of electricity, the closure of factories and a fundamental shortage of food, decent standards of living and prospects served to drive some young men towards the ranks of the insurgents. However, it is also true that the majority of Kyrgyz fled the IMU onslaught, fearful that the mountains would become a war zone, as has happened in Tajikistan during the civil war. Overwhelmed by the flood of IDPs, the government struggled to cope with the crisis.

The IMU campaign was short-lived, and, with winter threatening to close the passes, their units were withdrawn to the Tavildara Valley to reorganize. Understandably, the Tajik government was keen to move the IMU out of its territory. IRP leaders who knew or had fought with Namangani during the civil war were therefore sent to persuade the IMU to continue their withdrawal into Afghanistan. Consequently, in a helicopter fleet of Russian aircraft, 600 fighters and their families were extracted from Tavildara to Afghanistan, where they received a warm welcome from the Taliban.[15] Clearly Rahmonov was eager to avoid restarting the civil war, which would, undoubtedly, have meant the

Taliban making attacks across the Amu Daria and would possibly have brought down his government. The Tavildara base was also a strong position and would have meant considerable military and financial effort at a time when the government was still insecure. Nevertheless, while Tajikistan may have purchased some time, the IMU was also now in a position to recruit more men, refit and retrain for a fresh campaign the following summer. A new base was opened for them at Mazar by the Taliban in return for an assurance that the IMU would agree to attack the forces of Ahmed Shah Masoud.

The military results of the IMU's campaign were disappointing, but they were in a position to make their campaigns more effective, particularly using drugs revenue. Their attacks on the Kyrgyz had not resulted in any political changes, but timing their assault with the convening of the Shanghai Five meeting (the forerunner of the SCO; China, Kyrgyzstan, Tajikistan, Kazakhstan and Russia) had attracted international attention. They had exposed the deficiencies of counter-terrorism and counter-insurgency techniques in the Kyrgyz army, even if the amount of physical damage they could inflict was limited. To make improvements, the IMU's co-operation with the Taliban and Al-Qaeda increased over the winter of 1999. There was detailed planning of the next campaign, the securing of arms and ammunition, and the acquisition of more funds, much derived from drug-trafficking. The UN estimated that drug production increased in Afghanistan between 1998 and 1999[16], from 2,750 tons to more than 5,000 tons. This production was taxed, but the IMU was making more money by charging for its smuggling across the borders of Central Asia. Namangani exploited the contacts he had built up in the years after the Tajik Civil War, and, employing his links through the Taliban, he used Chechens to expand the smuggling operations. Conscious of the potential damage being done to Afghans, the Taliban decided to ban poppy cultivation in 2000, but, even with a drought, Afghanistan still produced 3,400 tons. Namangani's operations were unaffected. He and his associates had stockpiled 240 tons at Mazar and Kunduz, and some of this was ferried across into Tajikistan, where it could be refined. This is supported by the fact that raw *khanka* opium was sometimes intercepted by Russian and Tajik border guards. Inside Tajikistan, some of the drugs were distributed to local users, where they were taken as a boiled tea or injected. Most of the drugs moved from clan to clan, acquiring greater value as they headed towards Russia or the West. Afghan opium producers received the equivalent of US $30 per kilo in 1996, but in Osh the rate per kilo was $800. A kilo in Moscow cost $6,000.

The Tajik authorities are hard pressed to stem the flow of drugs. They lack the manpower and resources to search all vehicles crossing the border and cannot guard every pass. Blowtorches are used to cut open cavities inside trucks and fuel tanks are occasionally probed, but many tons get through. Destroying opium fields within the country is also an uphill struggle given the lack of helicopters and manpower. Ill-trained and poorly paid police are often tempted to join the smuggling, and it was alleged that Russian members of the border police and the Tajikistan-based 201st Motor Rifle Division were often eager to participate.[17] The scale of the corruption is considerable, and it is suggested that some of the hotels and casinos built in Ashkabad and Astana were funded on money laundered through narcotics. Warlords in Tajikistan were often deeply involved in drug-smuggling during the civil war, and many see no reason to end such a lucrative system in peacetime. The blockading of the Gorno-Badakhshan Autonomous Province by the government during the war (because of their support for the UTO), prompted many farmers to turn to opium as a cash crop, and this led to many drug barons becoming influential in the region. The civil wars in Tajikistan and Afghanistan left both countries awash with weaponry too, and these now arm the drug smugglers and their terrorist allies.

The IMU was also funded by Al-Qaeda and other agencies, and this money was used to acquire a considerable arsenal. Saudi donors gave them $15,000,000 with which to purchase sniper rifles, night-vision equipment, rocket-propelled grenades, heavy machine guns, flak jackets and radio sets.[18] More sponsors, many cultivated by Yuldeshev in Pakistan and across the Middle East, came forward with cash. It is estimated that Namangani received $26,000,000 from bin Laden in 2000 as well as two Mi-8 transport helicopters. Those who came into contact with the IMU believed their personnel were well paid, with estimates of $100–$500 a month each. Talk of these salaries acted as a magnet for young enthusiasts. Nevertheless, these details reveal that, as elsewhere in the world, the IMU and other groups affiliated with Al-Qaeda may use the ideology of jihadism to justify their cause, but their operations depend on the techniques of organized crime.

The response of the Central Asian states to the IMU's campaign of 1999 was weakened by divisions. The Uzbeks accused the Tajiks and Kyrgyz of doing too little to tackle the IMU, but they refused any meaningful co-operation. Instead, they increased their own border security, even to the extent of sowing minefields along their frontiers. Cross-border trade was severely affected, as was agriculture, particularly where grazing and irrigation channels had crossed political boundaries. Despite an increase in border posts and personnel, drug-smuggling and terrorist infiltration continued.

THE IMU TERRORIST CAMPAIGN OF 2000

In July 2000, the IMU had returned to the Tavildara Valley and begun the process of infiltrating across the borders of Kyrgyzstan and Uzbekistan. Their strategy was twofold: first, to launch attacks against the security forces of the two republics, and second, to smuggle weapons and ammunition to their sleepers so as to orchestrate a terror campaign from within Uzbekistan. If co-ordinated, this would result in the IMU being able to maintain a year-round resistance rather than relying on a summer campaign alone. By August, they had initiated a series of surprise attacks with units between 100 and 200 strong in southern Kyrgyzstan and in Uzbekistan's Sukhandarya Province. Once again, Sukh and Vorukh provided useful staging posts to attack targets in the Ferghana Valley.

The foray into south-eastern Uzbekistan was a new departure but one that was ultimately doomed. The 170 insurgents initially contented themselves with the establishment of a small base before making an attack on local Uzbek forces. They executed an ambush against a newly trained Special Forces unit with particular effectiveness, killing ten men. However, they were pursued with vigour and were eventually besieged in their base. After a month of bombardment and sniping, the position was stormed and only a handful escaped alive. No prisoners were taken. The incident revealed that, as with many jihadist fighters, there can sometimes be a preference for a sacrificial stand as opposed to classic guerrilla tactics. Once pinned to a position, they were vulnerable to the heavy weapons of regular Uzbek forces and were destroyed. It was clear from this episode and other aspects of the 2000 campaign that the IMU killed its own wounded rather than letting them fall into the hands of the Uzbek and Kyrgyz governments, to whom they might have 'talked'.

The treatment of local people by the Uzbek authorities reveals that hearts and minds are not high on their list of priorities. Uzbek herders from Sukhandarya Province alerted the security forces to the presence of the IMU unit, but the authorities were slow to react and accused the herders of selling produce to the insurgents. Destroying their flocks, they forcibly moved the locals into camps where the conditions were so bad that some died of the cold. A few who spoke out about their plight were beaten up, and, the following year, 73 were arrested on the charge of subversion or assisting terrorists.[19]

One IMU unit had been despatched deep inside Uzbekistan to attack the holiday resort of Bostanlyk some 100 kilometres north of Tashkent. When fifteen insurgents attacked and killed four soldiers and took four hostages, there was panic. No fewer than 4,000 civilians were evacuated. After pitched battles with the insurgents, the Uzbek security forces eventually wiped them out. Once again, this incident revealed some limitations in the Uzbeks' ability to offer security to the population, but it also indicated that even the most daring raids by the IMU were vulnerable if they fixed themselves to a location. There is no evidence that they made any attempt to win the support of the people, and yet, as Mao posited so succinctly, any guerrilla war is absolutely dependent upon insurgents being able to move among a supportive civilian population as 'fish through water'. For all the dedication of the jihadists, this fundamental failure to understand the practice of successful guerrilla warfare condemned them to failure.

Other operations in 2000 revealed further weaknesses. In Kyrgyzstan's Batken Province, inept IMU attacks on army outposts left 25 insurgents dead and inflicted only 24 casualties. The inexperienced if enthusiastic volunteers were then hunted by US-trained Special

Forces. On 11 August, one IMU team managed to ambush a Kyrgyz army patrol and killed 22 men (although it is possible that the wounded were murdered). The following day they kidnapped members of a climbing expedition, including four Americans and a Kyrgyz soldier. While being pursued by Kyrgyz Special Forces, the kidnappers murdered the soldier but gradually released their captives. Intercepted by 130 troops, the IMU detachment tried to fight it out: six of them were killed and two captured. One of the prisoners confessed to being a rapist on the run from the police, while the other claimed that he had only enlisted for the money. Of the survivors who fled to the Tajik border, their leader, Sabir, was shot by Tajik border guards. Among the IMU equipment that was captured was a video of the insurgent group. Many of the volunteers, some of whom now lay dead, were very young, and they were clearly drawn from across Central Asia. The fact that some were Chechens may help to explain the tactics, but the profile of the fighters in the video also suggests that simply being 'a fighter' may be as important as any ideological justifications. For all the rhetoric, jihadist recruits reflect common patterns of enlistment around the world.

As the winter of 2000 approached, Namangani's men once again pulled out of Kyrgyzstan and Uzbekistan, having lost at least 150 of their fighters. The IMU was no nearer its goal of toppling the governments or of creating their beloved caliphate. If they congratulated themselves for defying the republics as they pulled back into Afghanistan for a second time, then they failed to acknowledge that the campaign of 2000 had merely hardened the resolve of the governments. Indeed, the IMU operations had only succeeded in convincing other powers of the urgent need to assist the Uzbeks and Kyrgyz against terrorism. The US, for example, which had no particular affection for Karimov's regime, felt compelled to condemn the IMU as a terrorist organization because of the kidnapping incident, and it stepped up its assistance programme. The Clinton administration had already taken military action against Al-Qaeda in Sudan and Afghanistan, and the IMU's links with bin Laden reinforced its concerns. Russia, Turkey, France and China all sent counter-insurgency equipment; China donated night-vision equipment and sniper rifles. Russia offered Uzbekistan $30,000,000 in weapons, including 30 armoured personnel carriers, Mi-8 helicopters and radios. Russia also convened a joint strategy meeting although this was marred by suspicions between the Central Asian governments.

In the winter of 2000, the IMU continued to co-operate with the Taliban and integrate its efforts with Al-Qaeda. Reinforced with more recruits, the organization rose to a strength of 2,000 men including Uzbeks, Tajiks, Chechens, Arabs, Afghans and Uighurs from Xinjiang. Six hundred fighters were deployed in support of the Taliban, which itself was in the region of fifteen thousand strong. A third of these were 'foreign', including 4,000 from Pakistan and 600 members of bin Laden's 055 Arab Brigade. Backed with heavy artillery, armour and aircraft, and assisted by Pakistan's ISI and Special Services Group, the Taliban made a concerted effort to defeat Masoud decisively in the north-east of Afghanistan. Taloqan, Masoud's headquarters, had fallen on 5 September after a siege lasting one month, and his resistance was now pushed into the very fringes of the country. The Taliban and their foreign allies were delighted: eager to prove that the strength of their Muslim brotherhood was irresistible, they convinced themselves that no force could stand in their way. Some argued that, having beaten the Soviet Union and the United Front (or Northern Alliance, as it was known in the West) in the Afghan Civil War, and having humiliated America in Somalia, they could proceed to defeat Russia in Chechnya and destroy the US. The seeds of 9/11 were thus already being sown. This contact with extremists in Afghanistan further radicalized the IMU: some Pakistanis and Arabs, eager to gain more jihadist credentials, offered to serve alongside Namangani's men, but many members of Sipah-i-Sabah and Lashkar-i-Jhangvi who joined up had reputations for atrocities and massacres that would do the IMU's cause no good at all.

As Al-Qaeda gained greater publicity for its global terrorism, there was a corresponding growth of interest in the plight of the anti-Taliban resistance. Tajikistan was particularly alarmed by Masoud's defeat. The US and Russia imposed sanctions against any supply of arms to the Taliban in January 2001, and there was growing pressure on Mullah Omar to surrender bin Laden. China demanded that its ally Pakistan should insist that Uighur fighters be expelled from radical madrassahs and from the Taliban. Thus prompted by Islamabad, the Taliban simply moved its Uighur contingents over to the 'independent' IMU. Equally, when Musharraff insisted that the members of Sipah-i-Sabah and Lashkar-i-Jhangvi be extradited for crimes and murders inside Pakistan, the Taliban moved them to the IMU too. A Russian demand to have Chechens handed over was dealt with in the same way.

Intelligence reports that Namangani had returned to Tajikistan in November 2000 prompted Uzbek demands for his extradition, and they reinforced the diplomatic pressure by cutting crucial gas supplies in the depths of winter. They also insisted that Tajikistan create a land corridor to Sukh. Meanwhile, mining and wiring of the border areas continued, while Tajik nationals, suspected of terrorist sympathies, were deported, even though they were ethnically Uzbek. The Tajik government responded with some hostility, expressing irritation that Tajik dissidents such as Col. Makhmud Khudoyberdiev (who had led a raid into the country in 1998) remained at large in Uzbekistan. The spat over extraditions was resolved when the Tajik government persuaded Namangani and his fighters to withdraw to Afghanistan for the third time. The Uzbeks nevertheless believed that, not only were the Tajiks actually in league with the IMU (through IRP contacts) but that Russia too was secretly supporting the IMU against the republics. Karimov perhaps did not acknowledge the fragility of the Tajik govern-ment and the limits of its authority. Not did he appear to appreciate the strained relations between factions in Tajikistan caused by the pres-ence of the IMU. The use of Russian aircraft was not evidence of a conspiracy against Uzbekistan and Kyrgyzstan either. Russian–Tajik border units did not want to engage the IMU or spark an unnecessary conflict with their allies the Taliban. However, Uzbek concerns that Saudi Arabia and Pakistan might be backing the group as a means of gaining greater influence in Central Asia was not so far-fetched. At least, that had been the original intention. The problem for both of these countries was that, not for the first time, they had lost control of their protégés.

In the summer of 2001, the Taliban went on the offensive against Masoud and the IMU resumed their attacks on Kyrgyzstan and Uzbekistan. The Batken region of southern Kyrgyzstan bore the brunt of the attacks, and another offensive was launched in Surkhandarya. There was a change in IMU tactics though. Instead of relying only on infiltrating borders, now sleeper cells were activated inside the two countries. Terror and intimidation of the Uzbek and Kyrgyz populations, including attacks on a television transmitter, appeared to contradict the group's desire to gain support, even though both countries were facing an economic crisis characterized by a 60-per-cent rise in inflation, a cut in real wages and thousands unemployed – and therefore angrily dissatisfied with their respective governments. So concerned was Karimov's government that it announced the release of 25,000 prisoners (none of whom were Islamists). The IMU once again failed to grasp the need to gather mass support. However, by the late summer, its opportunity was slipping away. On 9 September 2001, Masoud was murdered by Al-Qaeda suicide bombers posing as journalists. Two days later, Al-Qaeda hijacked four planes in the US and crashed three of them into the World Trade Centre and the Pentagon, causing the world's worst terrorist atrocity. Such an attempt made it inevitable that the US, and its allies, would swing their military power against Al-Qaeda and their affiliates, including the IMU. The onslaught was not long in coming.

The initial reaction to American requests for bases in the Central Asian republics was unenthusiastic. They were alarmed at the prospect of greater American influence which might continue long after the Taliban and Al-Qaeda were dealt with – an anxiety shared by President Putin. But they agreed that the US should be offered some limited facilities. Kyrgyzstan, Turkmenistan and Kazakhstan granted the Americans the use of their air space and arranged to share intelligence. Uzbekistan offered the Khanabad air base but also made bases available for ground troops and allowed combat missions to be mounted from within the country, going far beyond what had been agreed with Moscow. Karimov had every reason to want to see the destruction of the Taliban as the hosts of the IMU, but he also saw an opportunity to use America as a means to neutralize Russian interference. The Uzbeks were soon rewarded with American technical backing for their armed forces and got secret assurances of support, including a guarantee of the inviolability of their borders, a clause clearly directed at Russia.

American assistance encouraged the IMF to offer its support, having pulled out earlier in the year because of the country's economic crisis. When the American-led Coalition forces swept the Taliban out of power, and the United Front opposition, including Uzbekistan's favoured warlord, Dostum, took control of Afghanistan, the Russians and the Uzbeks were relieved. Namangani had chosen to fight alongside the Taliban, hoping, no doubt, to replay the war against the Soviets. But the IMU leader miscalculated the Americans' military power, with apparently fatal results. It is thought he was killed in one of the devastating American air strikes that characterized the three-week conflict.[20]

For a time, Namangani's movement was clearly defeated. The remnants of the IMU fled, like many other Taliban fighters, into the tribal border areas of Pakistan where they could be sure of support from hard-line Pushtuns. However, Operation Enduring Freedom had scattered the movement and broken down its finance, smuggling, and command-and-control networks. Some of its members ended up in Kashmir (hosted by the banned militant group Lashkar-e-Toiba), others made their way back to Tajikistan (particularly Khushad, Khevaspor and Ayvanj in Gorno-Badakhshan), while the sleeper cells remained in existence in the Ferghana Valley. In late 2001, the IMU was re-titled the IMT in a gesture designed to widen its appeal, demonstrate its solidarity with non-Uzbeks, and clarify its aim to remove the national borders in Central Asia. The movement remained *hors de combat* until December 2002, when bombs were detonated in the Oberon market of Bishkek. The choice of target suggests that the IMT was not strong enough to penetrate the security of the border or take on the government. Indeed, the relative isolation of the incident illustrated that, despite their desire to keep resistance alive, this was a shadow of their strength in 1999–2000, when they had launched so many attacks. On 8 May 2003, there was another bomb attack in Kyrgyzstan, this time outside Bakay Bank in the city of Osh. It was thought that the perpetrators were two Uzbeks from the Ferghana Valley.

Since 2003, the Taliban and the IMT have been able to recover some of their strength and organization. In the tribal areas of the North-West Frontier Province, an Islamist coalition, the Muttahida Majlis-e-Amal, governs the area. One of its constituents is the Jamat-i-Ulema Islami, a

Deobandi ideological movement that backed the Taliban and the IMT. With detachments still in Kashmir, Afghanistan and eastern Tajikistan, the Pakistan border area represents its most secure haven. Already hard pressed to track down Al-Qaeda and jihadist Pakistani groups, the authorities in Pakistan do not have the resources to devote to locating IMT members as well. Using narcotics contacts built up in the late 1990s, the IMT has been able to re-establish some of its networks. Uzbekistan was subjected to a wave of terrorist attacks in the spring of 2003, including gun battles with Uzbek police. Then, in a new departure, fifteen suicide bombers attacked at several locations around the country. Thirty-three other IMU fighters were killed.[21] In July 2004, the American and Israeli embassies and the Uzbek Prosecutor-General's office in Tashkent were also attacked by suicide bombers. Three guards were killed and nine others wounded. The Uzbek security forces sealed off the capital with roadblocks and vehicle searches, but, in parallel with events in Afghanistan, the advent of suicide bombing was a clear indication that tactics employed elsewhere in the Middle East and promoted by Al-Qaeda had finally been imported to Central Asia. A group calling itself the Islamic Jehad of Uzbekistan claimed responsibility for the attacks, but this may be a front name for the IMT's foreign personnel or IIF allies. These foreign elements include Chechen fighters, Arabs and Pakistani jihadists from the Harkat ul-Jihad al-Islami.

In a predictable statement in September 2006, Yuldeshev announced that the IMT remained strong. He threatened revenge against Russia as well as the Central Asian republics, using the rhetoric usually associated with Al-Qaeda, but there was a reference to the Andijan shootings of 2005 which involved Uzbek security forces. Yuldeshev claimed the IMT was committed to bringing to an end the oppression of ordinary Muslims, thereby trying to make a specific link between the people of Central Asia and the fighters. Despite the presence of American and NATO forces in Afghanistan, the Central Asian republics still lack the means to combat terrorists, and co-operation between the republics remains limited, although China agreed to assist Tajikistan in training exercises in September 2006. Two Americans have been killed in Afghanistan by the IMT, and kidnapping for ransom is still a favoured tactic. It is also alleged that, now that Iran feels encircled by Western forces in Afghanistan and Iraq, its intelligence services have been secretly supporting insurgent groups, from Muqtada al-Sadr's Shia militia in southern Iraq to the IMT in eastern Tajikistan. The discovery of Iranian-made explosives and bombs by British forces in Iraq would appear to confirm these suspicions. It may also be true that, having found a common cause in Iraq, the exchange of expertise and a flow of funds and logistics may follow. Nevertheless, the IMT still has a chance to win support from the Uzbek public if the government fails to deliver economic improvements or political concessions. Karimov believes that Hizb ut-Tahrir and other Islamist organizations simply recruit for IMT by indoctrinating young men with their extremist interpretation of Islam. There may be some truth in this fear, but critics of the regime argue that, until the government ceases to suppress or muzzle the voice of the opposition, the situation will not improve.

Chapter 7

The Chechen and Caucasus Wars

The Chechen Wars were sparked by the collapse of the Soviet Union
and the emergence of a new, more assertive Russian state whose
ambitions to control the flow of oil from Azerbaijan and to check the
spread of Islamism on its southern flank clashed with smouldering
resentment of Russian influence and an invigorated nationalist identity. Two years of bitter fighting, from 1994 to 1996, failed to produce
a clear-cut victory for either side. Conservative estimates suggest that
35,000 civilians were killed, but others have claimed that between
80,000 and 100,000 may have perished.[1] The war was characterized by
guerrilla attacks on Russian personnel and ruthless reprisals, devas-
tation of urban areas – especially Grozny in 1995 – and the flight, if
not 'ethnic cleansing', of thousands of civilians. Fighting spread into
neighbouring Dagestan and Ingushetia, and two insurgent leaders
emerged as prominent warlords: Shamil Basayev and the Saudi
known as Khattab. Yet, despite numerical and technological superiority, Russian security forces grew demoralized by the Chechens' tactics
and their lack of progress. Russian President Yeltsin sought to avoid
a catastrophic humiliation by concluding a hasty peace deal.
Nevertheless, President Putin, is successor, was able to make political
mileage with the Russian electorate on the promise of dealing firmly
with Chechnya. In 1999, a second and more significant conflict broke
out. New waves of Islamist volunteers have joined the fighting, even
though the insurgents have been driven into remote bases and forced

to resort to random terrorism, including suicide attacks and bombings inside Russia. The conflict has degenerated into a civil war, with torture, murder, assassination and intimidation on both sides. The nadir of the whole struggle was marked by the Beslan siege in neighbouring Ingushetia, where 11 security personnel, 31 terrorists and 331 civilians, most of them children, were killed.[2]

The Chechen Wars have been likened, not least by the Russian government itself, to America's Global War on Terror. The Russians see their struggle with jihadists as identical to that of the Western coalitions, and, as a result, they find the West's criticism of Russian techniques in Chechnya condescending and hypocritical. Why, they ask, should the West condemn Russian aggression against Chechnya (part of its sovereignty) when the West has led assaults on Afghanistan and Iraq? There are, however, stark differences. While the American and British governments have tried – and, in some cases, convicted – servicemen who had abused or killed Iraqis during the occupation, the Russian government has failed to regulate or punish the excessive brutality of some of its troops. Indeed, the 2006 murder of the Russian journalist Anna Politkovskaya, known for her outspoken criticism of Russian policy and behaviour in Chechnya, fuelled suspicion that Moscow is concealing the truth about its 'dirty war'.[3]

The region has been destabilized by the conflict, and periodically terrorism, raiding and more conventional fighting have spilled over into other republics and Russian provinces. A separate war took place over the disputed territory of Karabakh between 1991 and 1994, but it too has yet to be resolved. Jihadists are eager to fuel these widely spread disputes so as to create a pan-Caucasian 'holy war' against Christian Armenians, Georgians and Russians. Russia, for its part, is just as determined to restore its influence in the region, to protect vital oil interests and pipeline routes, and to forestall the growth of militant Islamism and nationalism. It has even pressured Georgia economically to deter that country's growing relationship with the West, in particular its desire to join NATO.

The unilateral declaration of independence of Chechnya by Dzhokhar Dudayev, a Soviet air-force general, in the autumn of 1991 was given little regard in Moscow at the time. Faced with a battery of demands for independence or autonomy from many Soviet republics, and having narrowly headed off a hard-line Communist *coup d'état*, President Gorbachev had more pressing concerns in the capital. Boris Yeltsin soon challenged him to dissolve the USSR and called for Russian independence. By March 1992, Russia had not only disposed of the Soviet system; it had also drawn up a Federation Treaty that granted concessions over tax and autonomy to 86 of the 88 former Soviet states. Ironically, given that one of the architects of the law was Ruslan Khasbulatov, a Chechen, Chechnya and Tatarstan were not on the Federation Treaty list.[4] However, neither side seemed concerned. There were no negotiations, but Russian troops evacuated Chechnya in the spring of 1992. That summer, it seemed that Chechnya was, to all intents and purposes, independent. However, in Russia, the view was that the absence of any agreement did not imply independence at all.

Any misunderstanding of Chechnya's status was underpinned by deep-seated and historic suspicions. The Russians had begun to extend their imperial rule over the Caucasus in the eighteenth century, but the Chechens had not been finally suppressed until the 1870s. The Communists reasserted Russian control after a brief revolutionary interlude, but it was during the Second World War that one million Chechens, Ingush and other Caucasians were deported to Siberia as Stalin feared resistance might grow in the post-war period.[5] Even while Chechen conscripts were fighting the Germans on the Polish border, Stalin was convinced that they were were potential, if not actual, collaborators with the Nazis. Chechnya temporarily ceased to exist and hundreds died of neglect while in exile. In 1957, Khrushchev restored the republic and permitted the Ingush and Chechens to return, but the memory of colonialism, conquest and wartime coercion was impossible to erase.

Russian concerns were more short-term. Dudayev was an unknown quantity, but he had already established an alarming capacity for 'direct action'. He had led the storming of the All-National Congress of Chechen

People in September 1991, where Vitali Kutsenko, the Communist Party chief, had been killed and many others badly wounded. After Dudayev's declaration of independence, Yeltsin's troops had been prevented from leaving the airport by forces loyal to him. Ingushetia broke away from Chechnya in 1992 to rejoin the Russian Federation, but Dudayev did little to ameliorate the plight of thousands of non-Chechens who fled the state or to arrest the perpetrators of violence and lawlessness breaking out everywhere. When Russian engineers and other skilled workers were expelled from the country, the economy began to deteriorate rapidly. Anti-Dudayev factions emerged and violence against the President's rule escalated. Pitched battles with heavy weapons took place in rural and urban areas: Chechnya had tilted into civil war. The Russian view was that Dudayev was destabilizing the region, a fact underscored by ethnic violence which had spilled over into the Prigorodney district of North Ossetia. When Russian forces deployed there in October 1992 to restore order, what happened, in fact, was that nearly 70,000 Ingush fled. Dudayev argued that this was a prelude to a Russian invasion of Chechnya. He ordered full mobilization and declared a state of emergency, but one might speculate that this was a convenient moment for a leader who was rapidly losing control of his state.

It was almost two years later that a coalition of opposition forces, supplied with unmarked Russian aircraft and equipment and stiffened with 'mercenaries', began an offensive against the Dudayev regime. Grozny was bombed as a prelude to a ground assault. In fact, the attack of 26 November 1994, augmented by Russian forces, failed to secure the capital. Bad organization gave Dudayev's forces a chance to strengthen their defences. Worse, twenty Russian regular soldiers were captured, ending the pretence that Russia was not directly involved. Three days later, Yeltsin issued an ultimatum to the Chechens, ordering their surrender. Dudayev's refusal led to a massive air attack on military installations and on Grozny itself. In early December, Dudayev and the Russian Minister of Defence, Pavel Grachev, had agreed to end the fighting, but just five days later, a Russian ground offensive began. What drove this decision is unclear, but both Yeltsin and Russian army personnel favoured a surgical strike that would end the conflict swiftly. It is likely that both parties had little faith in

Dudayev's diplomacy either. But perhaps the real reason was the desire to acquire full control of the region's oil.

Chechnya lies astride the main oil pipeline from Azerbaijan, which holds out the prospect of lucrative transit fees. The signing of a 'deal of the century' contract between the Azeris and several large oil companies in the early 1990s added an impetus for immediate action. Moreover, Chechnya itself has considerable reserves. In 1980, it produced 7.4 million barrels from 1,500 wells, and by 1991 Grozny's installations were processing 17,000,000 tons of oil annually.[6] Despite Dudayev's declaration of independence, Moscow thought it could continue to do business with Grozny. West Siberian oil was pumped to the Chechen refineries; in 1993, the revenues from the industry were $800,000,000. However, the lawlessness and civil war that accompanied Dudayev's rule threatened the industry. Unscrupulous managers were selling oil from the pipelines on the black market, and the Russian mafia had made inroads into the business. The expulsion of Russian engineers meant the old industry there was in meltdown. Although officially denied as the reason for invasion, it was later argued by Gen. Alexander Lebed that Yeltsin had been forced to war by powerful financial interests. The fact is that he and his advisors went to war for a variety of coincident reasons. What they wanted was a short, decisive conflict. What they got was quite different.

THE FIRST CHECHEN WAR

The Russians opened the campaign with a major offensive, after a week-long air and artillery bombardment on Grozny, in January 1995. It is thought that several thousand civilians – the exact figure will probably never be known, but conservative estimates suggest 27,000 – died in the barrage and in subsequent street-fighting. The Russian losses were also quite high. Fighting in built-up areas has always carried a high butcher's bill, as combat tends to take place at close quarters in an environment that favours concealment and defence. In the New Year's Eve operation around the central railway station, the Maikop battalion of the 131st Motorized Infantry regiment was almost wiped out in 60 hours of continuous fighting. Far from a swift *coup de main*, the Russian armoured columns found themselves fighting for every street. The troops were shocked by the tenacity of the defence and by their mounting losses. Senior commanders were compelled to take up forward positions to direct the fighting, and paid the price: Maj.-Gen. Viktor Vorobyov was killed by a mortar bomb just days into the campaign. On 19 January, the Russians took possession of the ruined presidential palace, a position that had been defended for three weeks. This achievement marked a turning point. With the Russians holding a line roughly along the River Sunzha, the city was effectively divided in half. The Chechens withdrew their headquarters and their remaining defenders from the devastated capital to Novogroznensk, and a truce followed on 8 February.[7]

The Russians had used conventional tactics formulated during the Second World and Cold wars. Artillery saturation and the liberal use of air strikes were designed to paralyse the Chechens' defences, before ground forces swept along narrow axes to secure vital ground. Interestingly, Soviet experiences in the Second World War indicated that urban warfare was slow and costly, and gave defenders an advantage. As a result, Soviet doctrine had preferred the isolation of centres of urban resistance so as to achieve unhindered thrusts in depth. In episodes of counter-insurgency, however, the doctrine was to secure urban centres first, as it was thought that rural populations were generally less favourably disposed towards Soviet thinking. In the case of Chechnya, the focus towards the capital was designed to bring the campaign to a rapid conclusion, and the method was to employ overwhelming force. However, this version of 'shock and awe' failed to produce the desired result. From the outset, Chechens engaged in guerrilla tactics because of their asymmetrical position. The Russian forces lacked the training or experience to deal with these techniques. Artillery bombardments and air strikes were called for to neutralize relatively small pockets of resistance, but in the urban environment the Chechens could quickly change position.

The irregular nature of Chechen fighting, mounting casualties and the difficulty in engaging Chechen forces meant that the inexperienced Russian troops grew increasingly frustrated. Drawn from a tough training regime with a high incidence of physical penalties, Russian soldiers sought to punish Chechens whom they suspected of being fighters or their supporters. Repeating techniques used in Afghanistan in the 1980s, they resorted to *zachistka* (cleansing) raids: entire villages or small towns were cleared of their populations. In Samashki, it is alleged that Russian forces killed a hundred civilians while many others were beaten and tortured. Indeed, across the country, there were accusations that Russian troops had abused, tortured and summarily executed those they accused of being in, or giving succour to, the resistance.[8]

The Chechen fighters responded with an escalation of guerrilla attacks and acts of terror. Booby-traps were set and roads mined at night. Guerrilla bands coalesced for particular operations, including the audacious kidnapping of 1,500 hostages in the southern Russian city of Budyonnovsk. The conflict descended into new levels of bitterness. Fighters accused some Chechens of 'collaboration' with the Russians and executed them. They also mistreated civilian hostages and tortured Russian combatant prisoners. Hostage-taking for ransom increased (as it did in Iraq in 2004), and Russian troops made use of civilians as human shields for their convoys. Mercenaries in Russian employment were expected to augment their meagre pay with looting and extortion, and some regular troops indulged in the same practices.

In Russia, the media's coverage of the war contributed to a decline in the popularity of Yeltsin as President, and there was a general challenge to the legitimacy of the conflict. Significantly, other former Soviet republics criticized Russia's policy and felt emboldened to assert their independence. Watching the Russian forces struggling to suppress the Chechen 'bandits' actually encouraged the peoples of Central Asia, and reinforced their memories and impressions of Russia's war in Afghanistan. In Chechnya itself, the Russian offensive turned around Dudayev's flagging political fortunes. Former opponents rallied to his side. In addition, thousands of Muslim volunteers, many from the Middle East but also a number from Central Asia, flocked to join the guerrillas. Akhmad Kadyrov, the mufti of Chechnya, declared that Chechens were engaged in a holy war against Russia and encouraged the flow of foreign fighters into the conflict. Local militias also sprang up as civilians sought to defend themselves from all comers. There was a new risk of regional escalation, however, when Chechens took hostages in Kizlyar on the border with Russian Dagestan. The Russians responded by destroying the nearby village of Pervomayskoye inside the territory of Dagestan because they suspected it had Chechen sympathies. The incident elicited a sharp response from the Dagestanis and led to more doubts about the war inside Russia itself. Nevertheless, the fighting spread into Ingushetia in 1995, when Russian forces pursued Chechen insurgents there, and 200,000 refugees trudged across the borders, many of them ending up in North Ossetia in old collective farms or tented camps.[9]

Moscow was aware of growing discontent with the war inside Russia and in the former Soviet republics. Ingushetia's President, Ruslan Aushev, threatened to sue the Russian Defence Ministry for the costs incurred by raids across his borders. Some states refused to supply conscripts to fight in the conflict and passed their own laws to protect their citizens, or to deny the use of force altogether in the settling of domestic violence. This was, of course, against the background of recent history: none of the states wanted a return to the coercion of the Soviet regime. As Yeltsin's presidential election approached, Russian nationalists wanted to see a final resolution of the war so as to forestall more calls for separatism. The problem was that the fighting had bogged down and was unlikely to produce the 'quick victory' they wanted.

In fact, the situation deteriorated rapidly in 1996. Having taken fifteen months to capture the village of Bamut, a few kilometres southwest of Grozny, the lethargic Russian army was evidently suffering problems in logistics, counter-insurgency training, morale and organization. In March, about 2,000 Chechen insurgents infiltrated the capital and launched a three-day raid, which turned out to be so successful that parts of the city were overrun and significant supplies of arms and ammunition secured.[10] In April, the jihadist Khattab carried out an ambush of an armoured column of the 245th Motorized Rifle Regiment at Shatoy. The only success the Russians enjoyed was the killing of Dudayev by a missile that homed in on his satellite phone that same month. But the resistance continued.

The catalyst for a Russian settlement was the Chechen assault on

Grozny on 6 August 1996. Around 1,500 insurgents led by Shamil Basayev once again infiltrated the capital in trucks and cars and on foot. Acting on pre-arranged instructions, they laid siege to Russian outposts and bases. Even though some 12,000 Russian troops were deployed in and around the city, it was difficult for them to co-ordinate a response to myriad attacks. Russian troops in Argun and Gudermes found themselves pinned down and unable to manoeuvre. Armoured columns made up of Interior Ministry troops who were tasked to relieve these isolated units were ambushed and suffered heavy losses. The 276th Motorized Rifle Regiment lost 450 out of its 900 men in two days of intense and confused fighting as it tried to reach the city centre. Over five days, the Russian army estimated that two hundred of its men had been killed and a further eight hundred wounded. Thousands of Russian troops and security personnel, lacking ammunition, demoralized and unsure of their position, capitulated. Their weapons quickly fell into the hands of the insurgents. In mid-August, even though Chechen fighters were still in the capital, a local truce was organized. Furious, the Russian commander, Konstantin Pulikovsky, announced his intention to level the entire city and gave the fighters and the civilian population 48 hours to leave. However, just as the bombardment began, on 21 August, Lebed, the Russian national security advisor, concluded a ceasefire with the Chechens.[11] Ten days later a formal ceasefire was signed; the Khasavyurt Accords were concluded in the Kremlin on 12 May 1997. Despite all the destruction and all the losses (100,000 civilians and between 5,000 and 14,000 Russian personnel), the critical issue of Chechen independence had not been resolved. The Chechens believed they had a *de facto* agreement, but Moscow was clearly eager to avoid a diplomatic humiliation and perhaps envisaged a more favourable conclusion at some later date. It was a case of unfinished business.

THE SECOND WAR

Russia's attempt to conclude the Chechnya issue, not least the escalating terrorist attacks in Dagestan, led to renewed fighting in 1999 and a bitter winter struggle for Grozny. The legacy of the first conflict was that both sides employed greater brutality from the outset. The fighting for the capital was intense, but the battle for the countryside was protracted. Chechen fighters resorted to increasingly fanatical tactics, including terrorism inside Russia, and there was a strengthening of the more extreme Wahhabi doctrine in the resistance movement. That said, it has proved difficult for the Chechens to co-ordinate their resistance, and their raids are sporadic. By 2006, there was a stalemate: the Chechens were unable to assert their independence, the Russians unable to finally extinguish the resistance.

Relations between the two states had not improved after the first war. In 1997, a year after the Khasavyurt Accords, Aslan Maskhadov was elected, but Moscow had no grounds for optimism. Yeltsin's envoy, Valentin Vlasov, was kidnapped on a diplomatic mission in May 1998, and in February 1999, Mashkadov announced that Chechnya was to introduce Sharia law. A second kidnapping, of another envoy, General Gennadiy Shpigun, aroused more suspicions and irritation. Mashkadov, in fact, had his own problems. His anti-kidnapping official, Shadid Bargishev, was killed in a car-bombing on the eve of a major crackdown against hostage-takers in 1998, there were several attempts to assassinate the President himself, and the country's senior prosecutor, Mansur Tagirov, was seized and murdered. Worse, there were growing rifts between the militant jihadists and the National Guard, who were loyal to the government. In July 1998, shooting broke out in Gudermes between the two forces and about fifty civilians were killed. Russia had intervened in 1994 (just as the old Soviet regime had done in Afghanistan and Eastern Europe) precisely because the government in Grozny was apparently unable to maintain order, but the situation had arisen again. The question was: Would the Russians now adopt a different approach?[12]

There is some evidence to suggest that the Russians deployed Special Forces to influence the outcome of the power struggle developing in Chechnya, but, as so often happens, this clandestine intervention merely worsened domestic instability. Russia felt compelled to act because of a series of terrorist attacks inside Russia from 1996. Indeed, in Moscow's eyes, the Chechens were not honouring even the spirit of the Khasavyurt Accords. On 16 November 1996, a bomb destroyed a block of flats in Kaspiysk in Dagestan; 69 people, many of them relatives of border guards, were killed. On 23 April the following year, three people were killed by a bomb detonated in a railway station in Armavir, and in May another railway bomb killed two more.

The perpetrators of these attacks were clearly not part of the Chechen government. Regarding themselves as mujahedin, jihadists from Chechnya and Dagestan, and their Arab volunteer allies such as Khattab, were eager to keep the resistance alive.[13] Raiding the Buinaksk Russian army base in Dagestan, they regarded the destruction of several armoured vehicles and the killing of many servicemen as part of their jihad. This was not just for the 'liberation' of Chechnya, since, technically, Russia no longer controlled the state. Rather it was for the Islamization of Chechnya and for the fulfilment of the global jihad that would result in the creation of a new world order. Encouraged by the success of the Taliban and incensed by struggles elsewhere (including Palestine and Bosnia), the jihadists felt that they were engaged in a historic mission. Their deaths in such an endeavour would mean instant redemption. They found the guerrilla war empowering; it gave them the chance to strike at their enemies with force. Videos they produced of their attacks illustrate the depth of their passions most graphically. Sequences show ambushes of armoured vehicles, sometimes at close quarters. Their victims are shot down, executed and often mutilated. Amid exhortations that 'God is Great!', prisoners have their throats slit or are scalped.

The attacks in late 1998 and early 1999 in neighbouring states seemed deliberately designed to destabilize the region. In March 1999, for example, a bomb placed in the market of Vladikavkaz in North Ossetia killed 51 innocent people. That summer there were further attacks on border-police posts. The Russian government was clearly exasperated and grew suspicious when it emerged that Shamil Basayev had led a raid of up to 2,000 Chechen, Arab, Dagestani and Kazakh fighters inside Dagestan in August and September 1999. How far was the government involved in this raid? The attack was designed to relieve pressure on a series of border villages which were under siege from Russian forces, but the insurgents suffered a major setback when they came under air attack. Fuel Air Explosive was dropped on some of the settlements and a sustained counter-attack was launched that drove the insurgents back across the border. Many civilians were killed. Russia continued to exert pressure on Chechnya after the raid, making air strikes against the south-east where they suspected insurgents were based. By the end of September, these air attacks had been extended to targets in and around Grozny itself.

As the fighting on the border of Dagestan unfolded, a series of terrorist bomb attacks were made against Russian civilians in Moscow and Volgodonsk; some 300 were killed. Yeltsin immediately blamed the Chechens, although doubt was cast on this claim by Basayev, who denied responsibility. Given the factional nature of the insurgents, it was perfectly possible that another radical group was behind the attacks, but some Russians feared that their own security service, the FSB, had itself carried out the bombings to create a pretext for intervention. Two members of Khattab's Wahhabi jihadist organization were later apprehended and tried for the attacks in 2004. However, at the time, Moscow immediately demanded that the perpetrators be handed over by the Chechen government. Just 24 hours later, on 30 September 1999, Russian ground troops crossed the border. It seems the Russian government had little faith in the Chechen authorities being able to deliver the suspects, but one must also acknowledge that Moscow's leaders, now under the determined leadership of President Putin, believed that, given the increase of terrorist activity and the evident threat to regional stability, intervention was an absolute necessity.

The immediate response of President Maskhadov to the air and ground attacks was to impose martial law and declare a *gazavat* (holy war), essentially a statement calling for unlimited war.[14] By contrast, Putin tried to appear to be the moderate. He announced that the Russian forces would only advance to the River Terek, occupying just the northern portion of the state, in order to create a security zone against Chechen raiders. The Russian forces did indeed advance swiftly across the open northern plain but made a river crossing on 12 October before advancing on two axes towards the capital. The advance here was cautious, methodical and preceded by co-ordinated air and artillery saturation. Three weeks later, the Russians overran Bamut, which had been so difficult to secure in the first war, and their armoured columns gradually snaked around the capital. In the rear, Russian forces established 'filtration camps', processing refugees and detaining those suspected of being 'bandits'. An amnesty was designed to demilitarize the fighters, and this netted about 400 of them. It is alleged that many of these men subsequently 'disappeared', although it is not clear if they were killed by Russian security forces or by Chechens who accused them of collaboration, or if they were simply released.

The Chechens had spent the period before the Russian investment fortifying their capital, but the odds were formidable. The Russians enjoyed total air superiority, and, with 100,000 men, they significantly outnumbered the Chechen defenders. Just as important were the changes in Russian tactics. Intensive bombardments were used to neutralize each Chechen position in turn, and armour, APCs (armoured personnel carriers) and infantry were held back rather than thrown forward prematurely. Firepower was utilized to reduce casualties and effect a methodical, guaranteed victory. Yet the Russians were already considering the occupation to follow the fighting. The former mayor of Grozny, Beslan Gantamirov, was released from prison to lead a pro-Moscow Chechen force that would take part in the military operations but also assist in the security of the capital after the fighting. The Russian Interior Minister, Vladimir Rushailo, refused to supply the new militia with APCs, mortars or sniper rifles and equipped them only with obsolete assault rifles. He went on to accuse Gantamirov of failing to screen the Chechen personnel, but the militia played its part honourably in the fighting, suffering 700 casualties. Nevertheless, Gantamirov was dismissed and the force was effectively broken up soon after. The Russians simply found it difficult to trust the Chechens. They had had bad experiences in their war in Afghanistan, with defections, sale of equipment and weapons, and murders of Russian officers. The troops had little time for Chechen civilians either. Despite the suffering of some 40,000 civilians trapped in the capital, some refugees were fired on as they tried to escape, even in so-called 'safe corridors'. Russian soldiers found it hard to distinguish their enemies when the insurgents rarely wore uniforms and fought by ambush and raid.

The Russians may have had contempt for their opponents, but the Chechens displayed remarkable determination and skill in their defence of the capital. Interlocking fire zones were established, bunker systems constructed, mines laced through the streets, and snipers deployed in every effort to maximize the potential of the urban environment. Russian commanders tried to deter guerrilla operations by dropping leaflets demanding that all civilians leave the city. Failure to comply, they warned, would mean that they would be considered combatants. But this ultimatum was withdrawn in December 1999 amid international protest, not least from the US and Europe.[15] Nevertheless, the intense bombardment from aircraft, artillery and rockets reduced the city to ruins. However, the Chechens continued to try to wrest the initiative from the Russians. On 4 January 2000 they launched a raid from Grozny and temporarily took control of the village of Alkhan-Kala. The following week, Chechen fighters managed to open a corridor to the capital by retaking Shali, Argun and Gudermes until the Russians counterattacked. Ambushes of Russian convoys also took place, prompting Gen. Viktor Kazantsev to announce that only boys under 10, men over 60, and women and girls would be regarded as refugees.

The relentless Russian offensive inside Grozny was underway. A steady casualty toll was endured, and Chechens utilized every avenue, including sewerage systems, to ambush the Russian forces. However, by the middle of January 2000, it was clear that the capital would fall. Chechen fighters were short of food, water and ammunition, and only a desperate breakout would save the dwindling force. In the early hours of 1 February, the Chechens attempted to escape to the south-west. Many ran into the minefields the Russians had laid as they tried to skirt Russian units. Basayev's unit found itself under Russian artillery fire just short of the village of Alkhan-Kala, but volunteers agreed to run ahead of the main body to detonate mines in their path. Under the bombardment and unable to avoid setting off mines, the Russians estimated that about 400 fighters were killed and wounded. The survivors made their way towards the Argun and Vedeno gorges, where they could regroup and continue the resistance in the mountains. The Russian army thus took possession of Grozny and permitted civilians to return, clearly hoping that they had broken the back of the resistance.

Initially, there were grounds for optimism. In March 2000, a 1,000-strong party of Chechen fighters raided the settlement of Komosomolskoye and fought a pitched battle with Russian forces there for two weeks. However, fighting in this fixed position, as they had done in Grozny, proved costly, and it is estimated that the Chechen losses were between 500 and 600 – a catastrophic loss of manpower for a guerrilla army. Yet there was a grotesque end to this Russian military success. Of the 70 captives, it seems that very few survived. Anna Politkovskaya, the Russian journalist who was murdered in 2006, suggested that most of the prisoners were tortured and subsequently killed with entrenching tools in the Chernokozovo filtration camp. Three survivors could be accounted for. Two later hanged themselves, and the third went missing.[16] These claims of murder and accusations of atrocities by both sides have characterized the Chechen Wars.

INSURGENCY AND TERRORISM FROM MOSCOW TO BESLAN

The Chechen fighters have continued their resistance from the mountainous southern parts of the country, with raids and bomb attacks into urban areas. They favour assassinations of Russian or pro-Russian officials, ambushes of vehicle-borne military patrols, police vehicles and posts, and terrorist Improvised Explosive Devices against buildings or packed in cars. This campaign began immediately after the fall of Grozny. At the village of Ulus-Kurt, for example, a paratroop company was virtually wiped out after a three-day battle in February 2000: 86 Russian personnel were killed by a combination of Chechen and Arab fighters. Often it is impossible to get an accurate figure of the number of Chechen dead; both sides claim to have inflicted heavy casualties. In May 2000, a supply column on its way to an airborne unit came under attack at Serzhen Gurt in the Vedeno Gorge. After a four-hour gun battle, Russian sources admitted they had lost twenty-five men. The Chechens claimed they had killed 50 for no loss; the Russians stated they had recovered the bodies of four Chechen fighters. Claims about casualties are masked in other ways. On 1 March 2000, a 'friendly fire' incident caused the death of 22 men, but the Russian authorities initially argued that it had been a Chechen ambush. Although the Russian Foreign Minister, Vladimir Rushailo, claimed that the situation in Chechnya was 'being fully controlled' by the army, ambushes and accidents continued to take place.[17]

In counter-insurgency, the government has to prove and constantly reinforce its ability to govern, maintain order and guarantee security. It must be able to draw intelligence from the people as well as from its own military and police assets. It must have a physical presence throughout the territory. It must also be able to seize and retain the initiative, forcing insurgents into a reactive and defensive stance. Certainly the Russians possessed material advantages: control of the infrastructure, air supremacy, greater firepower and numerical strength. But winning the support of the local population was far harder, not least because of the record of Russian troops in the area, the numbers of lives lost and the levels of destruction inflicted. However, with the establishment of a new political authority in Grozny, the Russians were able to augment their strength with a Chechen armed police force. The Russians also deployed more Special Forces, and it was these troops who carried out a spectacular ambush against Chechen fighters on 4 May 2000 at Avtury. It was claimed that eighteen insurgents had been killed in an ambush initiated with machine-gun fire but backed up with an artillery bombardment. The Chechen police and Special Forces also combined in June that year to flush out fighters who had infiltrated back into the capital and who had been planting mines or firing rocket-propelled grenades (RPGs) at checkpoints. These tactics, and the lack of progress in the insurgency, prompted Ilyas Akhmadov, Chechnya's unofficial separatist Foreign Minister, to call for an end to 'this useless war' against Russia that same month.

Chechen fighters began to use terrorist tactics far more from 2001, a mark of their inability to overthrow the pro-Russian regime or to defeat Russian forces in the field. In Gudermes, for example, a bomb was detonated in a police station that specialized in fighting organized crime, killing six. The previous October, a bomb in the capital also had targeted a police station and been timed to kill a team of prosecutors. In June 2001, Russian Special Forces cornered Arbi Barayev, a 'warlord' leader, with about 50 fighters in the village of Alkhan-Kala near Grozny.

Despite a desperate resistance over several days, Barayev and seventeen other fighters were killed and the village overrun. This was a significant achievement for the Russians. Barayev, nicknamed 'The Terminator' for his ruthlessness, had murdered 170 people, including three Britons and one New Zealander in 1998. He was also a prominent figure in organized crime. The Russians continued the same sort of cleansing operations that had netted Barayev south of Grozny over the following months, a technique that often precipitated gun battles and casualties on both sides. However, throughout the period 2002–4, bomb attacks and assassination attempts against Chechen and Russian authorities went on.

The Chechen terrorist attacks killed a number of prominent figures. Sergei Zveryev, Russia's second-in-command in Chechnya, was killed in a remote-controlled bomb attack in May 2000. Adam Deniyev, a pro-Russian Deputy Chief of Administration with a chequered past, died of his injuries when a bomb exploded during his live television broadcast. In November 2001, Elza Gazuyev, a Chechen woman who had lost several members of her family, tried to kill the Russian military commander Gen. Gadzhiev while blowing herself up with a hand grenade. Many Chechens accused Gadzhiev of deliberating targeting civilians in his campaign, and he later died of his wounds. However, the Chechen resistance achieved their greatest coup with the assassination of the pro-Russian President Akhmad Kadyrov on 9 May 2004 in a bomb attack at the Grozny football stadium. Twelve other high-ranking officials were killed in the blast. There had been three previous attempts on Kadyrov's life, including two female suicide bombers the year before. There were other assassinations of Russian leaders in Dagestan and Ingushetia in 2006.

Suicide terrorism also escalated after the fall of Grozny. The first attack was carried out by a young woman, Khava Barayev, who drove a truck bomb into a pro-Russian Chechen checkpoint on 6 June 2000, killing several. Between 2 and 3 July that year, a hundred Russian servicemen were killed or wounded in a series of five co-ordinated suicide bombings in urban areas. A fifteen-year-old girl was shot dead as she tried to drive a truck filled with explosives into a Russian military building in Grozny in December 2001; the following year, suicide bombers wore Russian uniforms to get close to government buildings. Although guards opened fire as the trucks broke through a checkpoint, the detonation brought down a four-storey building and killed eighty people. In 2003, two suicide bombers used a truck bomb to destroy a Russian intelligence-services building, killing fifty-nine, and a lone female suicide bomber blew herself up alongside a bus in June that year, leaving eighteen Russian airmen dead. In August, a truck bomb driven by a suicide bomber attacked a military hospital in North Ossetia. Clearly designed to terrorize military personnel and Russian civilian opinion, the blast left 50 dead.

The Russians inflicted a steady attrition against the insurgents. The notorious Khattab was killed by a poisoned letter on 19 March 2002 in an operation orchestrated by the Russian intelligence services. Abu al-Walid, the Saudi successor of Khattab, was killed in an air attack on 16 April 2004. Kantash Mansarov, the imam of the militant Jamaat movement and possibly the co-ordinator of insurgent attacks in the capital, was killed by security forces on 19 February 2005. The following month, Rizvan Chitigov, a Chechen insurgent commander, was killed by pro-Russian Chechen security forces. In May, Vakha Arsanov, the former Vice President, was killed, as were Danilbek Eskiyev and Alash Daudov, two Chechen guerrilla leaders. Daudov was thought to have been the mastermind behind attacks on police checkpoints in Grozny, a hostage-taker and a terrorist who had planned to use chemical agents. He was killed by Russian intelligence agents. Finally, Rasul Tambulatov, the Chechen fighter who commanded insurgents in the Shelkovsky District, was killed, and several of his bomb-making associates were captured. However, it was the death of Akhmed Avtorkhanov, the former head of Chechen security under Maskhadov, that Putin described as a turning point. He was the last of the pre-war leaders, leaving the resistance only with militant Muslims and foreigners. The calculation was that the Chechen people were less likely to support these fanatical elements, and there was a degree of truth in that assumption.

In 2006, it seemed that the policy of targeting the rebel leadership had continued. The rebel 'President' since the death of Maskhadov had been Abdul-Halim Sadulayev, but he was gunned down by the FSB and a group of paramilitaries in Argun in June that year. Despite a Chechen insurgent ambush the following month which they claimed was in revenge for the death of Sadulayev, President Putin announced that 'combat operations' had effectively come to an end in Chechnya. The confident statement was reinforced a week later when Shamil Basayev, the former defender of Grozny, was killed when a truck in his convoy carrying 110 kilos of explosives exploded.[18]

Russia's methods for winning the war have been sharply criticized internationally and have been regarded as a form of 'state terror'. Human rights organizations, including Amnesty International, estimate that as many as 5,000 Chechens have 'disappeared' since 1999. They accuse the Russian security forces of using rape, murder and abduction as tools of coercion. The American Secretary of State Madeleine Albright addressed the UN Commission on Human Rights in March 2000 and expressed her 'alarm' at the 'persistent, credible reports of human rights violations' and feared that Russia was in danger of isolating itself because of international condemnation.[19] Amnesty argued that attacks on civilians were routine, including the widespread bombing or shelling of villages and towns. Refugees and those who got in the way of looting were particularly vulnerable. Amnesty also pointed out that both sides had executed prisoners. President Kadyrov was quick to blame Russian personnel for acting like 'death squads', for spiriting away civilians in the dead of night, and for summary executions and torture. Ironically, some of this activity was the work of his own son's militia and his own security police as the Kadyrov dynasty sought to assert itself.[20] In March 2006, a Chechen ombudsman appointed to look into the issue of 'disappearances' concluded that the local authorities could not solve the issue and that federal – that is to say, Russian – assistance was necessary. He implied that it was the Chechen government that was problem. The Russian human rights group Memorial estimates that 1,893 Chechens were kidnapped between 2002 and 2006. Of these, 653 were found alive, 186 were killed, and 1,023 'disappeared'. Their research covered only a third of the country, so the scale could be far larger.

Terrorist attacks have incensed Russian personnel and embittered the conduct of the war, and they have not been limited to the theatre of operations. In May 2002, a bomb was detonated at a military parade at

Kaspiysk in Dagestan, but most of the forty-two dead were civilians, including seventeen children. In July 2003, two Chechen girls were stopped trying to enter a rock festival at the Tushino air-base near Moscow. They blew themselves up, killing fifteen people. This was the first suicide attack deep inside Russia, but investigators could find no motive and no group claimed responsibility, leading to speculation that it was a random revenge attack for the deaths of Chechen civilians. However, in December, a male suicide bomber blew himself up on a packed commuter train at Yessentuki, 1,000 kilometres south of Moscow. Forty-four people were killed and two hundred wounded. Five days later, a female suicide bomber, using a specifically manufactured belt packed with ball bearings, exploded near the Kremlin, killing six people. These attacks were claimed by Shamil Basayev to be his work. The following February, the pattern of attacking busy transport systems was repeated as a bomb was detonated on a metro train at rush hour. Thirty-nine were killed and 134 wounded. The group that claimed responsibility called itself Gazoton Murdash and was led by Lom-Ali. The most daring attack, however, occurred on 24 August 2004, when two Chechen women blew themselves up on two Russian airliners, killing 90 passengers and crew.

These terrorist incidents, and many of the attacks carried out by Chechen insurgents during the two wars, have led Russian authorities to label almost all Chechen fighters as terrorists and bandits. Prisoners are not held as combatants but are detained on charges of possessing weapons illegally or participating in criminal armed groups. Fighters are imprisoned for murder or attempted murder and not accorded the status of prisoners of war. They cannot therefore be released at the end of the conflict. Salman Raduyev, a Chechen insurgent commander, was tried in December 2001 and found guilty of murder and terrorism. He died in a Russian prison camp a year later. The case of Salautdin Temirbulatov was more clear-cut. Sentenced to death for the murder of four Russian soldiers, Temirbulatov had filmed their execution, which had taken place in 1996. The video was one of many that became the stock-in-trade propaganda of the Chechen and Arab jihadists, but it was also used by the Russian army to illustrate to their troops what their opponents were like.

In 2001, Chechen terrorists targeted Turkey as a platform for their cause, seizing a Russian airliner as it left the country and forcing it to land in Saudi Arabia.[21] Saudi commandos stormed the plane, killing one hijacker but also two civilians. The following month, another terrorist cell took 100 Turkish hostages in a hotel in Istanbul. After twelve hours they surrendered, suggesting that they were trying to highlight their cause outside of the region. But these incidents appeared relatively benign in light of events that were to unfold over the next three years.

The ruthlessness of Chechen jihadists was brought home most starkly by the Moscow Theatre Siege in October 2002.[22] Forty terrorists took seven hundred people hostage and demanded that the Russians withdraw entirely from the Chechen Republic. Failure to comply would mean the systematic execution of all the hostages. Buying time with negotiations, the authorities were not able to save the lives of several Russians, who were murdered. However, as the condition of the hostages deteriorated, gas was used to incapacitate the terror gang. Special Forces stormed the building, shooting the Chechens dead before they could detonate their suicide belts and other bombs. Sadly, many of the hostages died while they were unconscious because of blocked airways. A desire to keep the identity of the gas a secret hampered efforts to revive the victims. What should have been a successful end to the three-day siege was blighted by the tragedy of 100 lives lost. Despite initial denials, Basayev later admitted that he had orchestrated the plot.

However, the most horrific hostage-taking incident related to the war was the siege of Beslan in September 2004.[23] More than 30 terrorists seized control of School Number One and held a thousand people hostage, most of whom were small children. As security forces positioned themselves around the complex over two days, there were occasional shots fired and more than one explosion. The terror group may have been trying to establish a perimeter zone, but they had wired the entire complex with explosives. They videoed themselves, brazenly showing the explosives dangling above the heads of terrified children. Before the Special Forces were ready, a series of explosions and an exchange of gunfire panicked the terrorists into detonating all their devices. In a desperate attempt to save the lives of the children and staff, the ill-prepared security forces and police stormed the complex. Explosions brought down the roof of the main building, killing many inside. A crossfire of automatic weapons killed more of the hostages but also almost all of the terrorists. Children were carried away in the arms of security personnel or ran for safety amid chaotic scenes. Three hundred and thirty-one civilians were killed and eleven Special Forces troops died in the rescue attempt.

Beslan had a profound effect on the Chechen cause. It hardened Russian domestic opinion against the Chechens, particularly when Baseyev admitted responsibility via a website two weeks after the siege. This did much to hearten Putin, who had consistently demanded a tough line. In October 2004, just one month after Beslan, the Duma approved a clause specifying that, in future hostage-taking incidents, the families of terrorists would be seized by the authorities, who would act towards them in exactly the same way as the terrorists did towards Russian hostages. But, more importantly, Beslan deterred insurgent groups from further hostage-taking missions.[24] Not only had practically all of the terrorists died without achieving their goals; they had lost popular backing. Many Chechens, including insurgent leaders, felt that the terrorists had gone too far.

ATTEMPTS TO SPREAD OR TO LIMIT THE WAR

Chechen insurgents, or more accurately, the jihadist elements that augment the insurgency, have made several attempts to widen the conflict and embroil the rest of the Caucasus region. The Russians have been just as determined to contain the fighting, although they have not been averse to pursuing their opponents across borders. The deaths of Chechen nationalist leaders has made way for radicals who use the ideology of militant Islam rather than Chechen national identity as their rallying cry. Maskhadov had called for Moscow to recognize Chechnya as an independent state, but the jihadists call for the Russians to be driven out of the Caucasus altogether. Regional aims have thus superseded national ones. In April 2006, the Chechen insurgent commander Doku Umarov insisted that any chance of negotiation with Russia had come to an end. Movladi Udugov echoed this new hardline stance, arguing that the Russians should expect attacks across their country. He insisted that it was now a case of 'total war' and that war should be waged wherever the Chechens' enemies could be reached. The implication of this statement is that terrorism could increase.

Taking Dagestan as an example, that threat of escalation already seems evident. There were relatively few incidents in the years 2000–2004. However, in 2004, there were thirty terrorist attacks, and, according to the Russian Academy of Sciences, in the first six months of 2005 there were seventy. But it was not just the number of operations. There was greater sophistication in the design of Improvised Exsplosive Devices (IEDs) in the latter years. It is estimated that there may be as many as 2,000 insurgents, of whom the bulk belong to the radicalized Jamaat Sharia, a group that claims to be the legitimate power in Dagestan.[25] Nevertheless, Jamaat Sharia received a significant setback when Russian security forces killed Rasul Makasharipov, its leader, on 12 July 2005.

Russia feels that Georgia, which has little reason to back the Chechens, is in fact secretly assisting the insurgents. Moscow argues that Georgians have failed to stem the flow of personnel or matériel across the border, and that the country is effectively a 'safe haven' for the fighters. The accusation was highlighted by the shooting down of a UN helicopter in Kodori Gorge in Georgia in October 2001. The Georgians claimed that they had no troops in the area, but this only led to speculation that a SAM missile had been fired by the Chechen commander Ruslan Gelayev, who, it was claimed, had been hired by the Georgians to deal with their own separatists in Abkhazia. The alleged collusion was never proven, but from February 2002, Georgia started to receive American support as a partner in the Global War on Terror. Yet, despite the obvious common cause in wanting to neutralize 'foreign fighters', relations with Russia remained frosty. In August that year, Georgia accused Russia of launching air strikes into its territory in the Pankisi Gorge area. Nevertheless, the following spring, Ruslan Gelayev was killed by Russian border guards as he tried to make raids into Ingushetia and Chechnya from a base inside Georgia.

The last Chechen attempt to broker a deal with Russia was made by Maskhadov in February 2005, but his call for a ceasefire was ignored and he himself was killed by Russian Special Forces the following month. His death marked the end of any moderate political force emerging on the Chechen side. His successor, Abdul-Khalim Sadulayev, made substantial changes in the political leadership of the resistance, but his death in June 2006 left Doku Umarov in command. Umarov's spokesperson announced that the goal was no longer the establishment of a liberal democracy or an independent nation-state but the creation of a North Caucasian Emirate founded on Sharia law and governed by an oligarchy of Islamist war veterans. The movement reorganized the political leadership into a militarized structure. Regions were divided in *jamaats* (sectors), or commands, and there was a clear intention to spread the fighting across the whole belt of mountains, regardless of national borders.

The result of the reorganization of command and strategy was an extension of attacks into neighbouring states such as Ingushetia. In 2004, Baseyev made a series of night attacks on the former capital, Nazran, and several other settlements, killing 80 security-forces personnel and several civilians. An attack was also made in broad daylight in October 2005 at Nalchik in the Kabardino-Balkar Republic; some 90 people were killed.

President Putin was not deterred by the continuing insurgency or the attempts to extend it across the region. He was eager to see the establishment of a government in Grozny that was favourable to Moscow. A referendum was organized to approve a new constitution, but many Chechens boycotted the vote, and there was some concern that the 40,000-strong Russian army garrison was included (out of 540,000 eligible voters). There was little support for Moscow's chosen leader, Akhmad Kadyrov, either. In the presidential elections of October 2003, Kadyrov used his militia to coerce his political rivals, and no separatists were permitted to vote.[26] Consequently, he won 80 per cent of the poll. But his assassination in 2004 led to a new presidential election. Despite a Chechen insurgent raid on the capital, which targeted polling stations and government buildings, the election went ahead, with Gen. Alu Alkhanov, a pro-Moscow candidate, emerging as the winner.

Nevertheless, Ramzan Kadyrov, the son of the murdered President, became Prime Minister and gradually established himself as the *de facto* ruler in 2005. His methods of rule are unorthodox. He runs a militia that has been accused of kidnappings and torture.[27] He exercises authority through clan members and a network of close political allies. Soon after he became Premier, he acquired control of the republic's oil industry and secured significant financial backing from Moscow. Much of this money was siphoned off into the hands of individuals. Despite the financial inducements, the Russians got little in the way of loyalty. The Chechen People's Assembly called for the withdrawal of all Russian forces except border guards, while Kadyrov himself criticized the Federal Police, known as the Operational and Search Bureau (ORB-2), and called for refugee camps to be closed down because they were nests of international spies.

Chechnya continued to be unstable. Militiamen loyal to Kadyrov clashed with armed gangs affiliated with President Alkhanov on 29 April 2006. The *Kadyrovtsy* militia had been repeatedly blamed for kidnapping, torture and murder, particularly of political rivals. This bloody encounter finally forced Kadyrov to disband his irregular private army, but the Prime Minister can still call on a loyal cohort of former soldiers and clansmen from the Tsentoroi area. As in other Central Asian states, loyalties are built up of layers of affiliation to ideologies, regions and states, but clan identity and heritage remain important bonds too.

Kadyrov has altered his policies to court greater popular support and thus cement his rule. In 2006, the most surprising development was his willingness to introduce greater Islamization. In January, he banned alcohol and gambling, and enforced the wearing of headscarves. He spoke in favour of polygamy, and suggested that teaching the Koran and Sharia law ought to be compulsory in Chechen schools. The following month, after public criticism of 'immorality' in the Chechen media, he introduced censorship. The international 'cartoons row' led to a ban on Danish humanitarian workers in the country. Alkhanov has joined this chorus, suggesting that he is in favour of the introduction of Sharia law. Not unlike the pro-Soviet Afghan governments of the 1980s, playing to the Islamic sentiments of the people was supposed to bring the administration greater popularity and undermine the jihadists' arguments. However, in Afghanistan, the governments consistently failed to persuade the people that they were sincere. Often their brutalities spoke louder than their protestations of piety. In Chechnya, it is too early to say whether Kadyrov, who, it is believed, wants to assume the title of President, will succeed in winning the hearts and minds of the people while centralizing power in his own hands. If he fails, it is unlikely that Russia will remain a passive observer for long.

Despite Russian attempts to have their war in Chechnya seen as part of a legitimate struggle against terrorism, the Council of Europe and the European Court of Human Rights have both been critical of Moscow's actions. In February 2005, the European Court ruled that the Russian government had violated rights to life and property, and had not honoured the ban on torture or inhuman and degrading treatment. The Court then ordered the Russian government to pay compensation to six plaintiffs. The hearing was based on three incidents. The first had occurred in October 1999, when the Russian air force had strafed a convoy of civilians who were trying to escape from Grozny. The second was the alleged extrajudicial killing of five men in the capital in January 2000. The third was the indiscriminate bombardment of the village of Katyr-Yurt in February 2000. No compensation was paid. In 2005 and 2006, further cases were brought to the attention of the court alleging that men and women had 'disappeared' or been blatantly executed by the Russian forces. As early as April 2000, the United Nations Commission on Human Rights (UNCHR) had called for a commission of enquiry into alleged abuses of Chechen civilians. The call for an enquiry was repeated in 2001.

Few independent observers have defended the Russian army's behaviour, and the sheer number of accusations strongly suggests that many Russian troops were ill-disciplined in their treatment of civilians. Worse, it appears that many Russian officers had little time for civilians who got in the way of operational objectives and perhaps even encouraged rough treatment. Nevertheless, in a war of this nature, troops under threat of ambush from insurgents who do not wear uniforms cannot easily differentiate friend from foe, or civilian from combatant. It is true that the Russian army has a reputation for ruth-lessness, and only the Russian government appears to deny that its soldiers have acted excessively, but neither side has a record of restraint. As in Afghanistan, Russian soldiers have contempt for enemies who mutilate their dead and wounded, or who attack through stealth or while posing as civilians. The Chechen fighters must accept some responsibility for the way the war has developed.

There are a few cases that have been brought to trial. In 2003 Col. Yuri Badanov was sentenced for kidnapping and murdering a Chechen woman. The hearings lasted more than two years, Badanov claiming that the Chechen woman concerned had been guiding fighters against his armoured unit. A far more high-profile case was heard in 2004. Four Special Forces personnel were accused of shooting dead six Chechens, one of whom was a disabled woman. The bodies were allegedly burned to conceal the evidence. The men were acquitted twice, even though, in the retrial, they admitted they had killed the victims. The court ruled that they could not be convicted because they had been following orders, but the verdict caused intense anger in Chechnya. Four other servicemen have been tried and received long prison sentences, but in each case the main determinant was military 'indiscipline' rather than any criticism of the way the war was being conducted and the fate of Chechen civilians.

There are many claims that witnesses to other incidents are silenced through fear. When, in April 2001, the mayor of Grozny, Bislan Gantamirov, announced that seventeen bodies had been recovered from a basement adjacent to the Oktyabrskoye police station, he accused the police of execution-style killings. Local residents inun-dated the office with enquiries about missing relatives. However, the basement was cordoned off, and soon after the building above it was destroyed. Gantamirov suddenly changed his statement and argued that the police had not been responsible. The Russian group Memorial believed that another basement near the same police station was used for routine tortures and executions until 2006. They estimate that 'hundreds' may have been killed there, but, once again, the building concerned has been destroyed. Several mass graves have also been uncovered. Corpses often bear marks of torture, mutilation or close-range bullet wounds. Pro-Russian Chechen authorities state that these are the result of insurgent killings, and some undoubtedly are. Yet there are doubts about several. In January 2003, for example, ten corpses were found that appeared to have been of people killed by explosives. Three were identified as individuals held in custody by the Chechen state security forces, although the authorities claimed that these too were the victims of insurgent executions. Other mass graves have been explained as groups of civilians who were buried hastily having been killed during the siege of 1999.

IN RETROSPECT

The figures for the numbers killed and wounded in the Chechen Wars are strongly contested. Russian sources such as the Defence Ministry state that 4,700 men were killed in the fighting from 1999 to 2002, while Russia's official news agency Itar-Tass believes that this is more likely to be the number killed in 2002 alone. Inexplicably, the official line is that, by 2005, 3,450 had been killed, but this figure excludes Interior Ministry troops, paramilitaries and intelligence-services personnel. Independent sources, such as Janes in the UK, estimate that 11,000 Russian and Chechen state forces had been killed in the two wars.[28] The Chechen government estimates that the number of civilians who died in the second war was in the region of 200,000. Insurgent sources state that this figure is more likely to be in the region of 250,000–300,000. They acknowledge the loss of 5,000 of their own side, but their claim that they have killed 50,000 security personnel seems grossly exaggerated. Again, independent sources think the number of civilian dead to be in the region of 80,000.

At the time of the First Chechen War, most Russians believed that Chechnya was an integral part of their national sovereignty. The Russian government tended to give the impression that insurgents were an unrepresentative fringe organization. Within the government, however, there were clearly concerns that Chechen separatism might prove an inspiration to other troubled areas, particularly in the Caucasus. There were already examples of states regaining their independence, including Georgia, Armenia and Azerbaijan, but a violent breakaway was a different matter. Whether Yeltsin felt he could execute a lightning war to snuff out unrest, or whether he felt pressed to act by increasing instability in Chechnya and powerful financial incentives, is impossible to tell. The numbers of troops committed to the first war were insufficient to take Grozny swiftly or to occupy the country effectively. The lack of training in counter-insurgency, the low morale, the logistical problems, the difficulties presented by the terrain and the heavy-handedness that alienated the Chechen people did not assist the Russian war effort. Insurgents fought the Russians to a standstill, and Yeltsin was eager to effect a quick settlement rather than escalate the conflict.

In the Second Chechen War, Putin was eager to apply greater force and to be less concerned with Western criticism. Having secured Grozny in a more methodical campaign, he enjoyed some support at home, but a steady attrition of troops caused some anxiety. After 9/11, he was able to draw attention to the links between Chechen jihadists and the ideology of Al-Qaeda, and this quietened some criticism from the US. Nevertheless, Europeans continued to be critical of Russia's human-rights violations. The Russian forces and their Chechen allies, including many fighters from the first war who now work for the government, have found it difficult to bring the conflict to a conclusion, and their cause has not been helped by brutality against civilians, corruption and dictatorship in the Chechen government, and the spreading of terrorist and counter-terrorist operations across the region. The Islamization and instability of the Chechen polity, two of the original reasons for the war, have not been resolved to Moscow's liking. Terrorist attacks continue, and, despite the disastrous outcomes of the Moscow Theatre Siege, suicide attacks on transport systems and the killings at Beslan, the insurgents continue to function with a degree of popular backing.

There are other, less 'political' effects of these wars which are nevertheless profound. Yuri Alexandrovsky, Deputy Director of the Serbsky National Centre for Social and Forensic Psychiatry in Moscow, believes that 70 per cent of the veterans of the conflicts are suffering 'cs', or 'Chechen Syndrome', a euphemism for post-traumatic stress syndrome.

Their behaviour has been altered by the experience of the counter-insurgency environment. Some of them have become violent, others withdrawn. In a depressing reflection of the Afghanistan war, some of these young men have turned to drug and alcohol abuse as a coping mechanism. Suicide rates are also very high.

Another by-product of the war is the greater brutality and criminalization of the Russian police. Their tours of duty in Chechnya have imparted habits of violence and corruption. Having been given license to beat up, even torture, suspects there, even if this is not officially sanctioned, policemen tend to feel that they should continue the tactics elsewhere. Testimonies and confessions can be obtained far more quickly and efficiently when accompanied by 'tough' tactics. The Russian Interior Ministry admitted in 2005 that crimes by police officers had risen by 46.8 per cent, although they gave no absolute figures. Most Russians now don't entirely trust the police, and some fear them.

For Chechens, there are other legacies. The World Health Organisation observed that almost 90 per cent of the population was suffering from either physical or emotional 'distress'. A third of these had the symptoms of post-traumatic stress. Many children have a constant fear of violence and tragedy. Yet there is little sympathy in Russia. Racist attacks on people from the Caucasus have increased there. The government acknowledged that incidents of racist violence had doubled from previous years in the period 2003–4 – that is, from twenty reported events to forty-five.[29] However, among the Russian people, there was a significant rise in nationalist sentiment. The far right enjoys the sympathy of between 12 and 24 per cent of the population. Putin still has the support of the people when he plays the nationalist card. Ironically, so does the Chechen government.

THE KARABAKH, ABKKAZIA AND SOUTH OSSETIA CONFLICTS

The Karabakh War, fought between Christian Armenians and Muslim Azeris, was at the same time an ethnic conflict, an attempt to resolve territorial irredentism from the Soviet era and a bid for regional power when the USSR collapsed. In the Revolution of 1917, there had been a brief period of inter-ethnic co-operation, exemplified by the establishment of the Transcaucasion Federation.[30] But the union of Azerbaijan, Armenia and Georgia was brief. The Azeris soon looked to Turkish support to oust the Armenians from Nakhichevan, while the Armenians were eager to eject the Azeris from Zanzegur. In Karabakh, however, the Armenians were divided between those who wished to support Dashnak, the pro-Armenian lobby, or the Bolsheviks. Both factions were brutally dealt with during the Soviet invasion of November 1920. Once the Soviets were established, the Azeris demanded that Karabakh be administered by them, which prompted a violent Armenian protest at Yerevan in 1921. Perhaps as a deliberate policy of divide and rule, the local Bolshevik leader, Josef Stalin, awarded Karabakh to the Azeris in 1923. The seeds were thus sown for a renewal of territorial demands at the end of the Soviet era.

When President Gorbachev granted greater autonomy to the Soviet republics in 1988, there were violent protests in Yerevan and Baku between the ethnic groups, a situation worsened by a clash at Askeran in Karabakh. At Sumgait, north of Baku, Armenians from Karabakh were set upon by gangs of Azeris and 100 people were killed; Gorbachev was forced to despatch troops to contain the violence, but the earthquake in Armenia quelled the unrest temporarily. Over a period of some months, ethnic tensions led to the flight of refugees into Azerbaijan or Armenia, and political leaders from the two states refused to compromise. In Azerbaijan, a Popular Front was formed. It clashed with Interior Ministry troops at Baku and elsewhere, but the Azerbaijani authorities continued to fuel the situation by closing traffic and trade with Armenia, knowing that it was dependent economically on hubs such as Nakhichevan. In 1991, Armenia declared itself independent while Azerbaijan chose to support the idea of a Union Treaty organization. Both sides began to build up arms. Azeri paramilitaries then entered Karabakh to 'disarm the militants' in Operation Ring (April 1991), a move approved by Gorbachev.[31] Loudspeakers bellowed that Armenians would be regarded as a threat unless they disarmed, but the locals calculated that the real intention of the Azeri forces was to ethnically cleanse the area. Resistance was initially disorganized and ineffective, but news of mistreatment of civilians and forced deportations led to an increase of Armenian volunteers willing to fight the Azeris, among them Monte Melkonian, who was to emerge as a prominent leader of the resistance.

Initially the Azeris possessed more advantages. The area was familiar to many Azeri commanders as it had been a potential battlefield of the Cold War, and they had more troops there: five Azeri divisions supported by five airfields against just three Armenian divisions with no air-bases. Moreover, the Interior Ministry forces (MVD), who had been engaged in selling or jettisoning their equipment in 1991, left the Azeris with 286 tanks, 842 APCs and 386 guns. Many members of the old 4th Red Army, and foreign donors from the Arab states, Turkey and Iran, also supported their cause. The Armenians were dependent on funds from Armenians overseas and their own resources, but they did make an appeal to the US. Nevertheless, weapons and fighters were moved into Karabakh via the Liachin Corridor and commenced an insurgency. At the siege of Stepanakert, the Azeris shelled the town freely, killing many civilians with heavy artillery and Katyusha rockets and reducing the city to a shambles, but the Armenians counter attacked. When they reached Khojaly on 26 February 1992, it is alleged that irregular forces carried out a massacre in revenge for the Sumgait pogrom, but the details remain murky.[32] Some 17,000 Azeris were killed in the fighting, twice the estimated number of Armenians. The Russians stepped in to broker a ceasefire when the Azeris had been forced back inside their own territory, but no peace settlement was convened. In 2006, the Armenians remained in occupation of some 14 per cent of Azeri territory, but border skirmishes are not uncommon.

Ethnic, political and territorial anxieties similarly drove the Abkhazia Conflict. In the late 1980s, as the possibility of Georgia's independence emerged, many Abkhaz grew fearful that their autonomy would be lost, and they began to lobby for an independent Soviet state of their own. However, on 16 July 1989, demonstrations turned violent and an estimated sixteen Georgians were killed in the unrest. Soviet troops were deployed to restore order, and Moscow blamed nationalist hardliners for the fighting. When Georgia's independence was finally realized in 1991, Zviad Gamasakhurdia, a former Soviet dissident, became its first leader. However, he was so unpopular that he was forced from power in January 1992 after a prolonged siege of his offices. His successor was the ex-Foreign Minister of the Soviet Union, Eduard Shevardnadze, but he was forced to accept a government dominated by Georgian nationalists. When this government adopted the constitution of 1921, the Abkhaz assembly believed it marked the end of their autonomy. They consequently declared themselves independent, although no government recognized them. Apparently acting against a group of kidnappers, Georgian forces rolled into Abkhazia, but the Abkhaz interpreted this as an act of aggression, and fighting broke out. After a week of violence with heavy casualties on both sides, the Georgians took control of the province and shut down the assembly in the capital, Sukhumi. The Abkhaz defeat prompted a furious response from the 'Confederation of the Mountain Peoples of the Caucasus', a group that included Chechnya and Ossetia but that effectively meant Russia. Volunteer paramilitaries including jihadists joined in the fighting against the Georgians. The large number of Russians led to accusations from Tbilisi that the Russian government was behind the effort, and the Abkhazian offensive that swept Georgian troops out of the north of that province bore all the hallmarks of Russian regular army operations.

However, there was stalemate until July 1993, when the Abkhaz made an effort to seize the capital. There was heavy shelling, but the rebels failed to secure the city. Another offensive was launched in September, and after ten days of intense fighting, Sukhumi finally capitulated. The fall of the city was immediately followed by one of the worst atrocities of the era. Thousands of Georgians were massacred by the Abkhaz rebels and their allies. The Georgians were unable to mount a counter-offensive as a new threat appeared. The supporters of Gamasakhurdia led an uprising in the province of Mingrelia (Samegrelo), but, fearing another massacre, the Georgian population fled. Some 250,000 people were displaced by the fighting in and around Abkhazia, and an estimated 10,000–30,000 Georgians and 3,000 Abkhaz were killed. International observers such as the Organisation for Security and Co-operation in Europe (OSCE) condemn the Abkhaz for ethnic cleansing and for gross violations of human

rights. The UN does not recognize the government of Abkhazia, arguing that it was perfectly legitimate for Georgia to have moved to restore
law and order in 1992 within its own sovereign borders. It also insists
that, if there is any referendum in the future on Abkhazia's independence, it must be done after the multi-ethnic (and primarily Georgian)
civilian population has returned. A UN observer group, UNOMIG,
currently monitors the ceasefire between the two belligerents. However,
Russian peacekeepers are regarded as an unwelcome intrusion by the
Georgians. A Georgian Special Forces mission to the Kodori Valley
caused particular controversy when Russia demanded they be withdrawn and not redeployed there in the future. The EU and the US are
unlikely to support Abkhazia since they regard Georgia as a more
important, and pro-Western, partner, but nor are they likely to replace
the Russians as the main peacekeeping force. However, in 1998
Washington offered $15 million for reconstruction and rehabilitation,
and progress was made on the peace process. Russia, for all its antagonism, is eager for Gazprom, the state company, to conquer the
Georgian markets, and they would like to see an opening to the Black
Sea for North Ossetia. The West wants to see Georgia become the
transit route of oil and gas to Turkey.[33]

Georgia has also faced unrest in the north of the country, again
involving Russia. In 1989, the South Ossetia Supreme Soviet, strongly
influenced by the South Ossetian Popular Front (Ademon Nykhas),
demanded union with North Ossetia, which lies inside Russia. The
Georgian Assembly overruled the South Ossetians, and suppressed
public demonstrations and newspapers on the issue. After Georgian
independence, more measures were brought in to prevent separatism.
The Georgian language became the only language of the administration, even though Russian, the tongue of South Ossetia, had been part
of the 1936 constitution. Protests grew increasingly violent during
1991. Ossetian villages were burnt down by angry Georgian nationalists, prompting Ossetian reprisals. As the fighting escalated, it is
estimated that 1,000 were killed and between 60,000 and 100,000
made homeless. South Ossetians who fled north found themselves
unwelcome, especially among the Ingush, because of fears over land
ownership and employment. However, the conflict was dampened by

Russia's threat to intervene in 1992. In November that year a peace-keeping force of Russians, Georgians and Ossetians was established. Order was maintained until 2004, when Georgian efforts to crack down on drug smugglers led to kidnappings, shooting incidents and terrorist bombings. The ceasefire is frequently threatened by the stand-off between Georgians and Ossetians.

Harri Kamarainen of the OSCE's Conflict Prevention Centre believes that, oil pipelines aside, the causes of the conflict in the Caucasus have been strong nationalist tendencies and weak institutional frameworks. This stands in contrast to Central Asia's republics, which have strong Communist Party and government structures but where nationalist sentiments are less pronounced than local, ethnic and clan loyalties.[34] The high incidence of civil violence, rather than inter-state conflict, seems to confirm this. Russia is eager to play the leading part in the region, and it regards the Caucasus as an important part of strategic and economic security. To secure energy resources, the West and Russia share the desire to see a peaceful resolution to the conflicts in the Caucasus, and it is this common ground that may herald co-opera-tion in the future. A desire to suppress and defeat terrorist organizations, however they are constituted, could also mean better co-ordination. The complexity of the conflicts, and Russia's tacit support of Abkhazia and South Ossetia, remain the most significant obstacles to a final resolution.

Chapter 8

China and Xinjiang Province

There has been a long history of unrest in the westernmost province of China, the product of differences between the local populations, the majority of whom are Uighurs, and the Han Chinese, who have been its overlords for extended periods in the past. The differences are racial but also religious, since the majority of Xinjiang's population is Muslim. Irrespective of their ethnic or religious origins, they regard the Han Chinese presence as an occupation that has brought mixed blessings. While many are undoubtedly profiting from an end to the unrest that plagued the first half of the twentieth century, there are deep suspicions of Chinese triumphalism about the 'development' of the province, particularly when so few seem to benefit. Chinese policy is driven by several concerns: the growing demands of the economy, an expanding population, separatism and security. Clearly, China's burgeoning economy means greater strain on the resources of its western region and a desire to acquire more from the neighbouring Central Asian republics. However, the constant refrain of development is also the result of a fear of separatism in China. There were calls for autonomy and independence, accompanied by widespread violence, from the inhabitants of Xinjiang in the 1920s and from the 1980s. However, there was support for Xinjiang separatism from the USSR in the 1930s and '40s, and the region was effectively under Soviet influence until the Chinese Communist victory in 1949. Nevertheless, the failure of China's policies also helps to explain the unrest of the last half century.

The Great Leap Forward and the Cultural Revolution produced economic chaos, deepened resentment of modernizing outsiders and led to crackdowns against local protestors. They also increased the migration of Han Chinese on a massive scale, fuelling local resentment of alien influence and power.[1]

Alongside these policies lies the more subtle but no less damaging attitude of new Chinese migrants, a combination of curiosity, condescension, hostility and arrogant high-handedness. Exclusion from jobs, alleged mistreatment of women and reforms regarded as interference produced the 1990 Baren Riot and the even more serious 1997 Gulja Riot, the direct consequence of which was a terrorist campaign orchestrated largely by local Uighurs with external backing. The Chinese blame this wave of terrorism on foreigners such as Al-Qaeda and the Taliban, a view that has affected relations with the Central Asian republics, Turkey and Pakistan, and also with the US. However, critics argue that the violence is really a reflection of local concerns about their treatment, overwhelming Han migration and a lack of jobs. Undoubtedly, China is eager to exploit Xinjiang's oil and cotton, and sees the province as a space to resettle its population from the east, but some suggest the plan is to deliberately swamp the Uighurs. The resistance is therefore partly generated by an ideology (the unrealistic notion that China can be forced to relinquish Xinjiang), mishandling of local issues by the Chinese (and a refusal to acknowledge the realities of their policies), and a legacy of violence and jihadism. The Chinese seek to eradicate unrest by development, by migration and through political controls. These measures may take a long time to take effect, and there are no guarantees of their success.

THE LEGACY OF VIOLENCE

The overthrow of the Manchus in the Wuhan Rising in 1911 marked the beginning of a long era of warlordism in China. The Civil War also affected western China, although Xinjiang was regarded as a minor theatre compared with the struggle taking place in the east. When, in the same period, the Bolsheviks seized power in Russia and gradually advanced across Central Asia, the heart of the continent was in turmoil. In Mongolia, for a brief period, the Russian Baron Ungern-Sternberg exercised a brutal reign of terror and massacred many hundreds of Chinese. Urga (Ulan Bator) was sacked in October 1920 with particular ferocity.[2] Attempting to invade Russia in May 1921, Ungern-Sternberg was defeated twice and fled to Chinese Central Asia. Pursued by the Red Army, his force was gradually destroyed. In the end, his own troops were so demoralized that plots were hatched to assassinate him, and he was eventually wounded, captured and tried by a people's court, whereupon he was shot by a firing squad.

Meanwhile, Sun Yat-sen, the founder of the Kuomintang (KMT), had established his capital in Canton as a rival base against the warlords of northern China, but when he received no help from the West, he turned to the USSR. As early as 1920, the Bolsheviks had sent emissaries to China to establish links with Communists there; they aimed to recruit cadres of men and women to study in Russia and to train in the revolutionary crafts of street-fighting and insurrection. So large were the numbers that they formed their own 'school' in the Soviet Union. Stalin, who had responsibility for relations with China, saw Sun Yat-sen as a tool, to be discarded once Bolshevik influence had been established. He despatched Mikhail Borodin to reorganise the KMT's party and armed forces using Soviet officers. This influence was critical, imposing discipline and encouraging grass-roots membership for the movement. However, the KMT also discovered that Stalin had ambitions to use western China as a springboard against British India to the south, and when Soviet consulates were opened there it appeared that Moscow planned to turn the region into a 'red republic'. There also appeared to be a plan to install the warlord Feng Yu-hsiang with Soviet funds as a pro-Moscow puppet, but there were soon tensions between the Chinese and Russians in Kashgar.[3] A secret convoy of goods was intercepted by the Chinese officials and impounded for two months. When the cargo was eventually examined, it was found to consist of gold and silver for some clandestine purpose. Later, the Russians tried to organize a rally in the provincial capital, but the Kashgar authorities prevented any Chinese from attending, fearing a *coup d'état*. A whispering campaign was orchestrated by the Soviets, and there was evidence of an increase in espionage and attempts to bribe Chinese officials. In sum, there appeared to be an attempt to extend Russian influence, but the Russians made no attempt to seize power by force. Perhaps they were waiting for the right opportunity. This finally presented itself with the death of Sun Yat-sen in March 1925.

In fact, in the central and eastern parts of China, the succession of Sun Yat-sen by Chiang Kai-shek was a setback for Moscow. Chiang Kai-shek curbed the Communists in the KMT, and, following a series of victories against the northern warlords, he purged the movement of 25,000 left-wingers in 1927. Borodin fled as the northern warlords stepped up their own attacks on Communists too. The Soviet embassy in the capital was sacked, and papers were unearthed which compromised the Russians' original plans (including an operation to orchestrate riots across European capitals). Faced with annihilation, the Chinese Communists attempted a coup against Chiang Kai-shek on 11 December 1927, but they commanded few followers, and, after two days of resistance in Beijing, they were defeated by KMT troops. This was followed by massacres of Communist civilians while Soviet consulates were closed down. However, as the KMT did not yet control Kashgar, the Soviet presence there was not affected. Chiang's victory had left Xinjiang isolated and vulnerable. For seventeen years, the province had been under the control of Governor Yang, a dictatorial figure who personally controlled the local currency, filtered information from China, and suppressed political factions, crime and dissent. However, sensing that the leader of Xinjiang lacked external support, Fan Yao-nan, Yang's deputy, assassinated the old governor in an attempt to gain power for himself in 1925. The Minister of the Interior, Chin Shu-jen, intercepted the conspirators and used the plot to seize control. Fan was executed and Chin governed for five years, increasing taxation but failing to tackle rising inflation or corruption. His tenure was thoroughly detested by the Uighurs. In 1930, in a bid to raise yet more revenue, he tried to annex Hami. He ordered an increase of taxation, seized land from local Uighur families (compensating them with low-quality alternatives) and failed to act against a tax collector who allegedly 'seduced' an Uighur girl. This last incident proved the final straw. The couple were lynched in a prelude to a wave of violence. Planning to inflict harsh reprisals, Chin despatched a military column to Hami, but the Uighurs appealed, fatefully, to a neighbouring warlord, Ma Chung-yin, for assistance.

Ma was a young bandit-soldier, an expert horseman and marksman, and a ruthless leader. He was a Tungan, so ethnically 'Chinese' and closely akin to the Turkis rather than the Uighurs, but, as a Muslim, he shared the faith of the people of Kashgar and Hami.[4] Having resigned from the KMT, he had established his own headquarters in Kansu, where he terrorized local people and lived from stolen goods. Settlements that resisted his demands were subjected to massacres of all men over 14. The under-14s were recruited and the women given over to the excesses of his soldiers. The appeal from the Uighurs gave Ma Chung-yin an inflated sense of his own importance, and he believed his mission gave him the status of a Central Asian *Mahdi* (deliverer, messenger). For four years, between 1931 and 1935, he waged war in Xinjiang, deepening the antagonism between the Han Chinese and the Uighurs, and giving a rough unity to local populations who had been banded together under that title. Turkis were the first to join him as he crossed the Gobi and seized Barkul. However, the Chinese garrison at Hami repulsed his assault, using a variety of modern weapons augmented by medieval fire-arrows. As the desert war ebbed and flowed, settlements were destroyed by both sides, although Ma's men tended to kill every living thing if they faced resistance, including women, children and livestock. A typhus epidemic accompanied the fleeing populations, further adding to the death toll. By 1933, the rebellion had spread across Xinjiang, and there were episodes of Chinese converting to Islam to save themselves, although that failed to stop their property being looted. Girls were seized, even converts, and there were many episodes of torture and mutilation. At Yarkand, the Chinese garrison held out for months but capitulated after bartering for their lives. The rebels failed to keep their word: the garrison was massacred along with their families, and their children were burned alive.

These atrocities, and the Chinese counter-atrocities, affected the region profoundly for generations yet also paved the way for the acceptance of Chinese Communist rule two decades later. The violence, warlordism and unrest caused such misery that any stability was welcomed. However, in 1934–5, it was not the Chinese who brought Ma's reign of terror to an end; it was the Russians. In 1934, Ma's forces made their third attempt to take Urumchi. They managed to seize houses close to the city walls, but the Chinese torched them, killing the occupants in the process. So desperate was the defence that the Chinese armed White Russians as auxiliaries, although they gave them inferior weapons for fear of an internal coup. In this they were right, for as soon as the Ma rebellion was crushed, the Russians did indeed attempt to seize the city from within. The Chinese governor, Sheng, had a more powerful ally, though, than the handful of Russian exiles. Crossing the border without insignia and in paramilitary uniforms, more than 2,000 men of the Red Army were secretly deployed to the city. When Ma's men made another attack on the walls, they were confronted with massed machine-gun fire supported by armoured cars. Ma was repulsed again, having suffered 2,000 casualties. His men fled south and westwards, plundering the local populations as they went and further alienating any base of support they might have enjoyed. Ma sought to continue the struggle, but, after visiting the Soviet consulate in Kashgar, he simply gave up and crossed into the USSR. There he disappeared, perhaps murdered in one of Stalin's purges. The remaining Tungan forces were driven out of Kashgar, Yark and and Khotan, and, as Red Army troops reached each settlement, they deployed 'advisors' to remain in place. In effect, the Soviet Union had taken control of the province.

Stalin's motives were grander than simply eradicating a minor warlord from a neighbouring state. He saw the potential for Ma to enlist Muslims from Soviet Central Asia and possibly re-ignite the Basmachi revolt. He was also aware that there were two Japanese attachés on Ma's staff. The Japanese seizure of Manchuria in 1931 and the attack on Jehol in 1935 appeared to threaten the Soviets in Mongolia, Siberia and, potentially, Central Asia. When, the following year, Japan concluded an anti-Comintern pact with Nazi Germany, Stalin felt that the USSR was being encircled as a prelude to an attack. The usual Bolshevik obsession with espionage grew to exaggerated proportions, and the purges of 1934–8 were invariably directed against 'spies'. In the meantime, Sheng diplomatically promoted some Uighurs and invited a second Soviet intervention in May 1937 against the remaining Tungan rebels. A reinforced Soviet regiment was sent to Hami to block any Japanese move and to keep the province isolated from the rest of China. Subsidized Russian goods were brought in, simply to undercut Chinese and British wares and thus extend Moscow's influence over this new buffer state. Russia acquired the province's mineral rights, its oil and its energy. Finally, in 1939, Soviet and Japanese forces clashed on the Mongolian frontier, and, defeated at Khalkin Gol, the Russians eagerly concluded a non-aggression pact with Tokyo in April 1941.

With elements of the Red Army deployed in Xinjiang, the province was effectively under Soviet control, and Russian engineers began to exploit the oil resources of the region, surveying and drilling wells. However, the years 1941–2 marked severe military setbacks for the USSR, accelerating the urgency for oil. Anticipating the final defeat of the Soviet Union and conscious of the Japanese military success in 1939, Sheng ordered the Russians out of Xinjiang. The advisors went but so did all the oil plant they had brought in, and 25 of the wells were capped. Undeterred, Sheng unleashed a reign of terror to re-establish his authority: 80,000 potential enemies were arrested and hundreds killed. Governor Sheng then turned to the KMT for support. However, Russian victories in 1943–4 prompted Sheng to purge his authorities of KMT members and invite Stalin's men back but without much success. Chiang, conscious now that Sheng would simply appeal to the highest bidder, 'recalled' him to the KMT government and gave him a minor post.

Even though Sheng had left, his police and armed forces acted with their usual ruthless efficiency against the last rebellion of Xinjiang in 1944.[5] The Ili Rebellion involved Kazakh exiles and local forces under the bandit leader Osman Batur, who were trying to establish the Eastern Turkestan Republic (ETR). The spark for the rising had been the execution of 400 Muslims, although the background was deepening resentment of new Chinese settlers. Uighurs joined the revolt, and there was a combined attack on the KMT at Nilka and Gulja. In panic, Chinese officials started shooting people randomly, prompting more Uighurs to join the resistance. The key leader to emerge in this community was Ahmedjan Kasimov, and he strove to unite Communists, Turkis and Islamists against the KMT. The Han Chinese were overwhelmed and many male officials were summarily shot. The ETR was formally declared on 15 November 1944 under the leadership of Ali Khan Ture, although real power still lay with Kasimov. Kyrgyz, Mongols and Russians joined the rebellion that winter, and the Soviets provided some assistance despite official denials. Local rebels were under no illusions, however: they were fighting not for the spread of Communism or for the interests of the Soviet Union but for the end of a Chinese occupation they regarded as humiliating. The KMT was driven back during a winter offensive in which the Soviet Red Air Force was instrumental, and, by January 1945, all of Xinjiang was in rebel hands. Once again, the fighting had been marked by gruesome atrocities.

Chiang Kai-shek demanded that the Soviets end their assistance to the rebellion and offered negotiations. These were accepted in October 1945. A ceasefire was concluded in the north, but Islamists in the south continued to fight the KMT. Nevertheless, the rebels got the autonomy they desired in January 1946. The new state was to be democratic with regular elections, civil rights, the use of the local languages alongside Chinese, freedom in the arts and a reduction of taxation. For security, the Uighurs were permitted an army of 12,000 men, but the remainder of eligible servicemen had to join the KMT. The USSR was, to all intents and purposes, the guarantor of this autonomy and had reasserted its influence in Xinjiang. Nationalists felt that the Communists of the region had nevertheless been contained. By contrast the Communists argued the ETR was a proto-Communist revolution to be lauded.

In reality, autonomous Xinjiang was in a fragile state and was soon destroyed by the Chinese Communists. The authorities of Gulja argued constantly with the government officials of Urumchi, revealing a fatal but typical fissure: the various settlements lacked any unity beyond their resentment of the Chinese. These divisions continued even as the Chinese Communist People's Liberation Army (PLA) overran Xinjiang from the east. In the summer of 1949, at the critical moment, Kasimov and the other leaders were killed in an air crash, the circumstances of which have generated controversy ever since.[6] Some speculate that either the KGB or the Chinese Communists murdered them, but the evidence is inconclusive. The incident nevertheless prompted a purge of 1,000 'suspects' by the Communists, but this only sparked a counter-attack against the local Chinese. An estimated 7,000 were massacred. Despite Soviet encouragements of Uighur separatism, it was now difficult for the USSR to intervene directly, particularly with such large numbers of PLA deployed in the province. Any action at this point, coinciding with a confrontation with the West in Europe, might lead to an unnecessary war. Mao's legions were thus permitted to occupy Xinjiang and to embed Communist rule at will.

POLICIES OF THE COMMUNIST ERA

The official Chinese explanation for the Xinjiang ETR was that it was a proto-Communist rebellion, but it was not successful because it was not fully developed along Maoist lines. The advance of the PLA into the province is styled a 'liberation', and, to some extent, Uighurs welcomed the Chinese troops as a relief from the warlordism and banditry that had plagued the previous decades. The Chinese official line also stresses the importance of unity. Literature repeats the word in mantra-like fashion, trying to convey the idea that Xinjiang was always Chinese even though the people there were clearly not. The fact is that the province more closely resembles a colony. The attitude of some Han Chinese towards the Uighurs seems to reflect the subordinate status of the latter despite Mao's entreaties not to separate the peoples. In a sense the sort of restrictions the Uighurs face, which are tantamount to those of a police state, are the same for all Chinese, so it is easy to exaggerate a situation facing one distinct group under Beijing's administration. That said, there is considerable resentment of Chinese rule in some quarters which under-mines Mao's original aspiration to integrate the Uighurs into the political system. Disdain for the local people on racial grounds and criti-cism of their religious beliefs have deepened the alienation. The use of coercion against protestors, the establishment of gulags, forced resettle-ment, a tidal wave of poor Chinese settlers and rumours of arbitrary arrests, torture and executions all fuel Uighur anger.

When the Chinese established Communist rule in 1949–50, they did so with typical thoroughness. Muslim noblemen were shot. Landowners were carted off to be 'reformed' and dispossessed. The belongings of those too politically sensitive to shoot were expropriated by the state. Commissars condemned Turki headmen as reactionaries. Imams, paid by the state, could not be elected and were supervised by the China Islamic Association. Mao's portrait was hung in every mosque; mosque teachings were to be converted into pro-Communist lectures, while mosque lands were confiscated and Islamic courts abolished. In orchestrated 'rent campaigns', peasants were encouraged to take their landowners to court against unfair rents or simply to denounce them. In 1952, a land-reform programme was initiated that redistributed land to peasants but then forced them into co-operatives, and, once the threat of resistance was thought to have passed, into collective farms. Former members of the KMT's army were organized into rural labour regiments whose task was to feed the PLA, or they were enrolled into units which could provide internal security or border patrols. Political prisoners were also organized into the first collectives, and technicians from the east were driven into Xinjiang to begin its 'development'.[7]

Despite Mao's calls for the involvement of Uighurs in the local administration to wean them from reactionary ideology, the Chinese officials believed they were 'not yet workers' and therefore could not be entrusted with political power. Although self-government was enshrined in the constitution, the unity of China and the inculcation of Marxist-Leninist thinking were the priorities, or so it was argued. Consequently, no Uighurs served in government at a national level, and Han Chinese dominated the provincial administration. At the factory level, Uighur officials were shadowed by trusted Chinese. However, Chinese technicians and workers ignored the directions of the Uighurs, whatever their rank or status. The borders of the autonomous provinces were deliberately drawn to prevent an Uighur majority being realized in any one of them. Everyone was taught to keep in line with Party directives, which were always unanimous and pro-Beijing. The conclusion one is forced to draw here is that what the Chinese Communists wanted was a region, and a country, that was quiescent and obedient. In

Xinjiang they wanted to keep Soviet influence out, exploit its mineral and agricultural wealth, and resettle people from the overcrowded eastern cities or its impoverished rural areas.

In 1956, there were calls for 'self-criticism' of the regime, a move designed to reveal public opinion when all organs for its genuine expression had been removed. In fact, the campaign had to be called off after a few weeks, such was the vehemence of public anger. The regime was concerned enough to carry out widespread purges. There were investigations of 100,000 people, 830 arrests and 53 executions in what was styled an 'anti-rightist' effort.[8] Chinese officials in Xinjiang interpreted the criticism as revealing a need for greater and more urgent assimilation of the Uighur population. The old, underlying fears of the Soviets resurfaced in 1958, though, when Zhou Enlai insisted on the abolition of the Cyrillic alphabet for the Uighurs in favour of a Roman one with a few Chinese words. Nevertheless, if the aim was to make the Uighurs more Chinese, then the policy was curious, particularly when the decision was changed again in the 1980s. However, the net effect was not unfavourable to the regime's interests – it weakened the sense of identity of the Uighurs, particularly across generations brought up with different alphabets.

A far more profound change occurred that year with the Great Leap Forward, a policy that led directly to a devastating famine the following year and a massive increase in the number of migrants pouring in from eastern China.[9] It was so damaging a policy was it that it was abandoned prematurely in 1961. The aim had been to accelerate the achievement of the five-year-plan targets in just two years. The policy would involve the collectivization of all the agriculture in Xinjiang and the establishment of 450 giant communes (with upwards of 20,000 people in each one) but also the forced industrialization and proletarianization of the people through the construction of blast furnaces, steel works and brick kilns. Much was made of the bumper yields the plan had achieved, but the reality was that production actually fell in some sectors. There was a widespread famine, although Xinjiang's smaller population shielded it from the worst of the hunger. Starving migrants nevertheless headed westwards: some 500,000 in 1959 alone. Pastures traditionally farmed by Kazakhs were simply taken away.

Those that resisted the collectivization policies were killed, but riots in Xinjiang and Ili were serious enough to alarm the authorities. In Khotan, 50 Han Chinese were killed in the unrest.

The Chinese allowed many Uighurs, Kazakhs and Kyrgyz to leave the country in light of the famine of 1959, the second mass emigration to the USSR in a decade (the first being during the takeover of the PLA in 1949). In 1962, an estimated 500,000 left China, a fact the Chinese conveniently blamed on Soviet propagandists, who were certainly active in their criticism. Even so, this explanation did not account for the large numbers streaming into Afghanistan and Pakistan. In 1963, the exodus was checked, and the Chinese planners, no nearer their goals than they had been in 1949, were forced to rethink their policies once again.

Xinjiang was soon subjected to the another major initiative emanating from Beijing. The Cultural Revolution was set off by a desire to root out those holding back radical reform but soon developed into factional fighting. Spearheaded by enthusiastic Red Guards, those showing insufficient zeal were potential targets for denunciation and punishment. Existing Communist leaders were especially vulnerable, but Wang Enmao, the Party Secretary at Urumchi, anticipated the onslaught of the Red Guards. He recruited his own 'Red Guards' and immediately denounced the newcomers as 'rightists'.[10] However, accusations against Uighurs were also common, particularly the suggestion that they were spies, and this produced a new wave of repression. Having relatives in the Soviet Union could result in a beating or prison sentence. Mosques were burned, imams were painted and paraded for public humiliation. Fear of being denounced was so strong that some Uighurs were eager to assert their revolutionary credentials, while others chose to resist, splitting the population in much the same way that the Chinese themselves were divided. As events in other authoritarian states have shown, policies of repression can pick up their own momentum and tear apart the cohesion of society with tragic consequences. The rioting across the region was so violent that the army was called in to restore order, and at Shihezi, north of Urumchi, old Communists fought the new radicals, leaving several of the latter dead. Wang Enmao urged the national government to bring its campaign to an end, warning that a revolt in the west was now imminent. Although the campaign was indeed called off on 25 February 1967, he was forced to 'admit his errors' publicly and was removed from office.

The failure of the radicals' policy was underscored by the reforms and concessions that followed in the years 1971–8. Farmers were permitted to carry out some private production on the side, and there were small free markets for them to sell their produce. Schools for Muslims were reopened, if strictly controlled. In 1978 there were land reforms with some debts being written off, and, while not transferring land into the farmers' hands, they were allowed to occupy and work it. Nomads were allowed to own livestock and land too. Poverty was still endemic for the Uighurs, but, by the end of the decade, Chinese attitudes towards them had improved. In the 1980s, there was official acknowledgement that the Uighurs were of Turki origin and not Chinese; mosques were reopened, Muslims enjoyed 'freedom of belief' to worship, and some Islamic literature was permitted. They also remained free of birth-control restrictions, namely the 'one child' policy designed to defuse the demographic time-bomb of China's rapidly increasing population.

However, the 1980s was also a period of new demands. Uighurs wanted, above all, jobs and greater political autonomy. These calls invited new impositions and surveillance from the Chinese authorities.[11] The undercurrent of unrest occasionally broke through to the surface: there were riots, for example, against films and nuclear testing at Lop Nor in 1985. Dissidents claimed that arrests and torture increased as a result. However, the period of concessions finally ended with the Tiananmen Square Massacre in June 1989 and its Xinjiang equivalent. The protest of pro-democracy students in Beijing was mirrored a march by Uighur students in Urumchi. Yet, in contrast to Tiananmen, the demonstration was not orderly or peaceful, nor was it, in effect, about democracy, Communist officials and the police were attacked from the outset, and property was destroyed as students railed against the publication of a popular book in China that purported to be about the sexual customs of Muslims.[12] This was a religious protest, and there were critical references to the history of Chinese policies against Muslims. The Chinese had abolished the *zakrat* (tithe), the Islamic courts, and the madrassahs. They had given imams menial work to do in the Cultural Revolution, forced them to declare an oath of loyalty and ridiculed them. If there had been a period of concession in the 1980s, that now came to an end. Mosques that had been built without permission were demolished by the state; there were threats, inducements and punishments for Uighurs to avoid religious observance. By the mid-1990s, government workers were being told that they would be sacked if they attended a mosque. Prayer in public was banned, as was fasting. Workers were given free lunches during Ramadan, and many were given free alcohol. Attending a religious class in secret could carry a heavy fine. In school holidays, Uighur children were ordered back onto the school premises on Fridays, so as to prevent them from attending religious services. Chinese scholars have been altering Uighur literature and histories to suit the new political agenda.[13]

Perhaps the most explosive issue was the birth-control policy. In the 1970s, all China had been subject to the restriction of the number of children per family except the Muslim Uighurs. While the policy was relaxed across China in the 1980s, it was re-imposed – to include Muslims – in 1988. The measure was seen as an attack on Islam,even though it applied to all Chinese, for whom large families have always been a tradition and an aspiration. What is more shocking, however, is the allegation that the Chinese authorities were carrying out compulsory sterilization and abortions. Some of the abortions were very late in term and had to be carried out by caesarean. There were fines for settlement elders or villagers if stowaways were found but rewards for compliance. The suspicion is that the policy was deliberately designed to limit the Muslim population to ensure the dominance of the Chinese.[14] However, it is difficult to assert this with any confidence. The vast numbers of Han Chinese migrating into Xinjiang make it unlikely that such draconian policies would be needed even if this was the intended outcome. Nevertheless, it reveals the depth of feeling in the Uighur population, the consequences of the secrecy surrounding policies of authoritarian regimes and the sheer volatility of the issue. Strong feelings are aroused, and these are reflected in similar reactions to rape cases, or accidents involving the death or injury of Uighurs at the hands of the Han Chinese.

Just one year after the breaking up of the student protest at Urumchi, there was a determination not to tolerate similar disturbances. Consequently, when a crowd gathered in 1990 at Baren, south-west of Kashgar, the authorities were waiting. Local opinion has it that there was a protest against the closure of a mosque, the culmination of weeks of smaller disturbances. The police claimed the vast crowd was making calls for a jihad and the expulsion of the Han. They believed there were foreign fanatics stirring up the mob. Eyewitnesses claim that the police went in with live ammunition from the start, and there are estimates that between 22 and 50 people were shot dead.[15] 'Mortars and helicopter gunships' were used against the fugitives, and many thousands were arrested. The Chinese media reported that trouble-makers, armed by the Afghans, were striving for separatism. Reporters also noted that the protestors were forced to take vows to fight, beat up policemen and stole weapons, hurled grenades at a local government building and killed seven police officers before the authorities took firm action. The conflicting testimonies leave us with great uncertainty about the narrative of events but also about the motives of both sides. It appears that local government buildings were besieged by a very large crowd in an ugly mood, and they were led by radicalized individuals. Accounts tend to agree that the police were unable to cope and that they suffered casualties. Yet the response was not based on the principle of 'minimum force', which suggests that the Chinese authorities wanted to make an example of Baren, perhaps to snuff out any idea of a provincial uprising from the beginning. The consequences were nonetheless far-reaching.

The Chinese stepped up their security measures after the incident. Cameras were set up in mosques, and Uighur spies were recruited by the secret police. Attendees of religious festivals were photographed and catalogued. Local newspapers were directed to condemn separatism. The numbers of police and militia were increased, including 28,000 more armed police and specialist riot-control units. However, this did not prevent the first bomb attack in 1992: a device was detonated on a bus, injuring 26 Chinese. Two more explosions and attacks against buildings elsewhere in Xinjiang were reported, although it seems there were no casualties. Nor did the new security measures deter a protest at Lop Nor in March 1993. Anti-nuclear demonstrators broke into a military base and burned several vehicles and aircraft. The PLA opened fire and killed some of the attackers, arresting hundreds more.

Against the background of a sustained anti-crime campaign between 1994 and 1996, relations between the Uighurs and the Han Chinese worsened, until, in 1997, there was the most serious riot of all at Gulja. The rioting and its suppression resulted in a new wave of bombings and repression that continued from 1998 to 2000 and, to some extent, has not yet abated. The disturbances were blamed, once again, on foreigners stirring up ideas of separatism. On 4 February 1997, police moved in on two *talib* (religious students) whom they suspected of indoctrinating young people with radicalism in a *meshrep* (religious youth club). However, the arrests took place at a mosque, and worshippers tried to prevent the men being taken away. Fighting broke out which developed into a full-scale riot.[16] Several were killed on both sides. Some Uighurs later claimed that the police had come to arrest thirty women and that three of them had subsequently been tortured and murdered, their bodies dumped on the street, but there is no evidence to support this claim. The story may have been designed to increase the sense of indignation and anger with the Chinese authorities, although it is possible that women were present at the original fighting at the mosque. The next day there was a protest march. The crowd set off chanting religious slogans, but after two hours, it were confronted by armed police and dogs, and the ringleaders were arrested. The marchers broke up. However, this was not the end of the incident.

On 6 February, riot police and troops made a show of force around the city. Any sign of defiance invited a beating and an arrest. However, as security forces poured in, some Uighurs chose to resist, and, in places the police came under attack again. The official death toll was five civilians and four police. Others claimed that the total figure was between 30 and 400. There were allegations, unconfirmed, that police had set dogs on the crowds, used rifles and machine-guns, and, apparently, a flame-thrower. The city was sealed off for two weeks and a curfew imposed. In that period there were further house-to-house searches, and possibly as many as 5,000 arrests were made. Some of these prisoners were left in detention without shelter for so long that a few got frostbite. In one incident a father was shot for brandishing an axe. The son escaped and joined another man in a rooftop position with a machine-gun. Both were shot, but so were the wife and daughter who were not involved in the resistance. There were many claims of incidents like this, but few can be verified. What is clear is that the city was far from pacified until the summer. In April, police had fired from a truck into a crowd fearing they were about to be attacked. In July, the authorities staged two trials and executions of twelve rioters in public in the city stadium. More than 5,000 people attended the events.

The Gulja riots and crackdown were followed by a series of bomb attacks across the province but also by a specific bombing in Beijing for which eight Uighurs were arrested and executed. The regime also responded by sending more officials to supervise the re-education of Xinjiang and by yet more arrests. Between February and June 1997, it is estimated that the authorities shot dead 162 people and sentenced hundreds to death. Sixteen hundred people were reported missing, although some had fled across the border rather than being casualties of the unrest. There were reports of attacks on police stations, prisons and other government buildings. At Karla, a guided-missile base was attacked and 21 soldiers were killed. In 1999, a motorcade of police vehicles was hit by a roadside bomb although officially it was reported as a road-traffic accident. A similar explanation was offered for another incident the following year. On 9 September 2000, 60 were killed in an explosion in Urumchi and a further 300 were injured. The media reported that this was the result of a truck carrying old explosives blowing up (farmers have a curious tradition of using explosives to settle land disputes), but it could also have been a deliberate truck-bomb attack.[17]

The Chinese security policy in Xinjiang appeared to be founded on a show of force, and the basis of its authority was its ability to exercise power through reprisals. It is true that they favoured being able to defuse trouble through education, supervision and employment, but there was a willingness to use force without much concern for the long-term effects of such a policy. The families of suspects had been arrested, and many were detained without trial. In some cases there were no defence lawyers, and verdicts were reached by 'adjudication committees' staffed by the authorities. Long sentences were handed down for 'dissent', and a common charge was 'treason'. Surveillance was increased, and every factory and school was appointed its informers or 'security committees'. Labour camps have also been common. It is estimated that as many as 10,000,000 have been detained since 1949 in Chinese gulags, and it is alleged that up to 2,000,000 were held in 2006. Often styled as 'farms' or 'works', these *laoga* are run by the Xinjiang Production and Construction Corps, an organization that owns much of the provincial industry and agriculture. It 'employs' thousands and offers a small wage, although the workers cannot leave, and many have been forced to work on highway and other infrastructure projects. Discipline is harsh. There are suspicions of routine torture and execution.[18]

Since 9/11 there have been more references to terrorism in Xinjiang. Islam is seen by many officials as a mask for treason and a front for separatism. There are anxieties about fanaticism and atrocities which are associated with religious groups. For the ultra-atheist Chinese regime, civic virtue is to be found in compliance, uniformity and obedience. Like many in the West, the Chinese are shocked that the merest 'slight' against Islam, or a perceived injustice, can produce such violence. There are concerns that jihadist terrorists are at work, establishing networks among the Muslim population. There is evidence that Uighurs did indeed leave Xinjiang to train in Afghanistan and Pakistan, and then return with terrorist training and expertise. The difficulty has been to identify the genuine terrorist among a disaffected population, to differentiate the dissident from the dangerous activist. Unlike the West, the Chinese media and authorities do not tend to address the cause of the unrest, pointing only to extremist behaviour and separatism. Local Uighur concerns are about their treatment by the Han, about overwhelming migration, jobs, corruption and the lack of a democratic voice. The regime calls for more training, education and efficiency. It really wants more 'right thinking', but it fails to see that it is continuing to alienate the Uighurs with its current policies.

The Chinese government hoped for a change of heart in 1999 with its Great Western Development Plan. There had already been a long drive to build railways and herd settlers westwards in order to 'open up' the western provinces, but the plan conceived by Jiang Zemin involved an investment of $13 billion and 78 separate large-scale projects.[19] Xinjiang makes up just one-sixtieth of the population of China but possesses one-sixth of the territory and three-quarters of its national mineral wealth. However, there is some doubt about the true aim of the policy. Is it really about the development or assimilation of the Uighurs, or is it about the exploitation of the area's resources and the pacification of its population against a background of globalization? China has been concerned about the considerable economic power of the us and the rest of the West and feels it has to prevent the demise of the 100,000,000 small farmers of China by developing economies of scale in industry. In Xinjiang, the investment has been in infrastructure and in oil and cotton. These, it was anticipated, would lead to the take-off of other related industries. However, so far, oil exploitation in the Taklamakan has been disappointing. Cotton production increased in the 1990s, but China was still importing at first and stockpiling its own production. Xinjiang was still in receipt of subsidies and financial support throughout the decade. New motorways, railways, airports, office blocks and hotels have sprung up, partly to serve the needs of tourism and the new migrants from the east, but, despite the impressive appearances, the realities have been disappointing. China still has 300,000,000 unemployed, and not all can be accommodated with jobs in Xinjiang. There was a budget deficit which led to spending cuts, and some state industries have been bankrupted. Taxation is high, and corruption flourishes at every level. A recession in the 1990s meant that many skyscrapers and office blocks remained unoccupied.

Foreign investors are still deterred by the remoteness of Xinjiang, the vast distances (which imply huge transport costs), the complexities of Chinese bureaucracy, and fears of sabotage and riots. When, in 2001, it was proposed to build a gas pipeline 4,160 kilometres across China from the Tarim Basin to Shanghai at an estimated cost of $18 billion, both BP and Shell showed some initial interest, but they pulled out when it became apparent their returns would be too small.[20] Of the oil and gas revenue being generated currently, the profits are small, and barely 2 per cent is reinvested locally in education and administration. Farmland is sold cheaply to new migrants, but the chief beneficiary is the Xinjiang Production and Construction Corps, not the Uighurs. There is some anxiety about future water shortages, and there is already intense competition on the margins of the Taklamakan between Uighur settlements and the new migrants or their industries. Climate change is worsening this problem. The retreat of glaciers and the diminishing of the water supply is increasing desertification of agricultural land. While 39,000 square kilometres were reclaimed for farming, 49,000 square kilometres were lost to the desert in the same period. Lakes are drying up, prompting demands for more reservoirs and putting yet more pressure on the existing supplies. The disastrous cotton production of Soviet Central Asia, with salination of the soil, poisoned water supplies, and the excessive use of pesticides and other chemicals, is being repeated. Corruption worsens the situation as pet projects are favoured and some developments are pushed forward for the personal gain of those in authority. To the anguish of Uighurs, traditional settlements are sometimes bulldozed to make way for new developments. Narrow streets are regarded as 'fire hazards' and are redeveloped, although widening of the roads makes them less defendable in an insurgency, and therefore security may be the real reason for the changes. That said, the flats the Uighurs are given in exchange are modern and well equipped, with flush toilets, electricity and running water. There are also opportunities to trade with the new Han migrants.

However, the Great Western Development Plan risks alienating, rather than assimilating, the local population. All new contracts tend to go to Han Chinese, and while some cities are booming, Uighurs are dependent on a 'kiosk economy'. Unemployment among them is proportionally higher. Less well-qualified Han are often promoted above Uighurs, and complaints lead to dismissal. Often it is the Han who get permits for private enterprises. The encouragement to new Han migrants also alarms the Uighurs and other minorities. In 1949 there were 300,000 Han and 5,000,000 Uighurs and others; in 2000 there were 7.5 million Han civilians, 2.5 million in the Xinjiang Production and Construction Company and 2 million members of the security forces – a total of 12 million compared with an Uighur and other minority population of 19 million. Although the Han Chinese have a lower birth rate, the influx of up to 7,500 per day threatens, as one Uighur put it, a 'demographic genocide'.[21] However, Chinese concerns that the slowing of this flow and of their birth rate might alter this trend could, according to Christian Tyler, explain the aggressive implementation of birth-control measures against the 10 per cent of the population who are 'minorities' in China.[22]

CHINA'S RELATIONS WITH CENTRAL ASIA

Not all Uighurs choose to resist. Some have elected to leave the country and have settled as widely as Europe, Turkey, India and Taiwan. It is estimated that as many as 1,000,000 may have emigrated in recent years. Of these communities, some have engaged in political lobbying against China. The most enthusiastic support has come from Turkey, prompting complaints from Beijing.[23] Indeed, the Uighur diaspora has affected relations with a number of countries, including the Central Asian republics and China's ally, Pakistan.

The Central Asian republics co-operate because they want China's valuable export contracts and they need co-operation against their own dissidents. They are also concerned about the consequences of defying the Chinese, who possess considerable military and economic power. Kazakhstan has agreed to keep watch on Uighur dissidents in return for favourable treatment of Kazakhs in Xinjiang. Despite some evidence of Kazakh resistance to the Chinese authorities, this deal has been honoured on both sides.[24] The Kazakhs have infiltrated some Uighur organizations and deported individuals, some of whom have subsequently been executed. Kyrgyzstan has also been under pressure from China to hand over Uighur suspects. Leaders of Uighur organizations have also been murdered in the republics, and the suspicion is that this has been the work of the government security services.

The Chinese, for their part, are eager to prevent their western neigh-bours from sympathizing with Uighur separatists. They are conscious of the existence of a historic pan-Turkism and know that the Turks tried to implement a new imperial dominion from Constantinople (Istanbul) to Kashgar as late as 1918. Jiang Zemin's visit to Turkey in 2000 got an angry reception which reinforced these concerns, but Zhu Raigji, the Prime Minister, encouraged the Turks to see the Uighurs as a problem akin to their own Kurdish separatist movement. The Turkish view remains that the Uighurs, if handled well, would be a community that could bring mutual benefit to the Chinese and the minorities of Xinjiang. There has been some co-operation between Turkey and China on the issue. In 1999, Turkish police arrested ten members of the East Turkestan Liberation Organisation after the murder of two Chinese restaurant owners and the petrol-bombing of the Chinese consulate. The suspects argued that their actions were retaliation for nuclear testing in Xinjiang. More alarming was the announcement of the Home of Youth organization – the so-called 'Hamas of Xinjiang' – which claimed that it had 2,000 active members in Turkey, including members of the armed forces. Home of Youth may have been able to do no more than fund radical elements in Xinjiang, but the Chinese were right to be concerned about financial support;[25] the prominent donors have been Saudi Arabia and Iran. While charities from these countries were anxious to ring-fence funds for schools and mosques, there are no guarantees that the money has not been siphoned off to pay the wages of radical imams.

The greatest threat does come, as the Chinese have long argued, from 'foreign elements' – that is, Uighurs trained outside China making attacks on Chinese interests. In May 2004, for example, three Chinese engineers were killed at the new oil-port installation at Gwadar by Uighurs trained by the IMT and the Taliban. Two other Chinese engineers were kidnapped in October that year while working on an irrigation project in Waziristan, and one was subsequently killed in the rescue operation mounted by Pakistan's Special Forces. In 2000, Pakistan had co-operated with China by expelling hundreds of Uighurs who were attending radical madrassahs, and the state closed the Kashgar Rabat and Khotan Rabat hostels in Islamabad. Twelve men were deported and were summarily executed just inside the Chinese border. However, critics accused the Chinese of playing a double game when it came to the Taliban. While calling for Uighurs to be kicked out of Afghanistan, they were accused of being eager to use the Taliban to destabilize the Middle East and therefore disrupt their economic rivals. This seems highly unlikely. The only agreement with Kabul appears to have been over American Cruise missiles, which, if brought down unexploded, China was eager to examine. Their main concern was the presence of 'Chinese' – that is, Uighurs – in the ranks of the Taliban and the IMU.

After the American-led operations in Afghanistan in 2001, the Uighur jihadists were scattered. China was keen to embrace the ideology of a war on terror as a means to improve relations with the US and deal with its own internal-security problems. After years of Western criticism of China's human rights record, it could now argue that it was simply fighting terrorism. The Chinese media eagerly grouped all forms of dissident activity as 'terrorism'. There was a new wave of arrests and executions, and complaints of torture from Uighurs. There were new restrictions on Uighur religious ceremonies and adornment. To its critics, China said it was merely stamping out criminal elements regardless of their ethnicity or religion. The Americans co-operated by freezing the assets of the East Turkestan Islamic Movement (ETIM).[26] The Uighur radicals believed that they were not terrorists at all but merely responding to the crackdown and injustices of the Chinese. Tyler argues that the Americans' categorization of the ETIM was designed to win over Chinese support for their impending operations in Iraq, but the criteria for such a listing are consistent with other groups, and the activities of the ETIM, so the relationship may be purely coincidental.[27] The fact is that Uighurs did join the Taliban, partly because they represented the best opportunity for training and funding but also because, like similar groups in Central Asia, the Uighurs felt an affinity with their aspirations.

The Global War on Terror may appear to some to be a convenient excuse for the Chinese to crackdown on Uighur dissidents, but a wave of bomb attacks against Han civilians and administrative personnel, designed to terrorize Beijing into a change of policy, is, by any definition, a form of terrorism. It is often the case that those in exile feel frustrated by their powerlessness to effect change. Frustrations are magnified, and this produces exaggerated and sometimes extreme solutions. Ideas of what can be done and what needs to be done can be reduced to black-and-white alternatives. Not all exiles react this way. Some embrace the opportunity to start a fresh life, to get jobs and improve their prospects. As it is for those still in Xinjiang, the picture is a mixed one: compliance and collaboration, despair and resignation, defiance and resistance. The Chinese are pushing ahead with the Xinjiang development programme, and they continue to press their own identity onto their westernmost province. However, the communities remain as divided as ever.

There are significant differences in the views of each. The Uighurs are stereotyped as a curiosity by the Han, and the continuation of ancient rituals in rural areas produces a sort of condescending fascination. The older Uighurs continue to wear traditional clothes as a mark of defiance, and they keep to local time despite official insistence on following Beijing time for similar reasons. Eating in a Chinese establishment is frowned upon by Uighurs and regarded as 'unclean'. Inter marriage is rare despite official encouragement and financial inducements. Language and religion remain barriers. New migrants often treat Uighurs with contempt and behave arrogantly even towards older Chinese inhabitants. However, younger Uighurs, like their Chinese counterparts, have embraced Western dress. They have a modern, if separate, nightlife. Some Uighur Muslims drink alcohol socially too. In urban areas, old rituals are disappearing, but what tends to keep resentment alive, and thus a desire to stick to the old ways, is the lack of jobs and prospects. There are also major anxieties about the sheer numbers of Chinese pouring in. The Chinese are more concerned with separatism and protest, conscious of the fate of the USSR as it tried to make the transition from a Communist command economy.

Radical groups are eager to exploit the situation in Xinjiang. Hizb ut-Tahrir has tried to recruit people to establish cells in the province. Uighurs influenced by jihadist thinking and trained by the Taliban or IMT still operate on the North-West Frontier Province of Pakistan and possibly in Kashmir.[28] However, the Pakistani security forces shot dead Hassan Mahsun of the ETIM in March 2004. They work closely with

Chinese intelligence staff, some of whom were deployed to Balochistan and Waziristan to assist in the identification of Uighur activists. Many of these men operate under the cover of construction engineers. On the other side, Uighurs and Uzbeks co-operate in kidnapping and terrorist operations, sometimes under former Taliban leaders such as Abdullah Mahsud. The fact that Chinese workers have also been killed in Afghanistan's reconstruction work (eleven were shot dead in June 2004) suggests that Uighurs are involved in joint operations there too. The recent trajectories of terrorism and counter-terrorism in China therefore seem to be in common with the rest of the region, which indicates the need for a regional strategy. Nowhere is this clearer and more sensitive than in the area of energy security, to which we will now turn.

Chapter 9

Hydrocarbons and the Great Powers

The Caspian Basin was one of the earliest sources of oil production in the world, with significant extraction beginning in the nineteenth century. Today, despite years of under-investment in the Soviet era, engineering difficulties and the problem of piping the oil and gas to markets outside of the region, the Central Asian fields are emerging as some of the most important in the world. This importance is not just based on the physical volume of oil and gas, estimated at 50 to 110 billion barrels of oil and 5 to 13 trillion cubic metres of gas (170 to 463 trillion cubic feet), but on the fact that the flow of Central Asian hydrocarbons could help to meet the burgeoning world demand and provide a surplus that would help regulate world prices in times of temporary shortage.[1] For decades, the Saudi-based oil companies generated sufficient reserves to assist in the regulation of prices, pouring more oil into the markets if prices increased or reducing their own production when more oil was being sold from other areas such as Nigeria, Russia or South America. However, the rapid growth in consumption in the Asia-Pacific region in the last years of the twentieth and early years of the 21st centuries, and conflicts in South-west Asia, have all but eliminated the surplus reserves available in the Middle East. Attention has therefore focused on processing more oil but also on developing new fields for extraction, and Central Asia is under the spotlight. Kazakhstan and Azerbaijan have been successful in attracting significant investment from the West, but Iran and China have also been eager to establish bilateral agreements with the republics. All are trying to achieve 'energy security' – access to 'sufficient supplies at reasonable prices, free from serious risk of disruption', and, where possible, 'strategic stocks' or reserves.[2]

The strategic importance of oil and gas is long established. In both world wars, the Central Asian and Middle Eastern fields were crucial to the Allied war effort. The Central Powers in the Great War and Germany in the Second World War tried unsuccessfully to wrest control of the regions. Hitler's Wehrmacht fought desperately to open up a route to the Caucasus in southern Russia, and the Allies occupied the Middle East, including Persia, as a precautionary move. More recently, there has been considerable speculation that America's policy of democratizing South-west Asia through expeditionary warfare in Iraq and Afghanistan is not just about neutralizing the foundations of extremism but is really an attempt to restructure the region for two ends. One is to ensure the dominance of American investment in the oil industry, and the second is to create 'energy security' for the US by encouraging production and sale of hydrocarbons on the world market.[3] However, this is a simplistic interpretation of the issues. Energy security depends on a variety of factors, and the globalization of the oil industry relegates the value of physically possessing oil reserves. Essentially, energy security is dependent on international prices, investment, security of demand, spare capacity and geographical diversification of production.

Globalization has tended to standardize oil prices around the world, ironing out the differences in cost produced by the quality of the crude, local taxation regimes, refining capacity and distances from producer to consumer. Prices have become the most visible aspect of energy security for millions of consumers globally, and sharp increases in price are contentious political issues. The Organisation of Petroleum Exporting Countries (OPEC) has been able to smooth out prices by increasing production in periods of relative shortage in supplies, and reducing production in times of plenty. In each case, their profits have not been affected: in periods of diminished production, they sold less oil but at higher prices.

Since the oil crisis of 1973, energy security has become one of the leading policy issues of the industrialized nations. With burgeoning demand, the physical supply of oil is the main security concern. Current world production is approximately 85,000,000 barrels a day (bpd), and, despite the predictions of the International Energy Agency (IEA) that, by 2020, the world will be producing 120,000,000 bpd, Thierry Desmarest, the Chief Executive of Total, believes the global production will be struggling to exceed 100,000,000 bpd by that date. The world has 2.2 trillion 'proven' barrels in reserve but will consume 1.5 trillion in the period 2006–30. The daily consumption figure for the year 2030 is estimated to become 115,000,000 barrels. To meet the demand, the industry estimates that it will require $3.1 trillion of investment ($2.2 million replacing spent reserves, $260 billion on tankers and pipelines, and $410 billion on refineries). BP and Exxon Mobile believe that new technologies and the vast reserves still available will enable the world to meet its soaring demands. However, there are some concerns. War and civil conflict can have a serious impact on production, as exemplified in Nigeria and Iraq in the early years of this century. Nationalist policies can also deter investment with Russia, Iran and Venezuela restricting access to foreign oil workers despite a general shortage of engineers and skilled workers. This has caused delays to vital oil and gas projects. There are some current technological problems still to be overcome. There is a shortage of deep-water drilling rigs, and costs for existing platforms are increasing. The need to repair or replace old infrastructure in existing fields is also a cause of delay and rising costs. Christophe de Margerie, Total's exploration chief and the next CEO, believed that it was not a question of reserves but a lack of engineers and problems in infrastructure that was likely to threaten the world's chances of meeting future demand.[4]

The IEA estimates that non-OPEC countries will increase production in the years 2006–15, but concerns about the scale of reserves mean they estimate a halving of the 55,000,000 barrels a day from these sources between 2015 and 2030. At the same time, the IEA believes that the costs of developing pipelines and tankers, and of developing Asia's oil and gas industries, will be in excess of $350 billion. The inter-relationship between oil prices and costs can have a significant effect on investment and production and, therefore, on growth. In the 1990s, for example, stable and low oil prices from the previous decade led to under-investment by the major companies. The effect of this was that the world industry was less prepared for the sudden increase in demand from the Asia-Pacific region and for the need to offset disruptions to the Middle Eastern supplies caused by the conflict in Iraq. Higher oil prices have traditionally encouraged national and international companies to invest, but the recent diversification of sources which have added new supplies to the market could cause prices to fall again. Such a situation means many countries are likely to depend more on OPEC to regulate production in order to keep prices, and therefore investment, stable. The development of the Central Asian industry could have a significant effect on this dependence.

The Caspian and Central Asian region has considerable potential, but there are some strong deterrent factors to investment and exploitation because of certain 'risks' caused by the political climate. In the 1950s, the Soviet Union neglected oil exploitation in the Caspian as it sought to develop its Urals-Volga and western Siberian fields, which were, in fact, strategically more secure. With independence, Azerbaijan, Kazakhstan and Turkmenistan have moved rapidly to attract investment and obtain markets for their supplies. The first challenge in this respect was to modernize the infrastructure of the industry in these countries. Lutz Klevemann, who visited the old Soviet Caspian platforms, noted:

> The offshore production site is in utter decay. The roads leading out to the open sea look like the aftermath of an intense artillery barrage. Our driver has to steer the Volga precariously around gaping holes, under which dirty, oil-soaked waves splash against the rotting stilts. Pipelines and oil reservoirs have rusted away, while crooked drilling towers of wood and steel are reminiscent of the first oil wells in Pennsylvania in the 1870s.[5]

There are also other concerns. There are serious disagreements about the legal status of the Caspian which threaten to disrupt production and development. There are fierce disagreements about the routing of oil and gas pipelines which carry financial and strategic implications. There are some anxieties about the political stability of the region, not least the potential for terrorist attacks on pipelines and installations, but there are also concerns about the lack of co-operation exhibited from time to time by Russia, the US, China and the Central Asian republics as each tries to assert its energy and strategic interests – a phenomenon sometimes referred to as the new 'Great Game'.

In the Friendship Treaty of 1921, and reiterated in the Treaty of Commerce and Navigation of 1940, Persia and the Soviet Union agreed to close the Caspian to all other vessels of the world and to reserve a 19-kilometre zone close to their coasts for exclusive fishing rights. However, no national 'borders' were agreed, and, since the collapse of the Soviet Union, the Central Asian republics have challenged the legality of the old agreements. Under the United Nations Convention on the Law of the Sea (UNLOSC), any nation may claim up to 19 kilometres from its shore as its own territorial waters and up to 320 kilometres as an exclusive economic zone (EEZ). In the case of the Caspian, this would mean that a border could be drawn up that traced a line equidistant from the national coasts, and this would also apply to the resources that lie on the seabed. However, if the Caspian is defined as a lake, the law of the sea would not apply and the resources would have to be developed jointly, as a condominium. Unfortunately, this very definition is a cause of dispute.

Until 2003, Iran's view was that all the littoral states should adopt a collective approach to the exploitation of the Caspian's resources. The simple explanation for this apparently well-meaning argument is that Iran's territorial waters, if defined by UNLOSC, would hold the least oil and gas reserves of all of the Caspian states. Tehran has maintained that the 1921 and 1940 agreements should hold good until new arrangements are settled between all the states, but this too suggests the prospect of giving Iran a larger share in any final deal. Iran has condemned bilateral agreements concluded by Russia and wants to see a sharing of the wealth generated. However, Iran appears to have accepted the division of the Caspian into national sectors while still claiming that it should have an equal share – 20 per cent of the surface and seabed – rather than a division based on UNLOSC. Nevertheless, it appears to have accepted that its policy line is in tatters. It has signed agreements with international companies for the exploitation of oil in its own sector and, from June 2003, began to develop the resources in its own portion. Faced with a rapidly growing population, a deteriorating economy and increasing energy demands, Iran could not continue with its principled and defiant position any longer.

Iran has also called for the demilitarization of the Caspian. This seemingly pacific gesture is largely the result of a fear that Russia, if it felt threatened, would use its vast military resources to face down Iran. Tehran, which has been confronted by the West over its nuclear programme and is anxious about Western military forces in neighbouring Afghanistan and Iraq, cannot afford to antagonize Russia or engage in an arms race. In 2002, this was starkly illustrated by an aggressive Russian naval exercise on the Caspian. Since 2001, Turkmenistan has acquired 20 patrol boats from Ukraine, while Azerbaijan and Kazakhstan have procured American naval hardware. The US Navy also provided personnel to Azerbaijan to advise on the protection of Azeri oil installations. Iran protests frequently about American influence in the region, but the fact is it can do little to assert itself politically or militarily against either the US or Russia.

Until 1996, Russia believed that UNLOSC did not apply to the Caspian, and it looked to maintain the 1921 and 1940 agreements. However, in that year Moscow concluded a number of bilateral agreements with other states and favoured the division of the sea into distinct national sectors some 70 kilometres from each coast. The remaining central portion, it believed, could be developed jointly, administered by a joint stock company that would represent the five littoral states. However, Turkmenistan, Azerbaijan and Kazakhstan rejected the proposal, so Moscow changed its position again. In 1998 Russia advocated the median-line approach (based on UNLOSC) and concluded a deal over the northern Caspian with Kazakhstan, even though this line cuts across several potential oil and gas fields. Curiously, Russia and Kazakhstan agreed to maintain common ownership over the surface waters to avoid complications with shipping, fishing and the environment. In January 2001, Russia concluded a similar agreement with Azerbaijan over the south-western Caspian. In 2002, Putin and Nazarbaev of Kazakhstan cemented their 1998 agreement with a deal to divide three gas fields on an equal basis. Just one year later, LUKoil and Gazprom, two of Russia's largest companies, announced their intention to start exploiting the Tsentralnoye gas field in 2007.[6] Iran and Turkmenistan protested about these agreements. Despite arms sales and co-operation over nuclear technology, the Caspian thus remains a bone of contention between Tehran and Moscow.

American concerns about Iran's nuclear programme centre on the combination of Tehran's fiery rhetoric against the West and Israel, and its apparent desire to acquire a WMD. However, Paul MacDonald argues that Iran is facing an energy crisis that makes its quest for nuclear power valid and pressing.[7] Iran has been unable to sell its heavier crudes, it has major technical problems in its newest fields which have delayed production, it has fewer reserves than it anticipated, and it has failed to meet its OPEC demands. Iran was in the curious position of having to import 150,000 bpd to satisfy domestic demand in 2005–6. It annual rate of increase in consumption is 5 per cent, but its production increased by only 100,000 bpd between 2000 and 2006.

The peak of Iranian oil production was in 1974, when it managed 6,000,000 bpd, but it has struggled to exceed this level, and its ambitious targets that were to be realized in 2005 have not been met. In the later 1970s, production levels continued to be driven up, but the 1979 Revolution and subsequent war with Iraq caused a sharp downturn in production. The anticipated recovery was slow to materialize, and production rose from 1.5,000,000 bpd to only 3,000,000 bpd in 1990. In 2006, production stood at 3.9 million bpd, still well below its heyday in 1974 and significantly lower than its target of 5 million bpd. One of the key problems was that re-injection of gas into oil fields was interrupted, leading to the ingress of water, known to the industry as 'coning', which caused the loss of millions of barrels of oil. Iran also overestimated its reserves to attract investment. Despite a survey carried out by the National Iranian Oil Company in the 1970s, which identified 62 billion barrels of proven reserves, the Revolutionary government raised its estimate to 93 billion barrels in 1988, and in 2003 it announced that it had an estimated 132.5 billion barrels.

However, it is thought that Iran's four offshore fields and some of its older onshore ones have already peaked in terms of capacity, and that, despite the discovery of new fields, its actual reserves may be about half that claimed by Tehran. In addition, heavy 'sour' crudes have proved unattractive to the market. 'Buy-Back' schemes, in which companies act as service providers in return for oil, have been delayed. Some investors have been deterred by Iranian politics or the offer of low rates of return, known as 'upstream difficulties' in the industry, and American companies are unable to co-operate with Iran under the Iran Libya Sanctions Act 1996 (ILSA). Iran is looking to use gas to offset its shortfall in crude production, but it cannot completely fill the gap. The South Pars field is expected to produce 125,000 bpd of condensates rising to 200,000 bpd in 2007 and 400,000 bpd in 2008. There is also the potential for Iran to increase its production via Gas-to-Liquids, but investment for these is expensive and may not be cost-effective. Iran may therefore be looking to nuclear power to close the gap in demand. The government in Tehran, which expects increasing opposition if the economic situation deteriorates further, seems utterly committed to nuclear processing for its survival. This may be in addition to its desire to regain some military strength in the region at a time when America appears hegemonic.

The Central Asian republics of Azerbaijan, Kazakhstan and Turkmenistan have a common policy line driven by their estimation that the seabed closest to their coasts contains more oil and gas than that of either Russia or Iran. Moreover, developing hydrocarbons is regarded as an essential component of generating national wealth, and therefore of sustaining political independence. The opportunities created by eager international investors are also too tempting to ignore (Kazakhstan attracted $40 billion in foreign investments in 2003), and they have given the republics more confidence in challenging the Russians.[8] Azerbaijan has consistently regarded the Caspian as a sea and called for the division of national sectors along a median line. In 1997 Azerbaijan and Kazakhstan agreed to delimit their sectors in this way. Kazakhstan then led a similar division with Turkmenistan. The following year, the Kazakhs concluded a deal with Russia to divide the northern seabed, and in 2001 Azerbaijan followed suit in the south. The only stumbling block seems to have been a dispute between Turkmenistan and Azerbaijan as to the exact positioning of a median line. Thus, while none of the Caspian states have ever agreed on the status of the Caspian, Iran has been faced with a *fait accompli*. Oil companies have also tended to ignore the lack of an agreement and forged ahead with developing the resources, but full exploitation has yet to be realized. Part of the problem lies in the shipment of oil and gas once it has been extracted and refined: the land-locked nature of the Caspian means that it is impossible to utilize the world's existing tanker fleet; instead pipelines must be established across thousands of kilometres in order to access the world's markets. With billions of dollars at stake, in terms of costs or potential profits, the pipeline issue has become one of the most contentious in recent years.

THE POLITICS OF PIPELINES

The routing of pipelines represents a considerable opportunity for the Central Asian states and their neighbours. Oil and gas are more readily available for domestic use if pipelines cross national borders. There are substantial amounts of foreign capital, the possibility of lucrative transit fees, more local employment and even strategic advantages: states which depend on the flow of hydrocarbons are vulnerable to the demands of those that have pipelines running across their frontiers. However, since Central Asia's pipelines need to cross a number of international borders and the stakes are so high, the negotiations are particularly fraught.

Formerly, Central Asian oil was routed into the Soviet Union. A pipeline crossed the Caucasus and terminated at the Black Sea coast of Novorosiisk. However, in 1991 the Central Asian states were concerned that continuing to route their oil and gas exclusively through Russia made them vulnerable and only promised access to Western markets. To take advantage of the burgeoning demands of Japan and China, it was proposed that a second pipeline be opened up eastwards from Kazakhstan to China, while a third pipeline could be constructed through Afghanistan to Pakistan, where it could be shipped on to Eastern markets. Another pipeline was proposed to run due south from the Caspian into Iran, while a final project envisaged a line from Baku across the Caucasus, where it would be routed either to Ceyhan on the Turkish coast or to the port of Supsa in Georgia. Each of these projects had to be prioritized, costed and debated between oil companies and governments. The positions of each player have been partisan.

From the 1990s, the US favoured the Baku-Tbilisi-Ceyhan (BTC) route as a priority.[9] This reflected their desire to avoid Iran and Russia, their regional rivals, rather than take costs and engineering into considera-tion. The project was approved in 2005, and the Americans envisage the BTC to be the Main Export Pipeline to the West's markets with a million barrels a day being pumped along its route. Most of the oil that the pipeline will carry will come from Azeri fields, such as Azeri-Chirag and Gunashi, but the Kazakhs also expect to be able to utilize the line. It is expected that a gas pipeline will subsequently be co-located, and this will terminate at Erzerum in Turkey, although Greece and Turkey have concluded a deal that will transport gas beyond Turkish shores into the European market. Turkey is particularly keen to act as the tran-sit state for Europe's hydrocarbons, which it sees as a means to enter the European Union 'club'. Equally, European states are anxious to see a diversification of sources for European energy. When President Putin reminded EU leaders in 2005 that Russia was the main provider of European gas and was likely to remain so, the response was frosty.

Russia, understandably, initially opposed the BTC project. In 2001, however, Moscow's position changed as it sought co-operation, not confrontation, from American oil companies. The stimulus was, in November 2001, the completion of the Caspian Pipeline Consortium (CPC) route. Running for 1,500 kilometres from Tengiz in Kazakhstan to Novorosiisk, the oil is subsequently pumped into tankers for global distribution. American expertise and funding, particularly from Chevron-Texaco, had been crucial in developing the Tengiz field (along with Exxon Mobil and Kazakhstan itself), and the logical next step was to get the oil from Kazakhstan by the most pragmatic and cost effective means. Kazakhstan, which lacks refining capacity for its enormous reserves, still depends on Russia for the bulk of its exports. The CPC is unlikely to be able to cope with the growing export capacity, however, and the Kazakh government have looked to China, which overtook Japan as the world's second-largest oil consumer in 2003, as a likely partner for its surplus. A pipeline deal has been concluded that will see a new route established from Atasu in Kazakhstan to Alashanku in China. Begun in 2003, the project is due for completion in 2008.

Kazakhstan has, like Russia, Turkmenistan and Azerbaijan, also engaged in 'swaps' deals with Iran. Despite the obvious advantages of a southern pipeline, including the short distance to the refining installations in the Persian Gulf, the US has consistently opposed any Iranian route. The solution has been to ship Central Asian oil to Iranian ports, particularly Neka, where the fuel is refined (in Tehran and Tabriz) in return for an equivalent volume of oil that can be picked up by the companies' tankers in the Gulf at Kharg Island (with quality differentials taken into account). This saves the Iranians having to pump oil from its southern fields to its population centres in the north, and allows the oil companies to avoid the expense of a pipeline. In 1997, the deal did not function entirely smoothly because of disputes over the quality of Iranian crudes, but the system resumed in 2002.

Kazakhstan's hydrocarbons industry stands out as the region's greatest energy success story. In 2003, production of crude oil and natural-gas condensate amounted to 51.2 million tons, an increase of almost 9 per cent on the previous year. Exports of oil and gas condensate amounted to 44.3 millions tons, valued at more than $7 billion. The proven oil reserves are calculated to be 4 billion tons with a further 2,000 cubic kilometres of gas. It is thought that this potential could translate into 3,000,000 bpd by 2015, lifting Kazakhstan into the top ten oil producers of the world. Its oil and gas exports now account for 65 per cent of the country's total, and generates 24 per cent of Kazakhstan's GDP. All this, and a carefully managed monetary policy, means that GDP is likely to triple in 2015 compared with 2000. The annual growth rate is over 9 per cent, making it the second fastest-growing economy in the world in real terms. That said, there have been significant delays in exploiting Caspian resources compared with land-based fields. Some doubts have been cast on the Kazakh forecast that it could, in conjunction with Azerbaijan, supply 100–120,000,000 tons of oil annually from the Caspian. This estimate did not include a further 50,000,000 tons pumped to the Black Sea coast.

The delays immediately led to increased speculation about the feasibility of the BTC route and its alternatives. American and Turkish estimates were based on the idea that, since the Bosphorus could ship no more than 70–80,000,000 tons a year, the BTC route was essential. However, investments were dependent on accurate calculations of the volume from the Caspian. Delays to the commissioning of the pipeline announced by the Azerbaijan State Oil Company (ASOC), and assessments that the construction would take at least 32 months, coincided with estimates in 2005 that Azerbaijan might only be able to produce between 15 and 17,000,000 tons a year: a volume regarded as 'too little to fill up the pipe'.[10] The situation was worsened by the speculation that Ukraine was about to start pumping oil from Odessa to Brody to Gdansk, that a pipeline might be built from Burgas in Bulgaria to Vlore on the Adriatic, and another constructed from Burgas to Alaxandroupolis in Greece, all of which would favour a Caspian-to-Black-Sea pipeline (via the northern coast), not the BTC. The Burgas–Vlore route allegedly attracted the interest of American companies like Exxon Mobil and Chevron-Texaco, both of which are involved in exploiting Kazakh oil and are eager to avoid the chokepoint of the Bosphorus. Yet the American and Turkish governments continued to press for the BTC and $130,000,000 was pledged for preparatory work. The ports of Vlore and Alexandroupolis have, in the industry's estimation, the same potential as Ceyhan. The rivalry over pipeline routes highlights Russia's determination to assert its influence in the region and to acquire a substantial share of the potential profits.

Turkmenistan, which possesses gas as its main hydrocarbon reserve, is far more dependent on pipelines than Iran or the US, and that has made it too vulnerable to Russia. Until the late 1990s, all Turkmen gas was routed via Russian pipelines, but Gazprom, the leading Russian gas company of the region and the owner of the pipelines, is a rival of the state-owned Turkmen gas industry. The Russians cut off access to these lines over a payment dispute in 1997. However, in 2003, the two countries signed a long-term contract, the terms of which allow Turkmenistan to sell an incremental volume of its gas to Gazprom. The volume of Turkmen gas exports to Russia has increased since then. Nevertheless, the government in Ashgabat has been unsuccessful in finding alternatives to this Russian stranglehold. Its hopes for a route to Pakistan via Afghanistan were dashed by the continuing conflict between the Taliban and its opponents. Despite the defeat of the Taliban in 2001, instability has deterred investment, and the chances of realizing the framework agreement, signed by Turkmenistan, Afghanistan and Pakistan in December 2002, looks bleak. The other alternative for Turkmenistan has been to develop its links with Iran. A 199-kilometre-long gas pipeline from Korpezhe-Kurt Kui was opened in 1997, but it lacks the capacity to export a great volume of Turkmenistan's surplus.

The pipeline controversy is further complicated by the issue of energy security. Clearly it is in the interests of both consumers and suppliers to diversify routes to avoid disruptions caused by technical problems or political disputes. It also makes states like Turkmenistan less vulnerable to Russian leverage. Yet, terrorism also means that alternative energy pipelines are essential. Terrorists threaten the region's political stability, but they can also be tempted to attack pipelines because of the disproportionate effect this can have on a government's economy, a point exemplified in Iraq after 2003. On the other hand, pipelines are an expensive burden on oil companies that affects profitability. This problem is worsened by the strategic interests of Russia, the US and the republics, as these can threaten to override the economic priorities. However, as the CPC example demonstrates, pragmatism can break the impasse. American and Russian companies look set to continue their co-operation to exploit Caspian resources, and Russia has shown its willingness to sign bilateral agreements with the Central Asian republics rather than maintain a position of principle that was economically damaging. As the volume of oil and gas production increases, and the demand continues to rise, it is likely that, in most cases, financial arrangements will assert themselves over strategic ones. The exception to this, at least in the short term, is likely to be the dispute between the US and Iran, which has deepened because of the nuclear issue.

POLLUTION

There is an eeriness about the approach to the Aral Sea. Rusting hulls of trawlers at Muynak, which once floated in coastal waters, now lie on sand dunes some 100 kilometres from the dying lake. On Vozrazhdenie Island, the Soviets had built a biological-weapons factory; they were eager to close the region to outsiders when Gary Powers flew his U2 spy plane over the sea and revealed the existence of the plant. This had the effect of concealing the environmental disaster that was unfolding. The sea had begun to recede from the late 1950s, when Soviet irrigation schemes were expanded, but the once-thriving fish-canning industry gradually dwindled, the 60,000 fishermen put out of business and the ships abandoned. The local population faces increasing infant mortality and rising cancer rates because the water supply is so badly contaminated. Sandstorms are more frequent, causing respiratory illnesses. It is estimated that the sea will disappear altogether by 2020.

The Aral Sea disaster is one of the greatest man-made environmental catastrophes. The construction of the Karakum Canal to feed the cotton fields of Turkmenistan, the impossible targets set by Soviet planners, the waste of water through unlined irrigation channels that are also open to the sun, and the construction of reservoirs upstream in Uzbekistan have all contributed to the sea's death. For years, Soviet planners were unconcerned because yields of cotton were so high. However, salination of fields have rendered many barren, and the toxicity of the water supply has killed off flora and fauna in the sea and the surrounding area – and caused acute damage to human health. Soviet planners believed that they could divert water from the Ob and Irtysh rivers to refill the Aral, a project that would have required the construction of a canal 1,600 kilometres long. The plan was stifled by bureaucrats. Uzbekistan argues that it cannot do without the freshwater supply for its cities, and Turkmenistan argues that the Karakum Canal is an economic lifeline. Both believe that they need water for their growing populations, so the sea continues to disappear.

Central Asia is badly affected by pollution after decades of exploitative agricultural and industrial activity. The storage of toxic waste in open sites, which are invariably unprepared, leads to a steady leakage of dangerous chemicals into the atmosphere, underground and surface water systems, and soil. In Kazakhstan, environmentalists identify several 'zones of crisis' caused by nuclear-weapons testing in the years 1949–61 and by petrochemical production.[11] At least twelve of the cities with a population exceeding 100,000 are subject to radioactive threats to health at a dangerous level. Radioactive slag heaps, totalling 50,000,000 tons, litter the landscape, and there are 267 sites where radioactive pollution lies between 100 and 17,000 microRads/hr. Kazakhs tend to regard the slag heaps as a source of housing or road materials and use them freely. Other dumps of industrial by-products, some from the metallurgy sector, also threaten water supplies, soil and human health. Even natural radiation appears to be hazardous. Half of the country has yet to be surveyed for radon, which can reach dangerous levels. The Soviet Union authorized the use of strong pesticides, and it is thought that over 500 tons of 'unfit' pesticides are still stored around the country.

Kyrgyzstan has fewer radioactive slag heaps, although the town of Mailuu-Suu in the west of the country is badly affected, and the mountainous nature of the country tends to funnel pollutants into areas of population. However, there are problems with the storage of dangerous pesticides throughout rural areas, and environmentalists are generally concerned that seismic activity makes surface storage of hazardous materials very risky. A similar situation prevails in Tajikistan, where pesticides have been used to increase yields in melon and cotton cultivation, although here there has been a sharp decline in their use in recent years. Nevertheless, there is a significant correlation between the use of these pesticides and the appearance of malignant tumours and other illnesses. Perhaps it is not surprising, given the intensity of farming in the Ferghana Valley, that soil and animal pollution from pesticides is also a problem for Uzbekistan.

Kazakhstan has responded to its environmental damage with surveys and monitoring of pollution levels, and an agreement with China (which had a nuclear test site at Lop Nor) to carry out collaborative investigations into the effects of nuclear-weapons tests on the environment. Monitoring of those regions rich in uranium ores has also been established. Kyrgyzstan and Uzbekistan have begun to reprocess or bury some of their toxic waste. However, there is a long way to go before the years of messy exploitation are cleared up. Central Asia is fortunate in that vast areas of beautiful mountains and austere deserts are unspoiled. But the consequences for the centres of human population are less encouraging. The cause of this damage was the hubris of Soviet planners, who were convinced of the need to 'modernize' and industrialize, partly in order to leap ahead of the West but also to support their social engineering of a loyal proletariat to replace a counter-revolutionary peasantry. In the end, they got neither an economy to match the West nor a loyal population. They ended up with a land that is sick.

CLIMATE CHANGE AND RECKONINGS

The inter-governmental panel on climate change's third assessment report was published in 2001 and outlined how, with an increased global surface temperature of 0.6 degrees centigrade since 1900, the world's climate is undoubtedly warming. Changes to inland use and increased emissions have, it is thought, made the earth warmer now than it has been for 5,000 years, and the rate of warming is faster than at any time in the last 10,000 years. The recession of glaciers in Central Asia's mountains, along with increased evaporation, are already altering the water supply of the region. Freshwater lakes are increasingly salinated. Lake Balkash in Kazakhstan covers 18,000 square kilometres and is one of the largest inland waters of Central Asia, but with a fall in the inflow from the River Ili, its main tributary, salination has now reached 4g/litre, thus rendering it virtually unusable for either drinking or irrigation.[12] Scientists now predict that droughts, such as the ones that have affected Tajikistan and Afghanistan in recent years, will become more frequent in the region. Farming economies are therefore at serious risk. There is also some concern that the steady, linear rate of change may shift abruptly and bring about catastrophic climatic events. Yet, this would mean not just the advent of short-term, if disastrous, incidents such as flash flooding, damaging storms,or hazardous temperature extremes. It might also mean rapid desertification, mass migrations of a more permanent nature, and conflicts over water. The Chinese economy, for example, currently pays an additional $30 billion per annum to deal with water shortages. To secure future supplies, China plans to divert more water from the Ili into Xinjiang's industry and domestic consumption. Climatologists think that, by 2020, precipitation in north-west China will have fallen by 20 per cent, a fact that will add to the pressure on the remaining supplies.[13] However, this will bring China into direct confrontation with Kazakhstan, which depends on the Ili for its own needs. If large-scale movements of climatic refugees are added to this scenario, existing ethnic and clan tensions could be pushed to breaking point. The existence of diminishing hydrocarbon resources in the same region will further complicate the problem.

The independence of the Central Asian republics led to considerable speculation about their oil and gas reserves in the early 1990s. Huge investments were made, and there were some exaggerated claims about the region's potential. However, disputes over the Caspian's status and the national boundaries of the littoral states; conflicts in neighbouring Afghanistan and Iraq; the technical, financial and diplomatic difficulties of the pipelines; terrorism, ethnic and civil violence, and political corruption; and uncertainty about the Iranian–American confrontation over nuclear weapons have all delayed or deterred the development of the hydrocarbon resources. Nevertheless, despite these problems, the reserves and capacity may turn out to be much smaller than originally predicted. The EIA estimates that, by 2025, Caspian production will reach 6,000,000 bpd. This seems buoyant until one considers that Persian Gulf production in the same year is expected to be 45.2 million bpd. The effect of Caspian production on world prices will therefore be far smaller than expected in the 1990s. That said, hydrocarbons from Central Asia will be regarded as an important addition to world supplies at a time of increasing demand. In terms of energy security, they may well assist the world in diversifying its sources, and they will certainly have a key role to play in developing the republics themselves. Nevertheless, they will also be the source of intense international rivalry; they may fuel domestic corruption and heighten inequalities of wealth and opportunity too. In addition, the expansion of the hydrocarbons industries threatens to repeat the environmental mistakes of the past. Sadly, the attraction of billions of dollars after years of Soviet stagnation will prove too tempting. In the long term, oil and gas are thus likely to be both a blessing and a curse to the region.

Chapter 10

Trajectories

During the Cold War, Central Asia appeared to be less important in strategic terms than the European Theatre or the Middle East. Its borders were largely frozen by the Soviet Union, and internal disputes were suppressed by the presence of the Communist Party apparatus. However, as Olaf Caroe, the former British Foreign Secretary of the Government of India and the last governor of the North-West Frontier Province, noted in his book *Wells of Power* (1951), the Central Land Mass Theatre of Asia was perhaps the most important geo-strategic zone on the planet.[1] The Soviets regarded Central Asia as their vulnerable southern flank and were eager to project their power into Afghanistan and the Middle East to protect the region. The Western powers regarded the whole of South-west Asia as an oil-rich zone vital to the West's economy that was within striking distance of the Soviets. China saw its westernmost province as the most likely to secede, particularly with Soviet encouragement. It was an area that retained its strategic interest to all the major powers. There were border disputes between China and the Soviet Union in the Ili Valley in the 1960s, nuclear testing in Kazakhstan and in Xinjiang, and a major confrontation between the Soviets and Afghans in 1979, in which America and several Middle Eastern states participated by proxy. The decision of the Soviet Union to withdraw from Afghanistan in 1989 convinced many Islamist thinkers that they alone had driven out an empire. The subsequent fall of the Soviet Union was a turning point for Central Asia that was to have profound consequences.

The issues that have arisen since 1991 are essentially three: stability; resources and their accessibility; and jihadist terrorism. In terms of stability, the Central Asian governments have struggled to make the transition from the Communist era to one of free-market economics, to contend with political opposition groups, and to manage the aspirations and grievances of their populations. Kyrgyzstan has attempted to follow a democratic path, but this has foundered in recent years. Tajikistan endured a bloody civil war before establishing a fragile coalition government. In the last few years this too has been undermined by demands for regional autonomy, the aspiration of certain clans which wield disproportionate amounts of power, an energy crisis, and pressure from external forces, including Uzbekistan and terrorist groups. The old Communist élites of Kazakhstan, Uzbekistan and Turkmenistan have managed to retain their power using a façade of democracy and the hard currency of coercion. In the Caucasus, stability is more elusive. Separatists, jihadists and clan factions have fought wars for Abkhazia, South Ossetia, Dagestan, Karabakh and Chechnya. None of these conflicts have reached a final resolution.[2]

The issues of resources and accessibility are closely linked. The reserves of oil and gas in the region are considerable, but it is proving expensive to extract and transport these hydrocarbons to the world's markets. More complex still is the political and diplomatic horse-trading over the routes the pipelines should take. The lucrative nature of the transit fees, the prospect of creating jobs, and the strategic value of controlling the flow from the region are highly attractive. However, there is growing disquiet that the majority of Central Asians will not benefit from the oil-and-gas bonanza.[3] While the economic and political élite enjoy unprecedented wealth, thousands of their compatriots are faced with high unemployment, a poor-quality diet and dependence on a casual and vulnerable kiosk economy.

Jihadists regard Central Asia as an arena where they can be influential, recruit volunteers and 'prove' their pan-Islamic credentials. After 9/11, Central Asia was regarded as the cradle of terrorism because of the abundance of training camps in Afghanistan and the fact that its trainees were drawn from across the Muslim world. After Operation Enduring Freedom, Afghanistan was eclipsed as the main arena for international terrorist groups, including the IMT, and this remains the case despite the resurgence of the Taliban. The centre of gravity of insurgency terror has shifted to Iraq since 2003, although Afghan and Iraqi 'alumni' have re-exported their terrorist techniques to Central Asia and elsewhere. Suicide bombings and mass-casualty terrorist atrocities, hitherto unknown in the region, have been evident there since 2004. A regional study certainly makes the connections between jihadist terrorists more apparent: Chechens have fought in Kyrgystan and Uzbekistan; Uighurs have killed Chinese engineers in Pakistan under Pushtun commanders; Saudis have ambushed and executed Russians in Chechnya. The links are explained by a shared ideology that is not, contrary to popular belief, directed exclusively against the West. These groups are waging war on what they perceive as threats to Islam and the Muslim *ummah*; they are waging war on the humiliations and injustices towards their 'brothers and sisters', and they object to arbitrary government, atheist policies and 'insults' to their beliefs. Above all they believe they are fighting for a pan-Islamic caliphate, which will restore the prestige of Islam and therefore, by definition, of themselves.

Not all see this final objective of a world caliphate as something that can only be achieved by terrorism and violence. The other-worldly aspiration of a united community, respectful of Islam and purged of heresy, is the approach of Hizb ut-Tahrir. A peaceful strategy has proven even more popular among thousands of disillusioned Central Asians. This yearning for a new order may not be abated simply by creating more democratic institutions, as some suggest. The experience of the Palestinian Authority, where the radical group Hamas achieved electoral success at the expense of moderates in 2005, indicates that democracy is not simply an antidote to extremism. The Central Asian republics and China have tried to cultivate a sense of national or socialist identity that can compete with the Islamist one. There have been attempts in China, as there once were in the Soviet Union, to stress the common ground between Islam and socialism, just as the West tries to do with democracy. The Chinese have also tried to undermine and subvert a sense of Uighur-Islamic identity while offering inducements to people to assimilate more comprehensively into a Sinicized society.[4]

Although American oil companies showed an interest in the Central Asian republics soon after their independence in 1991, with Chevron concluding a multi-billion-dollar deal with Kazakhstan for example, the US government did not regard the region as a post-Cold War priority. There was a more pressing need that year to establish workable relations with the Eastern European states and Russia, and to account for the nuclear arsenals at their disposal. It was not until the mid-1990s that there was a growing desire to get the oil and gas out of Central Asia and into world markets, but in doing so it was regarded as imperative to route the pipelines away from the jurisdiction of Russia and Iran wherever possible. However, by 1999, the emergence of the IMU, and the more prominent threat posed by Al-Qaeda and its other affiliates, forced President Bill Clinton to consider the terrorist threat in the region, and this implied seeking allies across Central Asia. However, the economic management of the region was not considered to be a matter for the American government, and it was content to let oil companies negotiate their own terms with the republics. Any idea of confronting Russia or any other state on this issue was regarded as a zero-sum game, and Americans believed that conflict resolution was essential for the prosperity of the region as a whole.[5] Washington expressed a hope that free societies would develop, but it was clear that it did not envisage any intervention. America did not intervene in the Afghan Civil War to bring that conflict to a conclusion, seeing the matter as an issue for the UN. Similarly, the US did not play a part in the conclusion of the Tajik Civil War, or the Azeri–Armenian conflict, which it saw as issues lying in the Russian sphere. Any deals with Iran were unlikely too, but equally there were no moves to establish military alliances with any of the new republics, although there was a transfer of limited military aid.

For the Americans, there was, however, a growing interest in the IMU – particularly its links to Al-Qaeda, its drug-trafficking and the growth of regional terrorism. A counter-terrorism conference was convened in Washington in 2000 which involved most of the Central Asian republics. Subsequently $3 billion worth of aid was sent to Uzbekistan, Kyrgyzstan and Kazakhstan for counter-insurgency. There were joint exercises with the armies of these states and the deployment of valuable high-tech surveillance equipment. Uzbek officers and Special Forces teams from each of the republics were given training in the US. In some cases there was training alongside the Russians too, and in 2000 there had been a joint Russian–American working group on counter-terrorism. Nevertheless, it was not until the administration of George W. Bush and the attacks on the US on 11 September 2001 that a willingness to intervene directly in the region became manifest.

However, those who tended to speak of a 'new Great Game' as a way to describe rivalry between Washington, Moscow and the Central Asia states at this time failed to acknowledge that, in fact, the label was inappropriate. The issues bear almost no similarity to those of the nineteenth century, and the idea of American–Russian co-operation in counter-terrorism, the spectacular financial deals over oil resources, and the global reach of jihadists from heavily defended but remote bases in Afghanistan have no equivalent in the older struggle.

Indeed, in contrast to all the old certainties of the Soviet past, Russia faced an uncertain future in 1991. Contending with economic dislocation, Boris Yeltsin regarded Central Asia as a drain and looked to the wealth of Europe for Russia's salvation. Although Russian nationalists and Communist hardliners wanted the Soviet empire back, Moscow cut the republics adrift. The attitude of the Central Asian leaders was ambivalent. On the one hand, they needed Russian support and commerce and were fearful of the democratic forces the collapse of the Soviet Union had unleashed. However, there was also a strong anti-Russian sentiment after seven decades of alien government. But Russian views of Central Asia began to change too, especially in light of events in Chechnya. Having lost 4,000 men in an effort to prevent the separatism of one strategically important province between 1994 and 1996, Russia was eager to keep out foreign influences and retain the Central Asian states in a commonwealth dominated by Moscow. Russians reinforced their distaste of Islamism in the Chechen conflict and were eager to face down the challenge posed by jihadist terrorists in the region. In fact, the heavy civilian casualties in the Chechen conflict and in Tajikistan's civil war produced fear and anger in both Russia and Central Asia. The pattern of conflict in Chechnya and Tajikistan had been one of internal disorder, Russian intervention, civil war and Russian control. Other Central Asian governments were concerned that this sequence of events could also happen to them.

There was indignation in Moscow that the West was critical of the conduct of Russian forces in Chechnya. There was also deep suspicion, a legacy of the Cold War perhaps, that the West was showing interest in pipelines and oil resources in the former Soviet Union. The Russians were eager to influence Kazakhstan and Azerbaijan, and, initially, they resented Western diplomatic overtures and economic ventures there. President Putin, however, saw the need for co-operation with the US. He was eager to gain support for the second war in Chechnya in 1999, but he failed to win much sympathy when he was so outspoken in his criticism of Muslim extremism. The Central Asian leaders were equally unsupportive.

Karimov was determined to keep Russia as an ally for Uzbekistan but also to assert the independence of his country. This has tended to produce inconsistency: in February 1999, he abandoned the CIS security pact in favour of GUUAM, the pro-Western alliance.[6] Nevertheless, in December that year, he concluded a new bilateral agreement with Russia. The following June he permitted Russia to control Uzbek air space, but just three months later he announced that Uzbekistan no longer required protection – and everyone knew he had directed his remarks at Russia. In May 2001, Karimov rejected membership of the CIS security pact and customs union, making critical remarks about Russian forces in Tajikistan. When Russia got Kyrgyz, Kazakh and Tajik approval for a rapid-reaction force to deal with the IMT, the Uzbeks refused to join it, which suggested Karimov that regarded it an excuse to deploy Russian troops anywhere in the region and perhaps lead to a permanent presence in his country. Karimov was just as inconsistent with his policy towards the Taliban. He accused the Russians of exaggerating the Afghan threat and decided to hold talks with Kabul. When his negotiations failed, he was vehement in his condemnation of the Taliban regime. Uzbekistan needed to co-operate with Kyrgyzstan and Tajikistan against the IMT, but the Uzbek security forces pursued IMT groups across the borders without permission and opened fire on their territories, causing fatalities. Yet Karimov has been critical and dismissive of the efforts of his two neighbours in their counter-terror campaigns. Russia too has been noticeably unsupportive of Kyrgyzstan, even though it has borne the brunt of IMT attacks.

Similarly, Turkmenistan refused to follow Moscow's line, insisting that it was a neutral state, but that has not left it immune from Russian pressure. It agreed to the deployment of Russian troops along the Iranian border, and it has faced the threat of its pipelines to Europe being cut off (they are routed through Russia) and its exports being refused entry to Russia, its chief market. Although Turkmenistan sold fuel to the Taliban regime, it tended to support the anti-Taliban United Front during the Afghan Civil War and hoped for the construction of a trans-Afghan gas pipeline to the Pakistani port of Gwadar to reduce its dependence on Russia. The death of Niyasov will be seen as an opportunity by Russia for greater influence, but it will also be regarded as a chance for the IMT, Hizb ut-Tahrir and jihadist fighters to influence the country or use it as a conduit. Iran too will want to ensure that a stable and friendly regime is established to the north, particularly as it already feels encircled by (pro) Western forces in Iraq, Afghanistan and Pakistan.[7]

The Kazakh government believes that its hydrocarbon wealth will provide useful leverage with Russia, the US and China. The government has tended to accept American investment but staunchly refused either to offer any more democracy to its people or to improve its record on human rights, or to tackle corruption, which appears to be worst at the very highest levels of the administration. Kazakhstan has a large ethnic Russian population and is dependent, at present, on Russian pipelines. Nazarbaev is conscious of Russia's military power poised across the border, but he is eager to use that power against any IMT threat. To balance this dependence, the government has looked for Western military assistance. Nevertheless, the Kazakhs cannot afford to alienate Russia entirely, and this tempers their dealings with the West and with China.

CHINA: EMERGING TRENDS

There is considerable difference of opinion on China's strategic trends with almost as many projections as there are policy researchers. The disagreement over China's intentions is deepened by the country's secretive approach to policy formulation and a degree of double-speak in official announcements. What is clear is that China's policy towards Central Asia is driven by the dual needs of maintaining its internal security against Uighur activists and providing for its burgeoning energy needs. The external supply of weapons and support to the Uighurs is of grave concern. In 2000, the Chinese authorities claimed to have confiscated 4,100 kilograms of dynamite, 2,723 kilograms of other explosives, 604 illegal small arms and 31,000 rounds of ammunition, and much of this they suspected had come from sources outside China.[8] With a proliferation of terrorist, separatist and other groups, Beijing deployed at least 200,000 additional troops to Xinjiang. There were particular concerns that Uighurs were being trained and slipping across the borders from Afghanistan and Tajikistan, and that sympathizers in the other Central Asian states were supporting them. There were warnings to the Central Asian governments that trade and investment could be jeopardized if no action was taken against Uighur groups. Kazakhstan, Tajikistan and Kyrgyzstan have complied with this demand on several occasions in the last decade. However, China is careful not to apply too much pressure to the Central Asian states lest they look towards the US and Russia for support. China's overriding concern is that, should any of their neighbouring states be overthrown by Islamists, as Afghanistan was, then there is a distinct risk that Xinjiang would also fall into the hands of extremists. China's Central Asian policy is, to a large extent, driven by this anxiety about its internal security. The Uighurs have interpreted China's policies as a thinly veiled attempt to destroy Islam in Xinjiang altogether, and there is certainly a strong secularizing element in Beijing's agenda.

China's energy needs also determine its policy in Central Asia and look likely to do so with even greater importance in the future. Oil and gas will be the energy sources that underpin all of China's industries for the next few decades because there is almost no investment in alternative sources. However, as Xinjiang's supplies have begun to dwindle, the projections are that, even at a conservative estimate of growth of 7 per cent per year, China will have to import 45 per cent of

its oil by 2010. However, some predict that China's consumption will exceed these estimates, leading to an energy crisis.

China has been eager to assert greater control over the hydro-carbon resources of Central Asia and will do, perhaps more aggressively, in the future. It has purchased several oil fields, the most important of which is China National Petroleum Company's (CNPC) acquisition in Kazakhstan for $5 billion elsewhere. It has invested more than $9 billion in pipelines to the borders, and it has begun to buy the shares of other companies. Sinopec Corporation (China Petroleum Corporation) paid British Gas $615,000,000 for a stake in Kazakhstan's gas fields, and CNOOC, China's third-largest oil company, bought an 8-per-cent share of the British North Caspian Sea Project for a similar $600,000,000 fee. However, despite these and future purchases, it is estimated that Central Asia will not be able to meet the needs of the Chinese economy. Central Asia will therefore become an important transit route for pipelines from the Middle East. It is believed that, by 2010, 45 per cent of the world's oil production will come from the Middle East, and there is a strong chance that Iran will play a key role in the development of the Chinese share. Beijing has been careful not to criticize Iranian poli-tics in the way the West has done, and it has been silent on the issue of an Iranian nuclear programme. There have been discussions on Sino-Iranian pipeline projects which Tehran believes could elimi-nate its dependency on Russian routes and Western markets. Chinese-built pipelines would link into the Turkmenistan and Kazakhstan systems, and cross over into Xinjiang. However, the astronomical costs of developing such a network, and the vulnera-bility of pipelines to terrorist attack, have led to speculation that China will try to develop the Iranian port facilities at Bandas Abbas and sea routes to East Asia. Such is the growing importance of Iran to China that it is likely to oppose American moves against Tehran. Moreover, if the sea route is selected, we may expect to see a far greater emphasis on the Chinese navy and its capabilities as it seeks to protect this line of communication. The enormous demand for oil and gas may make it imperative for China to develop both the Central Asian pipelines and the sea-lanes options simultaneously.

China appears to be extending its influence over Central Asia without recourse to military means by using the power of its commerce. China has begun to replace low-quality Russian goods with cheap manufactures. To penetrate the market, it has granted Kyrgyzstan a loan of $5.7 million, and Tajikistan $5 million, to purchase Chinese products. China has also invested heavily in Central Asia. The Xinhua News Agency claimed that China's investments in the region totalled $500,000,000, dwarfing the Central Asian republics own investments.[9] Chinese investors argue that they will increase their trade inside Central Asia by thirty to fifty times in the next ten years. Much of China's investment has been in infrastructure, particularly road and rail links, as it seeks to improve the avenues of commercial penetration. Weapons and specialist anti-terrorism equipment have also been the subject of investment as China pursues its goal of improving the relationship and co-operation between the Central Asian states against disruptive terrorist groups, and exploiting the resources of the region. However, this twin-track policy is not without its risks. The dominance of Chinese goods can cause resentment, particularly when local industries are destroyed. The supply of weapons can also create instability within the republics as it encourages military solutions to political grievances. Moreover, trading relationships and military support cannot entirely overcome popular sympathy for the Muslims of Xinjiang. Nevertheless, China seems to be trying to avoid the traditional appellation of 'sphere of influence' or even *dingwei* (living space) in Central Asia. It does not want the responsibility of directing the republics and prefers only to consider security co-operation and the acquisition of resources. Both of these are closely linked to China's domestic future: popular political unrest and an economic crisis would together bring down the regime and condemn the country to the sort of chaos that afflicted it between 1911 and 1949.

There is no doubt that China is growing in importance in the region. It has established bilateral trade agreements with the republics since 1991 but carefully avoided security alliances which might mean unwelcome commitments. However, the attacks of the IMT and their support of the militant Uighurs have forced China to review this policy. China has been successful in demanding that the Central Asian states act against Uighur critics and organizations, closing down offices and publications and arresting individuals. It has persuaded the Pakistani government to co-operate, to deport suspects and to permit Chinese intelligence operatives to work inside Pakistan. The borders of China are now closely monitored, but there has been a concerted effort to end old disputes with Russia and to reduce the garrisons there. There have been successful joint border commissions with Russia, Kazakhstan and Kyrgyzstan, and only the Tajik borders await a final demarcation – the delay being caused by the existence of gold deposits which both sides claim. One of the most successful meetings of the Shanghai Five in 1996 produced demilitarized borders, providing a 120-kilometre-wide transparency zone and joint patrols. There have been annual meetings ever since, agreeing policies against drugs, Islamic extremism and the secret transit of weapons and explosives from Afghanistan.

Jihadist violence has, ironically, generated a stronger unity among the Central Asian states, including China. China is now a source of military assistance, just like the US. In 2000 and 2001, China donated $1.3 million to Uzbekistan and Kyrgystan in military and technical equipment, including sniper rifles for border guards. From 2000 there has been a Chinese-inspired joint counter-terrorism centre in Bishkek. In 2001 Uzbekistan joined what is now known as the Shanghai Cooperation Organisation (SCO). Trade and investment have increased, and there is more co-ordination in military and security matters. Above all, the Chinese government knows that it has to tackle jihadist groups beyond its borders as well as internally. Whether it has the right combination of policies, however, remains to be seen.

Paradoxically, the jihadist threat has united Russia, America and China against a common enemy, although some of the old suspicions remain, and relations have been strained over energy security and coalition operations in Iraq. When American forces arrived in Uzbekistan and Afghanistan in 2001, the Chinese were quick to stage a large-scale military exercise in Xinjiang, and extra border troops were deployed. Visitors from Pakistan and Afghanistan, the most likely avenue for agents working for the West to use, were also banned for a short period. Russia too is anxious about any permanent American military presence in the region but is no less concerned about Chinese influence being extended. The Central Asian republics are eager to keep the larger powers at arm's length, and there has been a reluctance to co-operate when their own minorities' interests have been at stake. But they are also conscious of their need for the financial, technical and military support of America, China and Russia. Nevertheless, the US and China have shared intelligence on the IMT and the Uighur militants. The record of American and Russian co-operation over oil and gas resources also points to collaboration rather than confrontation being the way forward, and this can only be of benefit to the people of Central Asia. The critical question is whether China can also now reach this level of co-operation.

China's long-term intentions are concerned with other issues that affect its domestic security or that have remained unresolved for decades. The future of Taiwan and the possibility of an armed confrontation there, its relationships with North Korea and its old rival Japan, its influence in South-east Asia, and the decline of Russia's strength on the Pacific seaboard and in Central Asia are all considered important. However, despite the tendency of some American analysts to see China as a belligerent rival in what may be a new Cold War, China has certain priorities which allow us to read its intentions more accurately. Above all, the Chinese political élite is eager to protect its exclusive hold on power, and internal security will continue to be high on its policy agenda. Second, China must sustain its growth to meet the basic economic needs of the majority and thus avoid unrest, and this makes the acquisition of resources critical. Third, China will seek to preserve the military status quo of its neighbours and, where possible, reduce the presence of the US. China's assessment is that it is encircled by the US, particularly when the Central Asian republics appear sympathetic to Washington (bases were recently established in Uzbekistan and Afghanistan). Some American analysts argue that China is trying its best to oust America from Central Asia altogether and that its SCO is, in fact, an anti-American organization. The SCO's announcement that it opposed 'interference in other countries' internal affairs' and that 'models of social development [a reference to America's desire for global democratization] should not be exported' have been interpreted as a warning to Washington, but they could equally be a genuine expression of anxiety, particularly in light of America's recent interventionist operations in Afghanistan and Iraq.[10]

While the original charter of the SCO appears to be a classic example of collective security, each member is obliged to help only against terrorism, separatists or extremists – there is no mention of other powers. Joint military operations are small in scale compared with those that China carries out on its own, and hardly suggest an equivalent of NATO in Asia. The manoeuvres are designed to be confidence-building activities, and they help to cement a common desire to defeat insurgent threats; they also reflect China's fear that the US might exploit unrest in Xinjiang or Central Asia as a pretext for intervention. Ultimately, Beijing may come to realise that the best way to prevent American support for separatists and to secure its economic future is to grant concessions to the Uighurs, but for the foreseeable future it wants to remove the Islamist problem and therefore any reason for an American presence in the region.

In terms of capabilities, China is often regarded as far weaker than the US, and Chinese authors tend to disparage the 'China Threat Theory' as an 'elaborate and sinister deception' that would be used to justify American action against their country.[11] Some American analysts conclude that China is still too poor, too backward and too focussed on economic development to be a threat. The fact that the PLA was reduced from 7,000,000 in the 1980s to 3,000,000 in 2001 tends to support this idea. Nevertheless, traditionalists in the Chinese armed forces continue to advocate a strategy of 'people's war' – that is, a total-war approach to any conflict with another major power. They emphasize the need for a large standing army, an efficient mobilization system and technologies which do not depend on foreign imports. The technological level of the PLA and their likely performance nevertheless remain the subject of considerable controversy.[12] Indeed, it seems that there is also considerable debate within the Chinese military and political élite itself about the strategy to follow. Challenging the traditionalists are those who advocate a Revolution in Military Affairs, a technologically driven set of new strategies and doctrines which not only emulate but 'leapfrog' Western capabilities. Judging by the tone of their writings, this group was largely unsuccessful until the late 1990s. However, there is another school of thought, known as the 'Local War' advocates, who demand an evolutionary approach to military changes and that the basis of China's strategy should be the assumption that its wars are likely to occur on or near its borders. One of the key zones of interest for this group is the vulnerable coastal region, the historical invasion route for China's enemies.

The solution to the division of opinion over China's future strategy appears to be resolved by three issues: the decline of Russia in Central and East Asia; the doctrine of *Shi* (Propensity), which suggests that apparently inferior forces can defeat superior ones; and the secret development of a range of 'Assassin's Mace' weapon systems. The coincidence of these three factors looks likely to influence Chinese policy and planning for the next few decades.

For China, the decline of Russia as the dominant power in Central Asia serves as a reminder of how not to manage the process of transition from the Marxist-Leninist system. China regards Russia as an energy and trade rival in the region, but it has been satisfied with its ability to assert itself over Russian interests since 2000. The difficulty for Moscow in persuading Slavs to migrate into the Pacific territories of Russia and the economic decline experienced there have added to China's confidence that its northern and western borders are more secure than they were in the Cold War years. That said, the second-largest concentration of air and ground forces in China still protects the northern and north-eastern approaches. However, there is more emphasis on the 'Inferior Defeats Superior' doctrine when it comes to general defence. This doctrine places considerable emphasis on excellent intelligence (and thus the ability to anticipate an enemy's actions), deception, the disruption of coalitions, the development of a secret counter-coalition, and an effectively timed decisive strike. Increasingly the decisive strike appears to be framed in terms of the Assassin's Mace systems. These take the form of anti-satellite weapons, tactical laser weapons and stealth technology, as well as computer platforms or electromagnetic-pulse weapons to attack radio, radar, electronic and other communications or surveillance systems. The concept embraces the use of nuclear weapons, Special Forces and missile batteries but also the development of the next generation of biological weapons (known as Genetic or DNA weapons).

Despite the obvious concerns about a new Cold War, it should be remembered that China's strategic thinking is underpinned by anxieties about American encirclement, internal unrest (which might be exploited by Islamists, separatists or foreign powers) and the exponential growth of its energy needs. China needs to continue its economic integration with the world and wants to improve its relationship, both commercial and military, with the Central Asian states. It has more to lose by jeopardizing the status quo. Nevertheless, the regime will fight to retain its exclusive grip on power, and there is every indication that it will continue to bear down hard on Uighurs it suspects of separatism or terrorism. Moreover, the growing needs of the economy may force Beijing into a more assertive and hard-line stance in both its internal affairs and its foreign policy. The development of its military strategy and armed forces attempts to take account of every future contingency.

AFGHANISTAN, PAKISTAN, IRAN, TURKEY AND THE ARAB STATES

There are links between the ethnic groups of Afghanistan and the Central Asian republics, with Turkmen, Uzbeks and Tajiks making up the populations in the north. There are also cultural and historic connections which were truncated by the creation of the Soviet Union and the Cold War. The IMU was based and partly financed in Afghanistan, making use of common traditions of hospitality, resistance to outsiders and the patronage of their more wealthy backers like Osama bin Laden. Al-Qaeda regarded Afghanistan as an ideal base from which to project its power, its ideas and a 'holy war' into the wider world. The country was awash with weapons and drug-money. The Soviet War and civil war had provided the personnel with contacts across the Muslim world, making Afganistan an ideal starting point for a global jihad. It was also a location loaded with significance: the place where, they believed, they had defeated the Soviet Union. But the Taliban, and therefore Al-Qaeda, could never have become so well established without the backing of Pakistan, more specifically, the ISI.

The Taliban had been dependent on exploiting the funding of the US and Arab states in the Soviet War. They were also the beneficiaries of a particularly strident indoctrination in the Deobandi madrassahs of Pakistan. The civil war and its outcome nevertheless convinced them that their victory was part of a divine mission.

The Taliban, dominated by Pushtuns and augmented by 'foreign fighters', was never representative of all Afghans in the way that the Loya Jirga now is. The Taliban persecuted the Shia Afghans of Hazara, effectively drove out tribal elders from other clans and waged war on the ethnic groups of the north who were represented by warlords like Dostum and Masoud. The Taliban were only really supported because they overran most of the country and promised to end the endemic corruption that plagued it. Warlords and brigandage were common. But it was not long before the draconian punishments of the Taliban, with their own merciless version of Sharia law, became an unbearable regime of terror and oppression. Women and minority groups suffered particularly badly. The Taliban were rather ignorant of world affairs and barely understood the sort of aspirations held by bin Laden and his confederates. Yet they did share a desire to purge the Muslim world of heresies and foreign influences. What they failed to offer was anything constructive. There was no programme of reconstruction for a country in ruins. The Taliban offered only the waging of war against infidels and heretics, and a celebration of heroic death. Their defeat was a liberation for the Afghans, but the costs of rebuilding the country are vast, and there is some evidence to suggest that the opportunity to maintain the trust and support of the coalition powers that intervened so dramatically in 2001 will be lost. The Taliban are attempting to regroup, to recruit Afghans against the foreign forces and to disrupt the pace of reconstruction. The West has the capability to defeat the Taliban militarily, but whether Western leaders have the stamina to endure a long insurgency, particularly in light of the unpopular operations in Iraq, is another matter.[13]

Pakistan has played a crucial part in the region's affairs in recent years. Gen. Zia's Islamization policy of the 1970s did much to radicalize the armed forces, security services and religious parties. Fearful of separatism and the public's dislike of a military regime, Zia tried to popularize his government. The Pakistani military regime was responsible for the ISI's backing of the radical Afghan warlord Hekmatyr and then, through the orchestration of Gen. Musharraf, the Taliban. Musharraf's policy was deeply unpopular among the Central Asian governments, and it was with some relief, no doubt, that Pakistan was forced to cut off Mullah Omar's legions in 2001 following American pressure. Musharraf has had to pursue a delicate policy line since, avoiding the total alienation of his people by moving carefully and gradually against the madrassahs and religious groups while not appearing to follow Washington's dictates too closely. Despite accusations from some Western sources that he failed to pursue Al-Qaeda with vigour, there have been more arrests of their personnel in Pakistan than in any other country. Moreover, Musharraf has launched two campaigns into Waziristan against Taliban strongholds. However, he has been unable or unwilling to remove militant leaders from the North-West Frontier Province, or from Balochistan, because he knows that they enjoy considerable popular support. Pakistani forces were withdrawn from Waziristan in 2006 when it became clear that his troops were being drawn into a protracted dispute with local armed groups and tribal factions rather than the leadership of Al-Qaeda.[14] Nevertheless, it is evident that thousands of Pushtun fighters who belonged to the Taliban, members of Al-Qaeda and other jihadist groups have sought refuge in Pakistan's north-west.

The Pakistani madrassahs also continue to produce zealots for the Islamist cause. These huge complexes have always offered an education, but Saudi influence and funding encouraged more radical religious instruction to predominate. With the inspiration of the Iranian Revolution and a mythology of global Muslim oppression, Pakistani madrassahs produced a particularly passionate world-view. For the Pakistani government there were concerns over the possibility of Pushtuns breaking away to form an independent Pushtunistan, and the instability of Afghanistan on their western border required some resolution. Faced with a long-running dispute with India over Kashmir, and the much larger Indian armed forces, Pakistan's leaders were eager to create strategic depth by clandestine or proxy means. The Kargil Operations of 1999 in Kashmir and the support for the Taliban in 1996 had much in common. Intelligence and Special Forces were deployed alongside irregular units trained, equipped and supplied by the Pakistani army. In the case of Kargil, Musharraf was the chief planner, and, despite denials, Indian analysts believed they have exposed the subtefuge.[15] The most important outcome of both operations, however, was that the Pakistanis lost control of their protégés.

Not all of Pakistan's involvement with Central Asia has been so negative. Nawaz Sharif tried to build trade links with the Central Asian republics, and there were negotiations over pipelines, investment and development. Benazir Bhutto, the liberal Premier, also hoped that the Taliban would establish a peaceful order in Afghanistan, and that, if a good relationship could be maintained, it might be possible to extend trade and pipelines to Turkmenistan, if not the other states. However, Bhutto was undermined by her own intelligence services and by radical elements within the administration, especially at the provincial level. The ISI gave refuge to the IMU's leader, Yuldeshev, in the 1990s and allowed Namangani to visit Pakistan, where he was able to make contact with other jihadists. The ISI may have calculated that, by supporting the IMU, it could weaken the Central Asian republics but could promote Pakistan as a 'mediator', thus increasing its diplomatic leverage in the region. With so many in Pakistan sympathetic to Islamist thinking, the ISI had a distinct advantage. However, it never gained control over the IMU. Namangani and Yuldeshev were able to draw on Saudi funds, drug revenue and an arsenal of Afghan weaponry which made them independent of Pakistan's influence. Their agenda was also quite distinct from that of Pakistan anyway.

Musharraf's apparent shift to a pro-Western stance, embracing the Global War on Terror, has made any subsequent relationship unlikely. However, contrary to Islamist propaganda, the majority in Pakistan support his decision to oppose terrorism. Pakistan has been plagued with sectarian violence, and its people have been subjected to a number of terrorist outrages. Although Islamists have tried to mobilize the people with street protests and inflammatory literature, they have failed. Indeed, the prospects of a pipeline across Afghanistan or Iran to the new port at Gwadar make co-operation with the Central Asian republics more likely in the future. The rapprochement with India in

2004 over Kashmir, the banning of certain extremist groups and continuing investigations to hunt down Al-Qaeda figures in the country make collaboration with Central Asia over security issues more likely too.

Iran has also been active in Central Asian affairs. In November 1991, Foreign Minister Ali Akbar Velayati visited the five republics to establish diplomatic relations. Turkmenistan, as the closest of the Central Asian states, was offered an alternative outlet for its natural gas, a new pipeline and a rail link at the border. However, Karimov so disliked the Iranians that he cancelled several potential deals. This can be explained by Tehran's tendency for intervention. In the Afghan Civil War, the Iranians supplied and backed their own Shia Afghan faction. Following Taliban massacres, the Iranians were eager to monitor events in their neighbour's failed state. In the Tajikistan conflict, the Iranians also briefly backed the IRP but pulled out to avoid a clash with the Russians when they joined the fighting. However, what really riled the Uzbek authorities was Iran's willingness to permit the IMU to broadcast on its media. Iranian intelligence officers also met with Yuldeshev and gave him funds in the hope of using him against the Taliban and Pushtun Sunni radicals. The failure of this bid drove the IMU more firmly into the arms of the Taliban and, by default, towards Al-Qaeda.

Iran sought to project its influence to contain Sunni radicalism (which it regarded as a threat), to contain Iraq under Saddam Hussein, and to deter Israel and American from intervention in the Persian Gulf. Between 1989 and 1993, Tehran also developed close relations with Moscow, purchasing missile technology and nuclear-energy expertise. In 2006, Iran found itself subject to UN sanctions for refusing to heed restrictions to its nuclear programme, namely the alleged enrichment of uranium to weapons grade. Iran remains defiant. It has supported Hezbollah against Israel, supplying it with advanced military technology including batteries of missiles. It has test-fired weapons in the Persian Gulf. It has snatched Coalition troops close to its border (allegedly for espionage) and has been accused of supplying radical Iraqi Shia groups, including the notorious Sadr Army, with explosives and weapons with which to fight the British forces around Basra by proxy.[16] Nonetheless, Iran feels encircled by pro-Western powers. It believes that Israel is armed with American nuclear weapons and knows that Pakistan, also an ally of the US, is similarly armed. American and Western forces are deployed on almost every border, and US warships patrol the Persian Gulf. Internally, it is fearful of a CIA-inspired coup and anxious about growing public dissatisfaction with authoritarian, theocratic rule. With large numbers of Iranians too young to remember the Revolution of 1979, or care for its idealism, Iran feels isolated and under threat. Critically, its economy is also now also under pressure. Projected oil revenue has not been realized, unemployment has risen, and it now faces sanctions on other goods.[17]

Turkey, by contrast, has moved steadily closer to Europe and appears to be poised to join the European Union. It has tried to argue that, as a Muslim state, it can provide an important bridge between Europe and South-west and Central Asia. In 1991, it sought to influence Central Asia, hoping to exploit its linguistic, ethnic and historic connections. There were some who recalled with nostalgia and pride the Seljuks, the Ottomans and Pan-Turkic ideologues of the past. Enver Pasha, who had coveted ideas of a new Turkish empire from the Mediterranean to China in the early twentieth century, had tried to lead the Basmachi of Central Asia on the first step, a rebellion in the Pamirs that ended with tragic results. Afghanistan's Amir Amanullah had also been influenced by the Turkish model in his reforms of the 1920s, and many had once regarded Ataturk as a modernizing, secular leader within an Islamic context that could be emulated for success. In the early 1990s, it was hoped that Turkish businesspeople would have a distinct advantage when it came to making deals with the new republics. Central Asian leaders also appeared to favour the modern Turkish model of government. Some madrassahs were established along Turkish – that is, non-radical – lines. Turkish television channels were beamed into Central Asian cafés and homes. Scholarships were granted in Turkish educational institutions. The Turks loaned $1.2 billion for development and construction. Many of the exiles from the authoritarian persecution of Xinjiang and the republics also chose to live in Turkey.

However, Turkish Islamic radicalism has also increased in the last decade. Terrorist attacks on the Turkish state, and Western interests there, have been more frequent. These attacks have made Central Asian leaders cautious about adopting the Turkish model.[18] For its part, Turkey's intelligence services have shown considerable interest in the Central Asian opposition groups, not just in case of regime change but also because there are so many Central Asian exiles in their homeland. Turkey has offered the Central Asian governments military assistance, and the Turkish armed forces train Uzbek and Kyrgyz officers. On the civilian side, Turkish investment in Central Asia has been smaller than the government anticipated, partly because of corruption in the region but also because of concerns that so few democratic and economic reforms have been carried out there. However, as a NATO member and an ally of the US, Turkey, like Pakistan, has much to offer Central Asia, not least in providing a balance to Russian and Chinese influence.

Saudi Arabia has earned a reputation for supporting the most fundamentalist Islamic movements in Central Asia. After 1991, the Saudi government showed little interest in the region, but charities and Islamists were more proactive. They made funding available for the building of mosques and madrassahs, for Islamic literature and sponsorship of the hadj. Their intention was to recruit Central Asians to their conservative Wahhabi interpretation of Islam, and they saw their work as a missionary effort. However, some of their protégés have gone far beyond what their original sponsors would have sanctioned, joining movements like Hizb ut-Tahrir and even the IMT. Saudi citizens also filled the ranks of jihadist organizations, notably as 'foreign fighters' in Afghanistan, Tajikistan and Chechnya. The Saudi government has also tended to back more extreme Islamist factions: Hekmatyr in the Afghan Civil War; the Taliban (until it sided with Al-Qaeda in 1996), and elements of the IRP who went on to become IMT men.

The Saudi authorities have also made little attempt to prevent private funding for extremists as long as they are active outside the kingdom. There have been accusations that the Saudi regime buys off its potential opponents, including Palestinian radicals and its own dissident community. This policy, driven by a concern not to alienate the ulema of the country, may, if true, backfire on the regime.[19] The Arab members of the IMT and Al-Qaeda are committed to returning to Saudi Arabia to overthrow the monarchy. As in Algeria, Egypt, Iraq and Indonesia, the militants are turning against their government at home. The West, which is dependent on Saudi oil and conscious of the religious-cultural sensitivities of the country, is reluctant to intervene in internal politics. There were, however, serious concerns after 9/11 when it was realized that fifteen of the nineteen hijackers were Saudis. The Saudi government, as ever fearful of the domestic reaction, refused to allow an American investigation on their soil. Nevertheless, American complaints and the release of details of the government's funding activities forced the Saudis to carry out their own internal investigations. These events, and recent terrorist attacks in the kingdom, will make the Saudi government more cautious about its support for Islamist groups in the future.

The Gulf States will also be forced to review their polices in light of the Global War on Terror and operations in Iraq. In the past, the UAE has given haven to Al-Qaeda, Taliban and IMT personnel, and the state is accused of permitting money-laundering and arms- and drug-smuggling to take place within its borders. However, the fact is that the Gulf States are also favourably disposed towards the West, which they regard as their biggest consumer. By remaining neutral in the Global War on Terror, focussing only on their commercial status in oil production, refining and transit, the Gulf States hope to avoid the violence and disruption affecting other regions. However, overall there has been a disappointing reaction to Islamic terrorism in Central Asia from the OIC, which represents all Islamic nations. The reason for this is simply that the organization lacks unity. It may be that, until jihadist terrorism begins to make a critical impact on the governments of the Muslim world, there will be little co-ordinated action, a situation which, to a lesser extent, mirrors that in Central Asia.

SOCIO-ECONOMIC PROBLEMS

Oil production in the Caspian is expected to reach 4,000,000 bpd by 2010, a spectacular increase from barely 1,000,000 bpd in 1997. In addition the region is thought to possess proven reserves of 7–10 trillion cubic metres (236–337 trillion cubic feet) of natural gas. Heralded the republics as the new 'Oil Dorado', Western and Russian companies have been quick to conclude contracts with Kazakhstan, Turkmenistan, Azerbaijan and Uzbekistan. The landlocked nature of the region does, however, mean that, to reach the world's markets, there needs to be considerable investment in pipelines (an estimated $50 billion by 2010). The old Soviet lines are aged and in need of renovation or expansion, and the Americans are eager to route new pipelines out of Russian and Iranian orbits. For their part, the Central Asian states are also eager to diversify their pipeline routes, both for energy security (in case of natural disasters such as earthquakes and man-made problems like wars and terrorism) and to reduce their dependence on Russia. The first new pipeline, from Baku to Supsa on the Black Sea coast of Georgia, was opened in 1999. The Tengiz–Novorossiysk pipeline, which is within Russian territory, was completed in 2001.

Despite some dire predictions of conflict over the world's diminishing oil resources, there are encouraging signs of collaboration and co-operation so far.[20] Chevron concluded a $20 billion joint venture with the Kazakh government in 1993, and Exxon Mobil has subsequently joined the consortium. The CPC combines this Tenghizchevroil group with Russia's Lukoil. Azerbaijan's state oil company, SOCAR, has also embraced the collaboration of Amoco, BP, Lukoil, Unocal, Pennzoil, Statoil and some other businesses to create the Azerbaijan International Operating Company. French oil companies have joined American and British firms in exploiting other Azeri fields in the Caspian.

This co-operation reflects a similar improvement in American–Russian relations over the region. They remain competitors, and openly so, but perhaps not in the confrontational style of the Cold War. American government officials also disapprove, rightly it seems, of the analogies with the Great Game.[21] Although Russia and America have considered their strategic interests, including energy security, in their preferences for the routing of pipelines, commercial interests will influence the final decisions. The most cost-effective and financially realistic routes will be the ones that get built; the most profitable routes will be the ones that will be sustained. Russia and the US share a desire for stability in the region, since both stand to lose billions if terrorism and conflict disrupt the supply of oil and gas. It is this common aim that may force them, and others, to co-operate in the future.

Despite the financial bonanza oil and gas revenues have brought the economic and political élites of the Caspian and Central Asian states, the majority of the population live in relative poverty. The new rich import European and American cars, wear designer clothes and frequent fashionable bars and hotels. They own rural properties as well as urban ones, open overseas bank accounts and live in ostentatious luxury. In Kyrgyzstan, the World Bank report of 2001 revealed that, by contrast, 68 per cent of the people lived on less than $17 a month.[22] A subsistence annual salary was calculated at $295, but the average Kyrgyz salary per annum was $165. GDP fell between 1990 and 1996 by 47 per cent. Industrial output fell by 61 per cent and agricultural production by 35 per cent. On the Kyrgyz–Chinese border, one saw truckloads of scrap metal, stripped from disused factories, being shipped to China's smelting works, something Lutze Klevemann eloquently described as 'one empire robbing the corpse of the old'.[23] The poverty of Kyrgyzstan is not atypical. The Uighurs of Xinjiang, the urban poor of Uzbek cities, the kiosk-owners of Kazakhstan, the unemployed of Turkmenistan, and the refugees of Karabakh all share the same bleak future. In war-torn Tajikistan and Afghanistan, the conditions in some regions are so abysmal that some have died from hunger, cold and neglect.

Regional poverty brings with it a host of other problems, including trade in narcotics, organized crime and the trafficking of women. The International Organisation for Migration (the independent trans-national body supported by 120 countries worldwide) estimates that, in 1999, 4,000 Kyrgyz women and children were sold abroad as prostitutes in the UAE, China, Turkey and possibly Europe. The UN believes that human trafficking may now have exceeded tourism as the second-largest income generator in the country after narcotics.[24] The trafficking of women also affects other Central Asian countries, but women's rights in rural districts of Afghanistan are still a cause for concern. Many are treated like property; there are reports of beatings, rape and honour killings. The smuggling of heroin from Afghanistan has also proved attractive to criminal elements across the region, and this activity is closely linked to human trafficking and terrorism. Gangs use their revenue to buy arms, transport and loyalty. They also use the money to bribe those in authority. The UN Drugs Control Programme estimates that thousands of kilos are transitted through the Central Asian states every year, fetching enormous street prices in Europe and Russia. Local heroin addiction has also incapacitated a large number of young people, rivalling the alcoholism epidemic of the Soviet era. In Kyrgyzstan, there are 4,500 registered addicts, but the actual number of regular users may exceed 50,000. Accompanying this rise in addiction is the spread of AIDS. Hizb ut-Tahrir object to warnings from NGOs that people should use condoms: they argue that these warnings simply encourage prostitution. The drugs/AIDS problems have also now spread more widely across the region. In the 1980s, drugs tended to be transferred from Afghanistan to Pakistan, but by 2000 there were conduits through Iran, China, the Arab states and Central Asia. Pakistanis, Arabs and Chechens are the most prominent in forming drugs syndicates which fund terrorism.

The world is not indifferent to the situation, particularly the storm centre of the Ferghana Valley. The UN Development Programme has a specific Ferghana Valley development project, and there are an independent Soros Foundation programme and an American Ferghana Valley Working Group. All these organizations stress the need for co-operation between the Central Asian states that control the area. The Uzbek government has, in the past, prevented joint development work, but it is now a member of the SCO, which co-ordinates and encourages action. In Afghanistan, there is considerable effort being made in reconstruction. However, some NGOs have expressed frustration at the expense of the UN operations compared with the actual amount of reconstruction achieved. Among the more successful schemes, both in Afghanistan and in the Ferghana Valley, have been micro-credit programmes. Small funds, for crops, orchards, irrigation networks and animal husbandry, are used to help families achieve independence. In Afghanistan, women who were discouraged from going out to work were given chickens.[25] These provided a food source and eggs for sale, but the real beauty of the idea was that it was a low-cost project and the women could earn an income while remaining at home. The British army has also been successful in its Provincial Reconstruction Teams work. In contrast, vast prestige projects such as dam construction have been criticized for costing too much and producing poor-quality workmanship.

Water supplies are likely to prove a source of conflict in the future. Soviet systems once carried snow melt out to large cotton plantations or extended ancient networks. The independence of the republics, and civil wars in Afghanistan and Tajikistan, have disrupted many of the old systems, initially causing a 50 per cent drop in supply. As a result, 20 to 30 per cent of arable land was put out of use. In Tajikistan, the figure was closer to 50 per cent. In Xinjiang, water is already a contested resource between the Uighur farmers, old settlers, new migrants and industry. When Uzbekistan used the severing of gas supplies as a diplomatic lever against Kyrgyzstan and Tajikistan, these two countries responded by cutting water supplies to the Uzbeks in the Ferghana Valley. A severe drought that began in 2000, and that affected Tajikistan and Afghanistan particularly badly, caused a 50-per-cent fall in cereal production and left millions without an adequate diet. A further fall of 15–20 per cent in 2001 left thousands starving. In Tajikistan, people sold the doors and windows of their houses to pay for food.[26] Children could be seen dressed in rags and without shoes, a situation that made the winter of 2001 particularly hard. An ongoing energy crisis in Tajikistan has left the government with insufficient revenue to tackle the problem of poverty, especially in rural areas, and many are still dependent on foreign aid. In Afghanistan, the situation is very similar. Schoolchildren frequently drop out of their studies, even when the buildings are reconstructed, because they need to take up employment in public-works projects like road-building to pay for food.

The behaviour of the Central Asian regimes towards public protest has also attracted international interest. There are accusations that the Global War on Terror is used as an excuse to crack down on political opponents and that the regimes fail to recognize that their own hard-line strategy is fostering unrest, even to the extent of pushing young men towards extremist groups. This is a compelling argument, posited by experienced observers like the journalist Ahmed Rashid. Yet the situation is complex. Extreme and otherworldly ideologies like those promoted by Hizb ut-Tahrir seem more attractive when the economic situation seems so dire. Equally, when governments appear to ignore genuine grievances, or act with brutality towards protestors, there does seem to be a strong motive to join a terrorist group – to strike back at the regimes that oppress.

However, the apparatus of government in several Central Asian states is not unlike that of the Soviet Union, and, in case of Xinjiang, it is almost unchanged from the early days of Chinese Communism. The Central Asian peoples were always the poor relations in the regimes under which they lived. What has changed is the political and religious landscape of Islam. Radicalized by external contact with extreme ideologies, particularly Salafest Wahhabism and Deobandism, and by events in the Middle East, Iran and Afghanistan since the 1970s (including the Arab–Israeli dispute, the Iranian Revolution, and the Soviet–Afghan War and civil war that followed), a minority of Central Asians have drifted towards violence. In the case of Chechnya and Tajikistan, the breakdown of internal order and external intervention radicalized the conflict further. The breakdown of these states, and the collapse of Afghanistan in particular, proved a magnet for 'foreign volunteers' eager to assert their Islamist credentials in a world that seemed increasingly Westernised, globalized and irreligious. Central Asia has been seen by jihadists as a platform upon which to recon-struct a new world order, purged of infidels and apostates, where the Muslim *umma* could reassert its superiority over the West and China. The motives of the terrorists in Central Asia are only in part due to the heavy-handed policies of their governments, or to regional poverty. Rather, they see themselves engaged in an ideological struggle. At a personal level, the fighters are also driven by a desire to attack injustice and humiliation, and to give themselves a sense of righteous mission and life purpose. A few of the IMT are simply criminals, deeply involved in drugs, human trafficking or banditry.

The conflicts in Central Asia have often been characterized by clan warfare and ethnic violence. Even in the case of Chechnya, it was never just a war between Russians and Chechens. Political and clan factions were just as capable of fighting each other, and some Chechens chose to collaborate with the Russians to bring the conflict to a conclusion. In neighbouring Dagestan, the people were equally divided. In the Soviet War in Afghanistan, Afghans fought on the Russian side, as did many Central Asians, including Namangani, the joint founder of the IMT. The fault-lines of the country were even more clearly demarcated in the civil war. In the Tajik Civil War, there were massacres and atrocities of shocking severity, with clan and ethnic divisions overlaid by ideological differences. There was a similar pattern in the Karabakh conflict.[27]

Terrorism has generated instability and fear in Central Asia. Hostage-taking for ransom, bomb attacks (including suicide bombings), ambushes and raids of state forces, looting and the trafficking of drugs, arms and people are the scourge of the region. External forces have fuelled these problems. Pakistan and Saudi Arabia supported extremist factions in the Afghan Civil War. Islamists from South-west Asia, North Africa, western China, Turkey and Pakistan have joined the ranks of the IMT and Al-Qaeda. Russia, China and the US have backed the Central Asian governments, providing them with military assistance. America wants the resources of Central Asia to be available to world markets and wants to wage war against terrorist movements, Russia wants to secure its economic future and to maintain its strategic influence in the former Soviet Union, while China wants to acquire resources for its growing economy and to crush any domestic Islamist threat.

Counter-terrorism requires sound socioeconomic conditions as much as good intelligence and effective security measures. The Central Asians need to be provided with jobs, decent housing and sufficient food so they do not become, as Mao once put it, the 'water' to insurgent 'fish'. If civil violence is to be avoided, this will require the broader dissemination of the new oil and gas wealth. The oil companies are indeed encouraging the construction of schools, hospitals, roads and ecology projects, but there needs to be better co-ordination between each of the republics and other foreign agencies. Economic development, political representation, accountable government, efficient security and policing with consent are essential. If these are achieved, then the jihadists and their extreme ideology may be isolated and contained long enough for them to wither away.

References

1 Regional Issues and Contemporary History

1 Andrew Osborn, 'Uzbek Leader Silences Critics of Massacre', *Independent*, 13 May 2006.

2 Allison Gill, 'Its Time to Save Lives', *International Herald Tribune*, available at Human Rights Watch, http:www.org/english/docs/2007/05/06/russia/ 15859.htm.

3 Council on Foreign Relations, Ferghana Valley Working Group Report, *Calming the Ferghana Valley: Development and Dialogue in the Heart of Central Asia* (New York, 1999).

4 Karimov speech to the Uzbek Parliament, 2 May 1998, cited in Ahmed Rashid, *Jihad: The Rise of Militant Islam in Central Asia* (New York, 2002), p. 146.

5 Karimov cited in Amnesty International, *Human Rights Report: Uzbekistan* (June 2001).

6 Tohir Abdouhalilovitch Yuldeshev, Interview, *Voice of America*, 6 October 2000.

7 Noor Ahmed Khalidi, 'Afghanistan: Demographic Consequences of War, 1978–87', *Central Asian Survey*, x/3 (1991), p. 107.

8 Denis Sinor, *The Cambridge History of Early Inner Asia* (Cambridge, 1990).

9 Olivier Roy, *The New Central Asia: The Creation of Nations* (London and New York, 2000), pp. 1–10.

10 W. E. D. Allen and P. Muratoff, *Caucasian Battlefields: A History of the Wars on the Turco-Caucasian Border, 1828–1921* (Cambridge, 1953).

11 Peter Morris, 'Russian Expansion into Central Asia', in Peter Morris, ed., *Africa, America and Central Asia: Formal and Informal Empire in the Nineteenth Century* (Exeter, 1984), p. 76.

12 Peter Hopkirk, *Setting the East Ablaze* (Oxford, 1984), pp. 152–61.

13 Peter Hopkirk, *The Great Game* (Oxford, 1990), p. 278.

14 John Keay, *Where Men and Mountains Meet* (Oxford, 1993); Robert Johnson, *Spying for Empire: The Great Game in Central and South Asia, 1757–1947* (London, 2006), pp. 109–10.

15 Sir Percy Sykes, *A History of Afghanistan* (London, 1940), pp. 198–200.

16 Edward R. Giradet, *Afghanistan: The Soviet War* (London, 1985), p. 126.

17 Yaacov Roi, *Islam in the Soviet Union from the Second World War to Gorbachev* (London, 2000).

18 Svat Soucek, *A History of Inner Asia* (Cambridge, 2000), chap. 17.
19 R. H. Dekmajian, *Islam in Revolution: Fundamentalism in the Arab World* (New York, 1985).
20 Ahmed Rashid, *Jihad*, p. 3.
21 *Ibid.*, p. 10.

2 The Central Asian Republics before and after 1991

1 Shirin Akiner, *The Formation of the Kazakh Identity* (London, 1995).
2 Svat Soucek, *A History of Inner Asia* (Cambridge, 2000), p. 236; Olivier Roy, *The New Central Asia: The Creation of Nations* (London and New York, 2000), p. 87.
3 Roy, *The New Central Asia*, p. 115.
4 'Kazakhstan's Nazarbayev Wins Re-election With 91% of Vote', 5 December 2005, http://www.bloomberg.com/apps/news?pid=10000087&sid=a2ml 5vt5j2_Me-refer=top_world_news. Accessed January 2007.
5 Martha Brill Olcott, *Kazakhstan: Unfulfilled Promise* (New York, 2002).
6 Lutz Klevemann, *The New Great Game: Blood and Oil in Central Asia* (London, 2003), p. 82.
7 us Department of State, Joint Press Conference with Nursultan Nazarbyaev, President of Kazakhstan, 9 December 2001, http://www.state.gov/secretary/former/powell/remarks/2001/dec/6778.htm. Accessed January 2007.
8 Edward Allworth, ed., *Central Asia: 130 Years of Russian Dominance* (Durham, NC, 1994).
9 Profile of Islam Karimov, Human Rights Watch, http://www.hrw.org/press/2002/03/karimovprof.htm. Accessed January 2007.
10 http://www.kreml.org/interview/100931204, accessed January 2007.
11 Craig Murray, *Murder in Samarkand: A British Ambassador's Controversial Defiance of Tyranny in the War on Terror* (London, 2006).
12 'Principles of Our Reform', Islam Karimov interview with *Rossijskaya Gazeta*, 7 July 1995, http://2004.press-service.uz/rus/knigi/9tom/3tom/_12.htm. Accessed January 2007.
13 'Uzbekistan in for the Long Haul', International Crisis Group, 16 February 2006, www.crisisgroup.org/home/index.cfm?id=3952&1=1. Accessed December 2006.
14 'Presidential Elections in Tajikistan a Farce', Human Rights Watch, 1999, http://hrw.org/english/docs/1999/10/28/tajiki1668.htm; 'OSCE: Tajikistan Elections Fall Short of Standards', Radio Free Europe, 2007, http://www.rferl.org/specials/tajikelections/. Accessed January 2007.
15 Kyrgyz means '40 girls', after the original 40 tribes of the Mongols.
16 Akayev's webpage is at http://www.askarakaev.kg/; a more critical portrait is at http://news.bbc.co.uk/2/hi/asia-pacific/4371819.stm. Accessed January 2007.
17 Bakiev's profile is examined at http://news.bbc.co.uk/1/hi/world/asia-pacific/4660317.stm. Accessed January 2007.
18 Edward O'Donovan, *The Merv Oasis* (London, 1882), pp. 71ff.
19 L.V.S. Blacker, 'Travels in Turkistan, 1918–20' *Geographical Journal*, LVIII/3 (1921), pp. 178–97.
20 Obituary at http://news.bbc.co.uk/1/hi/world/asia-pacific/6199021.stm. Accessed January 2007.
21 Overview of the economy at https://www.cia.gov/cia/publications/factbook/geos/tx.html#Econ; details of the gas industry's potential and its problems in

'Turkmenistan: Potential "Super-Giant" Emerges on Energy Scene' at Radio Free
Europe, http://www.rferl.org/featuresarticle/2006/11/CB06DCDE-C0D7-40C7-
B0E9-8AC1BD48F6F2.html. Accessed 7 January 2007.
22 Ahmed Rashid, *Taliban: Militant Islam, Oil, and Fundamentalism in Central Asia*.
(New Haven, CT, 2001).
23 S. Wheeler, *The Amir Abdur Rahman* (London, 1895).
24 Amir Amanullah Khan's biography is at http://afghanland.com/history/amanul-
lah.html. Accessed January 2007.
25 William Maley, *The Afghanistan Wars* (London and New York, 2002).
26 Afghanistan's National Development Strategy is at http://www.af/ands.html;
Afghanistan Development Forum with its international partnerships is at
http://www.adf.gov.af/; 'Nato Struggles in Afghanistan', BBC report, September
2006, http://news.bbc.co.uk/1/hi/world/south_asia/5345452.stm; 'Herat: A City
Reborn', BBC report, December 2006, http://news.bbc.co.uk/1/hi/world/south_
asia/6206258.stm. Accessed January 2007.

3 Islam and Islamism

1 Yaacov Ro'i, *Islam and the Soviet Union* (New York, 2000).
2 Sergei Poliakov and Martha Brill Olcott, *Everyday Islam: Religion and Tradition in
Rural Central Asia*, trans. A. Olcott (New York, 1992).
3 S. Akiner, *Islam in Post-Soviet Central Asia: Contested Territory* (Hamburg, 2002);
Mehrdad Haghayeghi, 'Islamic Revival in the Central Asian Republics', *Central
Asian Survey*, XIII/2 (1994), pp. 249–66.
4 Mehrdad Hagheyeghi, *Islam and Politics in Central Asia* (London, 1996).
5 R. H. Dekmejian, *Islam in Revolution: Fundamentalism in the Arab World* (New York,
1995). For a contrasting view, see H. J. Oliver, *The Wahhabi Myth: Dispelling
Prevalent Fallacies and the Fictitious Link with Bin Laden*, http://www.thewah-
habimyth.com/files/thewahhabimyth.pdf. Accessed August 2004.
6 Ahmed Rashid, *Jihad: The Rise of Militant Islam in Central Asia* (New Haven, CT,
2002), p. 118.
7 Abdul Qadeem Zaloum, *How the Khilafah was Destroyed* (Lahore, 1998).
8 Chris Marsh, 'Hizb ut-Tahrir and Islamic Militancy: How Much a Threat to
Central Asian Regional Stability?', unpub. MRes, 1 September 2004, Kings
College London, p. 5.
9 An-Nabhani, 'Economic System', 1997, http://hizb-ut-tahrir.org_/english/
_books/pdfs/economicsystem.pdf; F. Fukuyama, 'Has History Started Again?',
Policy, XVIII/2 (Winter 2002), p. 6; I. Rotar, 'Central Asia: Hizb ut-Tahrir Wants
Worldwide Sharia Law', *Forum*, XVIII, http://www.forum18.org/Archive.php?
article_id=170, 2003.
10 Marsh, 'Hizb ut-Tahrir and Islamic Militancy', p. 31.
11 Rashid, *Jihad*, p. 123.
12 http://hizb-ut-tahrir.org ; www.khilafah.org ; www.1924.org; http://wwwmind-
spring.eu.com are examples of Western-based sites.
13 See US State Department, *Uzbekistan: Human Rights Practices 2000* (Washington,
DC, 2001); *Independent Human Rights Organisation of Uzbekistan, About Political
Prisoners in Uzbekistan* (July 2001).
14 Olivier Roy, 'Changing Patterns among Radical Islamic Movements', *Brown
Journal of World Affairs*, 6, 1 (Winter–Spring 1999), pp. 109ff.
15 Marsh, 'Hizb ut-Tahrir and Islamic Militancy', p. 22.

16 Sura 3, v. 104; sura 3, v. 110–14.
17 Rashid, *Jihad*, p. 124.
18 *Independent Human Rights Organisation of Uzbekistan.*
19 International Crisis Group, *Central Asia: Islam and the State* (Osh and Brussels, 2003).
20 T. Makarenko, 'Hizb ut-Tahrir on the Rise in Central Asia', *Jane's Intelligence Review*, 12 November 2002, pp. 30–33.
21 A. Cohen, 'Hizb ut-Tahrir: An Emerging Threat to US Interests in Central Asia', (2003), at http://www.heritage.org/Research/RussiaandEurasia/BG1656.cfm. Accessed July 2004.
22 Cited in Rashid, *Jihad*, p. 134.
23 J. Burke, *Al Qaeda: Casting a Shadow of Terror* (London, 2003), p. 234.
24 Rashid, *Jihad*, p.134.
25 *Ibid.*
26 *Ibid.*

4 The Tajik Civil War and the Islamic Renaissance Party

1 Boris Rumer, *Soviet Central Asia: A Tragic Experiment* (Boston, MA, 1989).
2 Ian Bremmer and Ray Taras, eds, *New States, New Politics: Building Post-Soviet Nations*, (Cambridge, 1996), pp. 607–8.
3 *Ibid.*, p. 606.
4 Ahmed Rashid, *Jihad: The Rise of Militant Islam in Central Asia* (New Haven, CT, 2002), pp. 101–2; Shirin Akiner, *Tajikistan: Disintegration or Reconciliation*; S. Olimova, 'Islam and the Tajik Conflict', in Roald Sagdeev and Susan Eisenhower, eds, *Islam and Central Asia* (Washington, DC, 2000).
5 'Tajikistan Civil War', www.globalsecurity.org, 1999. Accessed November 2006.
6 Dilip Hiro, *Between Marx and Muhammad* (London, 1995).
7 Human Rights Watch, 'Tajikistan', 2001. Accessed 4 November 2006.
8 Rashid, *Jihad*, pp. 112, 118.
9 *Ibid.*, p. 235; Sergei Gretsky, *Civil War in Tajikistan: Causes, Developments and Prospects for Peace* (Washington, DC, 2006).
10 Gretsky, *Civil War in Tajikistan.*
11 Meryem Kirimli, 'Ubekistan in the New World Order', *Central Asian Survey*, XIII/1 (1994), pp. 19–32; Roy Allison, ed., *Central Asian Security: The New International Context* (2001).
12 Rashid, *Jihad*, pp. 164, 172.
13 Resolution 968 (1994), 16 December 1994.
14 Gretsky, *Civil War in Tajikistan.*
15 Rashid, *Jihad*, p. 107.
16 Andrew Meier, 'Opium Highway', *Time Magazine*, 24 February 1997, pp. 50–55; Rashid, *Jihad*, pp. 107, 243.
17 Rashid, *Jihad*, pp. 97–102.
18 Gretsky, *Civil War in Tajikistan.*
19 Ahmed Rashid, 'Western Powers Bolster Tajikistan', *Central Asia Analyst*, 23 May 2001.
20 'Tajikistan Election' VOA News, 21 November 2006, http://www.voanews.com/uspolicy/2006-11-21-voa2.cfm?renderforprint=1; Roxana Saberi, 'Putting Tajikistan on the Map', 21 November 2006, http://news.bbc.co.uk/2/hi/asia-pacific/6154368.stm. Accessed 22 November 2006.

5 The Afghan Civil War and the Taliban

1 'Afghanistan: Government to Have Greater Control over Aid Pledged in London', IRIN news.org, 2 February 2006, http://www.irinnews.org/report.asp?ReportID=51510&SelectRegion=Asia&Sele ctCountry=AFGHANISTAN. Accessed February 2006.
2 William Maley, *The Afghanistan Wars* (London and New York, 2002) pp. 30–31.
3 *Ibid*, p. 23.
4 *Ibid*, p. 30.
5 Rob Johnson, *A Region in Turmoil* (London, 2005) p. 163.
6 Russian General Staff, *The Soviet-Afghan War*, trans. and ed. Lester W. Grau and Michael A. Gress (Lawrence, KA, 2002), pp. 18–19.
7 *Ibid.*, pp. 25–6.
8 *Ibid.*, pp. 252–3.
9 *Ibid.*, p. 69.
10 Mohammed Yousef and Mark Adkin, *The Bear Trap: Afghanistan's Untold Story* (London, 1992) p. 177.
11 Russian General Staff, *The Soviet-Afghan War*, pp. 62–3; Ali Ahmad Jalali and Lester Grau, *The Other Side of the Mountain: Mujahideen Tactics in the Soviet Afghan War* (Quantico, 1998).
12 Maley, *The Afghanistan Wars*, p.133; Henry S. Bradsher, *Afghan Communism and Soviet Intervention* (Karachi and Oxford, 1999), p. 277.
13 Johnson, *Region in Turmoil*, p.191.
14 Ahmed Rashid, *Taliban: Islam, Oil and Fundamentalism in Central Asia* (London, 200); Peter Marsden, *Taliban: War and Religion in Afghanistan* (London and New York, 2002), pp. 51, 55.
15 B. Raman, 'Pakistan's Sponsorship of Terrorism', 25 February 2000, www.saag.org/papers2/paper106.html; B. Raman, 'Pakistan and the Taliban', 10 November 2001, http://www.saag.org/papers4/paper358.html; B. Raman, 'Bin Laden, Taleban and India', 29 September 1999, www.saag.org/papers/paper83.html.
16 William Maley, ed., *Fundamentalism Reborn? Afghanistan and the Taliban* (London, 1999), p. 2; S. Kapila, 'Pakistan's Proxy Wars, Islamic Jehad and the Taliban', 12 March 2001, http://www.saag.org/papers3/paper209.htm.
17 Marsden, *Taliban*, p. 55; Maley, *The Afghanistan Wars*, p. 233.
18 Walter Lacquer, *No End to War: Terrorism in the Twenty-First Century* (New York, 2003), pp. 56–7, 159.
19 'Biography, Office of the President, Islamic Republic of Afghanistan', http://www.president.gov.af/english/president_biography.mspx; 'Hamed Kharzai', *Afghan Observer*, http://afghanobserver.com/Articles/Karzai_Bio.htm. Accessed December 2006.
20 'Security', Office of the President, Islamic Republic of Afghanistan, http://www.president.gov.af/english/np/security.mspx. Accessed January 2007; 'The Afghan Economy' The Economist.com, 23 February 2006, http://www.econ-omist.com/background/displayBackground.cfm?story_id=4494134; Ashraf Ghani, 'Afghanistan Has the Assets to Regain Momentum' FT.com, 19 June 2006, http://search.ft.com/searchArticle?page=13&queryText=afghanistan&javascript Enabled=true&id=060619007392. Accessed January 2007. The American government's perspective is at http://www.whitehouse.gov/infocus/nationalsecurity/rebuildingafghanistan.html.

21 *Financial Times*, 10 June 2006.
22 Rachel Majoree, 'US Envoy Warns on Efforts to Rebuild Afghanistan', 3 February 2006, http://search.ft.com/searchArticle?queryText=financial+aid+afghanistan &y=11&javascriptEnabled=true&id=060203000900&x=10. Accessed January 2007.
23 Simon Chesterman, 'Tiptoeing through Afghanistan: The Future of UN State Building', International Peace Academy, September 2002, http://www.ipacademy.org/PDF _ Reports/afghanistan0902.pdf; Carolyn Stephenson, 'Nation Building', in Guy Burgess and Heidi Burgess, eds, *Beyond Intractability*, Conflict Research Consortium, University of Colorado, Boulder, posted January 2005, <http://www.beyondintractability.org/essay/nation _ building/>. Accessed January 2007.
24 Rob Watson, 'Mission Too Important to Fail', 31 July 2006, http://bbc.co.uk/go/ pr/fr/-/hi/world/south _ asia/5232766.stm. Accessed January 2007.
25 Amin Tarzai, 'South Asia: Pakistan-Afghanistan Conflicts Continue', 29 September 2006, http://www.rferl.org/featuresarticle/2006/09/260c90a0-1f41-4ab6-a580-21bcc8a914f5.html.

6 The Islamic Movement of Uzbekistan/Turkestan and Regional Insurgency

1 'Islamic Movement of Uzbekistan, MIPT Terrorism Knowledge Base, 10 December 2006, http://www.tkb.org/Group.jsp?groupID=4075; US Department of State, 'Patterns of Global Terrorism, 2000', April 2001; Mark Burgess, 'In the Spotlight: Islamic Movement of Uzbekistan', Center for Defense Information, 25 March 2002, http://www.cdi.org/terrorism/ imu.cfm; Walter Lacquer, *No End to War: Terrorism in the Twenty-First Century* (New York, 2003), pp. 191–2.
2 Ahmed Rashid, *Jihad: The Rise of Militant Islam in Central Asia* (New Haven, CT, 2002), p. 148, n. 16.
3 B. Raman, 'Terrorism in Afghanistan and Central Asia, 24 November 2004, www.saag.org/papers12/paper1172.html. Accessed May 2005.
4 Rashid, *Jihad*.
5 Burgess, 'In the Spotlight: Islamic Movement of Uzbekistan', http://www.cdi.org/ terrorism/imu.cfm; Raman, 'Terrorism in Afghanistan and Central Asia', http://www.saag.org/papers12/paper1172.html. Accessed January 2007.
6 B. Raman, 'International Terrorism Monitor: Paper no. 22, Jihadi Terrorism in Central Asia: An Update', 1 February 2006, http://www.saag.org/papers17/paper1691.htm.
7 Rashid, *Jihad*, p. 143.
8 United States Mission to the OSCE, 'Statement on Freedom of Thought, Conscience, Religion or Belief', 28 September 2005, http://osce.usmission.gov/ archive/2005/09/HDIM _ On _ Freedom _ of _ Thought _ 09 _ 28 _ 05.pdf. Accessed January 2007.
9 Raman, 'International Terrorism Monitor', www.saag.org/papers17/ paper1691.html. Accessed January 2007.
10 Raman, 'Terrorism in Afghanistan and Central Asia', 24 November 2004, www.saag.org/papers12/paper1172.html. Accessed May 2005.
11 Kadir Alimov, 'Uzbekistan's Foreign Policy: In Search of a Strategy', Eisenhower Institute, 2006, http://www.eisenhowerinstitute.org/programs/globalpartnerships/securityandterrorism/coalition/regionalrelations/ConflictBook/Ali

mov.htm; Erich Marquart and Yevgeny Bendersky, 'Uzbekistan's New Foreign Policy Strategy', PINR, 23 November 2005, http://www.pinr.com/report.php? ac=view_report&report_id=404. Accessed January 2006.

12 Rashid, *Jihad*.

13 'Patterns of Global Terrorism 1999: Eurasia Overview', [US] Department of State Publication 10687, 2000, http://www.fas.org/irp/threat/terror_99/eurasia. html.

14 William D. Shingleton and John McConnell, 'From Tamerlane to Terrorism: The Shifting Basis of Uzbek Foreign Policy', *Harvard Asia Quarterly*, v/1 (2001), http://www.asiaquarterly.com/content/category/8/32/.

15 Rashid, *Jihad*.

16 Rashid, *Jihad*, p.165.

17 Andrew Meier, 'Opium Highway', *Time Magazine*, 24 February 1997, p. 54.

18 Rashid, *Jihad*.

19 *Ibid.*, p.169.

20 Mark Burgess, 'In the Spotlight: Islamic Movement of Uzbekistan', www.cdi.org/terrorism/imu-pr.cfm Accessed 11/3/2006.

21 Raman, 'Terrorism in Afghanistan and Central Asia', www.saag.org/papers12/paper1172.html. Accessed May 2005.

7 The Chechen and Caucasus Wars

1 Carlotta Gall and Thomas de Waal, *Chechnya: Calamity in the Caucasus* (New York, 1998); Anatol Lieven, *Chechnya: Tombstone of Russian Power* (New Haven, CT, 1998).

2 'Beslan: Tracing a Tragedy', *Guardian*, 30 September 2004; see also 'Bomber's Justification: Russians Are Killing our Children', *Guardian*, 6 August 2004.

3 Andrew Osborn, 'Dangers that Stalk the Enemies of Putin', *Independent*, 20 November 2006. See also Anna Politkovskaya, *A Dirty War: A Russian Reporter in Chechnya* (Harvill, 2004).

4 Tatarstan's President, Mintimer Saeymiev, concluded a separate deal with Yeltsin in 1994 that offered the state autonomy within the Russian Federation.

5 Carlotta Gall and Thomas de Waal, *Chechnya: A Small Victorious War* (London, 1997,) p. 60 (first edn of the book re-published as *Calamity in the Caucasus 2005*, New York, 1998).

6 Rosemarie Forsythe, *The Politics of Oil in the Caucasus and Central Asia* (Oxford, 1996); *Moscow Times*, 21 May 2002.

7 Richard Sakwa, ed., *Chechnya: From Past to Future* (London, 2005), pp. 117–30.

8 The 61st Session of the UN Commission on Human Rights, http://www.reliefweb.int/rw/rwb.nsf/db900SID/RMOI-06AD8A9? OpenDocument&emid=ACOS-635PN7&rc=4. Accessed November 2006.

9 Lutz Klevemann, *The New Great Game: Blood and Oil in Central Asia* (New York, 2003), pp. 51–2.

10 Timothy Thomas, 'Battle for Grozny', *Slavic Military Studies*, 10 (March 1997); Gall and de Waal, *Chechnya*, p. 205.

11 Radio Free Europe (Radio Liberty), 'Lebed–Mashkador sign new ceasefire agreement', 164, 1, 23 August 1996.

12 Radio Free Europe (Radio Liberty), 'Chechnya: Why did the 1997 Peace Agreement Fail?', 11 May 2007, http:www.rferl.org/specials/chechnya. Accessed May 2007.

13 The Salafest Wahhabis were never very popular even among those who regarded their struggle as a 'holy one'. See Walter Lacquer, *No End to War: Terrorism in the Twenty First Century* (London and New York, 2003), p. 187.

14 Lacquer, *No End to War*, p. 188; 'The Islamisation of the Conflict in Chechnya', www.nupi.no/IPS/filestore/00445.pdf.

15 Michael Orr, 'Chechnya', (Sandhurst, 2000), http://globalsecurity.org/military/library/report/2000/JIRArticle.htm. Accessed December 2006.

16 Human Rights Watch, 'Mistreatment and Abuse of Detainees', http://www.hrw.org/campaigns/russia/chechnya/filtration95.htm. Accessed May 2007.

17 See http://www.jamestown.org/publications_details.php?volume_id=416&issue_id=3848&article_id=2371431. Accessed November 2006.

18 See Klevemann, *The New Great Game*, p. 47, for Basaev's notoriety in Abkhazia.

19 The 61st Session of the UN Commission on Human Rights, http://www.reliefweb.int/w/rwb.nsf/db900SID/RMOI-06AD8A9?OpenDocument&emid=ACOS-635PN7&rc=4. Accessed November 2006.

20 On Kadyrov and his assassination, http://www.jamestown.org/publications_details.php?volume_id=416&issue_id=3848&article_id=236677. Accessed December 2006.

21 'Saudi Forces Storm Hijacked Jet', CNN.com, 16 March 2001, http://archives.cnn.com/2001/WORLD/europe/03/16/turkey.hijack.02/index.html. Accessed January 2007.

22 'Moscow Theatre Siege', 25 October 2002, http://news.bbc.co.uk/1/hi/world/europe/2362609.stm; 'The October 2002 Moscow Hostage Taking Incident', Radio Free Europe, 18 December 2003, http://www.rferl.org/reports/corruption-watch/2003/12/42-181203.asp. Accessed January 2007.

23 'Beslan: Tracing a Tragedy', *Guardian*; Amnesty International, 'Joint NGO Statement on the Beslan Hostage Tragedy', 8 September 2004, http://web.amnesty.org/library/index/engeur460502004. Accessed 14 December 2006.

24 Lacquer, *No End to War*, p. 188; see also www.jamestown.org/docs/Al-Shishani-14Sep06.pdf.

25 Lacquer, *No End to War*, pp. 188–9.

26 'Torture by Units under the Effective Command of Chechen Prime Minister Ramzan Kadyrov', November 2006, Human Rights Watch, http://hrw.org/back-grounder/eca/chechnya1106/3.htm#_Toc150776966; see also http://www.jamestown.org/publications_details.php?volume_id=416&issue_id=3848&article_id=236677. Accessed December 2006.

27 'Torture by Units'.

28 'Chechnya: Rebels Give Count of Losses', Radio Free Europe, 25 May 2000, http://www.rferl.org/features/2000/05/F.RU.000525083820.asp; 20 February 2003, CDI Russia Weekly, http://www.cdi.org/russia/245-14.cfm; Lawrence Uzzell, 'Russian Authorities Said to be Under-reporting Combat Deaths', *Chechnya Weekly*, v/8 (25 February 2004), http://www.jamestown.org/publications_details.php?volume_id=396&issue_id=2913&article_id=23561. Accessed January 2007.

29 'Racial Violence Escalates in Russia', 5 September 2006, Jane's, http://www.janes.com/security/international_security/news/jir/jir060905_1_n.shtml. Accessed December 2006.

30 Thomas de Waal, *Black Garden: Armenia and Azerbaijan through Peace and War* (New

York, 2003), pp. 126–31.

31 David E. Murphy, '"Operation Ring": The Black Berets in Azerbaijan', *Journal of Soviet Military Studies*, VI (March 1992).

32 Brian Killen, 'Massacre Leaves Dozens Dead in Azeri Region', *Chicago Tribune*, 3 March 1992.

33 Dimitry Polikanov, 'Transdnestria, Abkhazia, Chechnya: Pro et Contra EU Intervention', January 2003, www.Eurojournal.org. Accessed December 2006.

34 Laurence Broers, 'East: Frozen Conflicts Not So "Frozen" after All', 10 November 2006, www.rferl.org. Accessed December 2006.

8 China and Xinjiang Province

1 Michael Dillon, 'China Goes West: Laudable Development? Ethnic Provocation?', *Analyst*, 6 December 2000.

2 Peter Hopkirk, *Setting the East Ablaze* (Oxford, 1984), p. 147.

3 Andrew D. W. Forbes, *Warlords and Muslims in Central Asia: A Political History of Republican Sinkiang, 1911–1949* (Cambridge, 1986).

4 Hopkirk, *Setting the East Ablaze*.

5 Forbes, *Warlords and Muslims*, pp. 142, 182; Sadri Roostam, 'The Islamic Repubic of Eastern Turkestan: A Commemorative Review', *Voice of Eastern Turkestan*, III/9 (April 1986).

6 Christian Tyler, *Wild West China: The Untold Story of a Frontier Land* (London, 2003), p. 124.

7 Donald H. McMillen, *Chinese Communist Power and Policy in Xinjiang, 1949–1977* (Boulder, 1979), p. 91.

8 *Ibid.*, p. 91.

9 Tyler, *Wild West China*, p. 145.

10 McMillen, *Chinese Communist Power*, p. 190.

11 Amnesty International, 'People's Repubic of China: Gross Violations of Human Rights in the Uighur Autonomous Region', 21 April 1999.

12 Tyler, *Wild West China*, pp. 153–4, 156.

13 *Ibid.*, p. 159.

14 *Ibid.*, p. 161.

15 Amnesty, 'Gross Violations', pp. 164–5.

16 *Ibid.*, p. 19; Tyler, *Wild West China*, pp. 169–71.

17 Tyler, *Wild West China*, p. 173.

18 Laogai Research Foundation, 'The World Bank and Forced Labour in China', 23 October 1995, p. 5.

19 Nicolas Becquelin, 'Xinjiang in the Nineties', *China Journal*, XLIV (July 2000), pp. 75–6.

20 *Ibid.*, p. 83.

21 Tyler, *Wild West China*, p. 213.

22 *Ibid.*, p. 214; becquelin, 'Xinjiang', p. 69.

23 *Ibid.*, p. 241.

24 *Financial Times*, 17 June 1998.

25 *Taipei Times*, 10 November 1999.

26 *New York Times*, 13 September 2002. Tyler, *Wild West China*, p. 244.

27 *Ibid.*

28 *Daily Times* (Pakistan), 'China asks Pakistan to investigate Xinjiang Terrorist list', 17 January 2004.

9 Hydrocarbons and the Great Powers

1 Lutz Klevemann, *The New Great Game: Blood and Oil in Central Asia* (London, 2003) p. 3.
2 Barry Barton, C. Redgwell, A. Ronne and D. N. Zillman, *Energy Security: Managing Risk in a Dynamic Legal and Regulatory Environment* (Oxford, 2004) p. 5.
3 Rosemarie Forsythe, *The Politics of Oil in the Caucasus and Central Asia* (Oxford, 1996), pp. 17–21; Stephen S. Blank, *US Military Engagement with Transcaucasus and Central Asia* (Carlisle, PA, 2000); Michael T. Klare, *Resource Wars: The New Landscape of Global Conflict* (New York, 2002), p. 8. America's objectives regarding pipelines were outlined by Bill Richardson, Energy Secretary, in 1998, and are cited by Stephen Kinzer, in 'On Piping out Caspian Oil, US Insists the Cheaper, Shorter Way Isn't Better', *New York Times*, 8 November 1998.
4 Gawdat Bahgat, 'Central Asia and Energy Security', *Asian Affairs*, xxxvii/1 (March 2006), p. 3.
5 Klevemann, *New Great Game*, p. 12. Ahmed Rashid, *Taliban: Militant Islam, Oil and Fundamentalism in Central Asia* (New Haven, CT, 2000) p. 6; M. Ehsan Ahrari, *Jihadi Groups, Nuclear Pakistan and the New Great Game* (Washington, DC, 2001), p. 2; M. E. Ahrari and James Beal, *The New Great Game in Muslim Central Asia*, McNair Paper 47 (Washington, DC, 1996); Dianne L. Smith, *Central Asia: A New Great Game?* (Carlisle, PA, 1996); Ariel Cohen, 'The New "Great Game": Oil Politics in the Caucasus and Central Asia', *Heritage Foundation*, 25 January 1996.
6 The joint project, Tsentrkaspneftegaz, was reported in 'LUKoil Gazprom May Spend $12 Billion to Tap Caspian Field', *Moscow Times*, 8 July 2003.
7 Paul MacDonald, 'Oil Production Outlook Means Iran May Need Nuclear Power', *Petroleum Review* (April 2006), p. 20.
8 'Kazakhstan's Vision Sets It up as an Investment Gateway to Central Asia', http://www.dinarstandard.com/current/KazakVision032906.htm.
9 Michael T. Klare, *Resource Wars: The New Landscape of Global Conflict* (New York, 2002), pp. 102–4.
10 Ivan Gribanov, 'No Bosphorous Please: Four Projects to By-pass the Turkish Straits Spring to Life Simultaneously', RusEnergy.com, p. 3.
11 Ministry of Ecology and Bioresources, *Environmental Situation of the Republic of Kazakhstan* (Almaty, 1997); V. A. Vronsky, *Pollution in Central Asia* (Rostov on Don, 1996).
12 Stephan Harrison, 'Climate Change, Future Conflict and the Role of Climate Science', *RUSI Journal* (December 2005).
13 Harrison, 'Climate Change'.

10 Trajectories

1 Olaf Caroe, *Wells of Power: The Oilfields of Southwestern Asia – A Regional and Global Study* (London, 1951); Peter John Brobst, *The Future of the Great Game: Sir Olaf Caroe, India's Independence and the Defense of Asia* (Akron, 2005).
2 Richard Sakwa, ed., *Chechnya: From Past to Future* (London, 2005), pp. 265–87; Gail W. Lapidus, 'Conflict Resolution in the Caucasus', in Aspen Institute, *US Relations with the Former Soviet States* (Washington, DC, 1998) p. 26.
3 Michael T. Klare, *Resource Wars: The New Landscape of Global Conflict* (New York, 2002), pp. 105–7; Lutz Klevemann, *The New Great Game: Blood and Oil in Central Asia* (London, 2003), pp. 77–8.

4 Christian Tyler, *Wild West China: The Untold Story of a Frontier Land* (London, 2003); Klevemann, *The New Great Game*, p. 105.
5 Strobe Talbott, 'Remarks on US Foreign Policy in Central Asia at the Paul Nitze School of Advanced International Studies', US State Department, 21 July 1997.
6 Ahmed Rashid, *Jihad: The Rise of Militant Islam in Central Asia* (New Haven, 2002).
7 Roger Howard, *Iran in Crisis? Nuclear Ambitions and the American Response* (London and New York, 2004) p. 69.
8 Niklas Swanstrom, China and Central Asia: A new Great Game or traditional vassal relations?', *Journal of Contemporary China*, 14 45 (2005), pp. 571–2; Dewardic L. McNeal, 'China's Relations with Central Asian States and Problems with Terrorism', CRS Report for Congress, 17 December 2001, pp. 7–8.
9 *Xinhua*, 21 October 2006, http://news3.xinhuanet.com/english/2006-10/21/content__5232492.htm
10 *People's Daily*, 15 June 2006, cited in 'China and Shanghai Cooperation at Five', China brief, *The Jamestown Foundation*, 13, vol. VI, 21 June 2006.
11 Michael Pillsbury, 'China's Military Strategy Towards the US: A View from Open Sources', 2 November 2001, p. 2, at http://www.uscc.gov/researchpapers/2000–2003/pdfs/strat.pdf. Accessed 12 March 2007
12 See the collection of papers at 'Chinese Military Power', the Commonwealth Institute, http://www.comw.org/cmp. Accessed 12 March 2007.
13 'The War on Terrorism: Afghanistan and Terrorism', East Carolina University, Joyner Library, http://www.ecu.edu/lib/govdoc/afghanistan.cfm. See also Einnews.com updates, http://www.einnews.com/afghanistan/newsfeed-afghanistan-terrorism. Accessed January 2007.
14 Pamela Constable, 'Pakistan Reaches Peace Accord With Pro-Taliban Militias', *Washington Post*, 6 September 2006, http://www.washingtonpost.com/wp-dyn/content/article/2006/09/05/AR2006090501249.html. Accessed January 2007.
15 'Nawaz Blames Musharraf for Kargil', 28 May 2006, *Times of India*, http://timesofindia.indiatimes.com/articleshow/1581473.cms. Accessed June 2007.
16 Howard, *Iran in Crisis?*, pp. 43, 51–4, 56–63, 80.
17 *Ibid.*, pp. 119–62.
18 Dilip Hiro, *Between Marx and Muhammad: The Changing Face of Central Asia* (London, 1994).
19 'Country Reports on Human Rights Practices: Saudi Arabia', US Department of State, 25 February 2004, http://www.state.gov/g/drl/rls/hrrpt/2003/27937.htm. Accessed January 2007.
20 Klare, *Resource Wars*, p. 89.
21 *Ibid.*, p. 88.
22 IRIN, 'Interview with UN Chief in Kyrgyzstan', Bishkek, 28 August 2001.
23 Klevemann, *The New Great Game*, p. 97.
24 IRIN, 'Interview'.
25 'Silence over Afghan Women's Rights', BBC, 1 June 2006.
26 ICRC, *World Disaster Report, 2001* (Geneva, 2001); IRIN, 'One Million People Face Starvation in Tajikistan' Dushanbe, 29 August 2001.
27 Richard Sakwa, ed., *Chechnya: from Past to Future* (London, 2005); C. W. Blandy, *Dagestan: Birth of a Presidential Republic* (Conflict Studies Research Centre, Caucasus Series, 6/25, Defence Academy of the United Kingdom, briefing paper, June 2006).

Select Bibliography

General

Allworth, Edward, *The Modern Uzbeks: From the 14th Century to the Present: A Cultural History* (Stanford, CA, 1990)

—, ed., *Central Asia: 130 Years of Russian Dominance* (Durham, NC, 1994)

Bacon, Elizabeth, *Central Asians under Russian Rule: A Study in Cultural Change* (Ithaca, NY, 1966)

Brower, Daniel, and Edward Lazzerini, eds, *Russia's Orient: Imperial Borderlands and Peoples, 1700–1917* (Bloomington and Indianapolis, 1997)

d'Encausse, Hélène Carrère, *Islam and the Russian Empire: Reform and Revolution in Central Asia* (London, 1988)

Dragadze, T., 'The Domestication of Religion under Soviet Communism', in C. M. Hann, ed., *Socialism: Ideals, Ideologies and Local Practice* (London, 1993)

Dudoignon, Stephane, and Komatsu Hisao, eds, *Islam in Politics in Russia and Central Asia (Early Eighteenth to Late Twentieth Centuries)* (London and New York, 2001)

Edgar, Adrienne, *Tribal Nation: The Making of Soviet Turkmenistan* (Princeton, NJ, 2004)

Glenn, John, *The Soviet Legacy in Central Asia* (London, 1999)

Haugen, Arne, *The Establishment of National Republics in Soviet Central Asia* (New York, 2003).

Hauner, Milan, 'Central Asian Geopolitics in the Last Hundred Years: A Critical Survey from Gorchakov to Gorbachev', *Central Asian Survey*, VIII/1 (1989), pp. 1–20

Hopkirk, Peter, *The Great Game: The Struggle for Empire in Central Asia* (Oxford, 1984)

—, *Setting the East Ablaze: On Secret Service in Bolshevik Asia* (Oxford, 1984)

Kappeler, Andreas, Gerhard Simon, Georg Brunner and Edward Allworth, *Muslim Communities Reemerge: Historical Perspectives on Nationality, Politics, and Opposition in the Former Soviet Union and Yugoslavia* (Durham, NC, 1989)

Keller, Shoshana, 'Islam in Soviet Central Asia, 1917–1930: Soviet Policy and Struggle for Control', *Central Asian Survey*, 11/1 (1992), pp. 25–50

—, *To Moscow, Not Mecca: The Soviet Campaign against Islam in Central Asia* (Westport, CT, 2001)

Khalid, Adeeb, *The Politics of Muslim Cultural Reform: Jadidism in Central Asia* (Berkeley, CA, 1999)

Manz, Beatrice, ed., *Central Asia in Historical Perspective* (Boulder, CO, 1994)

Olcott, Martha Brill, 'The Collectivization Drive in Kazakhstan' *Russian Review*, XL/2

(1981), pp. 122–42

—, *The Kazakhs* (Washington, DC, 2002)

Rakowska-Harmstone, Teresa, *Russia and Nationalism in Central Asia: The Case of Tadzhikistan* (Baltimore and London, 1970)

Ro'i, Yaacov, *Islam and the Soviet Union* (New York, 2000)

Rumer, Boris, *Soviet Central Asia: A Tragic Experiment* (Boston, MA, 1989)

Sabol, Steven, 'The Creation of Soviet Central Asia: The 1924 National Delimitation', *Central Asian Survey*, XIV/2 (1995), pp. 225–42

Saroyan, Mark, 'Rethinking Islam in the Soviet Union', in Susan Gross Solomon, *Beyond Sovietology: Essays in Politics and History* (Armonk, NY, 1993)

Shahrani, Nazif, 'Central Asia and the Challenge of the Soviet Legacy', *Central Asian Survey*, XII/2 (1993), pp. 123–36

Soucek, Svat, *A History of Inner Asia* (Cambridge, 2000)

Suny, Ronald Grigor, *The Revenge of the Past: Nationalism, Revolution, and the Collapse of the Soviet Union* (Stanford, 1993)

Post-Soviet State-Building

Anderson, John, 'Constitutional Development in Central Asia', *Central Asian Survey*, XVI/3 (1997), pp. 301–20

—, 'Creating a Framework for Civil Society in Kyrgyzstan', *Europe-Asia Studies* LII/1 (2000), pp. 77–93

—, 'Social, Political, and Institutional Constraints on Religious Pluralism in Central Asia', *Journal of Contemporary Religion*, XVII/2 (2002), pp. 181–96

Emadi, Hafizullah, 'State, Ideology and Islamic Resurgence in Tadjikistan', *Central Asian Survey*, XIII/4 (1994), pp. 565–70

Haghayeghi, Mehrdad, *Islam and Politics in Central Asia* (New York, 1996)

Heinen, Joel, Chinara Sadykova and Emil Shukurov, 'Legislative Policy Initiatives in Biodiversity Conservation in Kyrgyzstan', *Post-Soviet Georgraphy and Economics* XLII/7 (2001), pp. 519–43

Huskey, Eugene, 'The Rise of Contested Politics in Central Asia: Elections in Kyrgyzstan, 1989–90', *Europe-Asia Studies*, XLVII/5 (1995), pp. 813–33

International Crisis Group, *Central Asia: Islam and the State* (Osh and Brussels, 20030

Iwasaki, Ichiro, 'Observations on Economic Reform in Tajikistan: Legislative and Institutional Framework', *Post-Soviet Geography and Economics*, XLIII/6 (2002), pp. 476–92

Kuru, Ahmet T., 'Between the State and Cultural Zones: Nation-building in Turkmenistan', *Central Asian Survey*, XXI/1 (2002), pp. 71–90

Luong, Pauline Jones, *Institutional Change and Political Continuity in Post-Soviet Central Asia: Power, Perceptions, and Pacts* (Cambridge, 2002)

—, ed., *The Transformation of Central Asia: States and Societies from Soviet Rule to Independence* (Ithaca, NY, 2003)

O'Kane, John, and Touraj Atabaki, eds, *Post-Soviet Central Asia* (London and New York, 1998)

Shirazi, Habibollah Abolhassan, 'Political Forces and Their Structures in Tajikistan', *Central Asian Survey*, XVI/4 (1997), pp. 611–22

Weinthal, Erika, *State Making and Environmental Cooperation: Linking Domestic and International Politics in Central Asia* (Cambridge, MA, 2002)

Post-Soviet Politics

Akbarzadeh, Shahram, *Uzbekistan and the United States: Authoritarianism, Islamism and Washington's New Security Agenda* (London, 2005)
Anderson, John, 'Authoritarian Political Development in Central Asia: The Case of Turkmenistan', *Central Asian Survey*, XIV/4 (1995), pp. 509–28
Bremmer, Ian, and Cory Welt, 'The Trouble with Democracy in Kazakhstan', *Central Asian Survey*, XV/2 (1996), pp. 179–200
Collins, Kathleen, *The Logic of Clan Politics in Central Asia: Its Impact on Regime Transformation* (Cambridge, 2005)
Dawisha, Karen, and Bruce Parrott, eds, *Conflict, Cleavage and Change in Central Asia and the Caucasus* (Cambridge, 1997)
Fierman, William, 'The Communist Party, "Erk", and the Changing Uzbek Political Environment', *Central Asian Survey*, X/3 (1991), pp. 55–72
Gleason, Gregory, *Markets and Politics in Central Asia: Structural Reform and Political Change* (New York, 2003)
International Crisis Group, 'Cracks in the Marble: Turkmenistan's Failing Dictatorship', International Crisis Group Asia Report 44 (2003)
—, 'Repression and Regression in Turkmenistan: A New International Strategy', International Crisis Group Asia Report 85 (2004)
Kazemi, Leila, 'Domestic Sources of Uzbekistan's Foreign Policy, 1991 to the Present', *Journal of International Affairs*, LVI/3 (2003), pp. 205–20
March, Andrew, 'From Leninism to Karimovism: Hegemony, Ideology, and Authoritarian Legitimation', *Post-Soviet Affairs*, XIX/4 (2003), pp. 307–36
—, 'The Use and Abuse of History: "National Ideology" as Transcendental Object in Islam Karimov's "Ideology of National Independence"', *Central Asian Survey*, XXI/4 (2002), pp. 371–84
Matveeva, Anna, 'Democratization, Legitimacy, and Political Change in Central Asia', *International Affairs*, LXXV/1 (1999), pp. 23–44
Olcott, Martha Brill, *Central Asia's New States: Independence, Foreign Policy, International Affairs*, 72, 4 (1996), pp. 862–3.
Schatz, Edward, *Modern Clan Politics: The Power of 'Blood' in Kazakhstan and Beyond* (Seattle, WA, 2004)

Ethnicity, Nationalism and Nation-Building Post-1991

Akbarzadeh, Shahram, 'A Note on Shifting Identities in the Ferghana Valley', *Central Asian Survey*, XVI/1 (1997), pp. 65–8
Diener, Alexander, 'National Territory and the Reconstruction of History in Kazakhstan', *Post-Soviet Geography and Economics*, XLIII/8 (2002), pp. 632–50
Edmunds, Timothy, 'Power and Powerlessness in Kazakstani Society: Ethnic Problems in Perspective', *Central Asian Survey*, XVII/3 (1998), pp. 463–70
Foltz, Richard, 'The Tajiks of Uzbekistan', *Central Asian Survey*, XV/2 (1996), pp. 213–16
Glenn, John, *The Soviet Legacy in Central Asia* (London, 1999)
Khalid, Adeeb, *The Politics of Muslim Cultural Reform: Jadidism in Central Asia* (Berkeley, CA, 1999)
Khazanov, Anatoly, *After the USSR: Ethnicity, Nationalism, and Politics in the Commonwealth of Independent States* (Madison, WI, 1996)
Kubicek, Paul, 'Regionalism, Nationalism, and Realpolitik in Central Asia', *Europe-Asia Studies*, XLIX/4 (1997), pp. 637–755

Kuzio, Taras, 'Nationalist Riots in Kazakhstan', *Central Asian Survey*, VII/4 (1988), pp. 79–101

Lane, David, 'Ethnic and Class Stratification in Soviet Kazakhstan, 1917–39', *Comparative Studies in Society and History*, XVII/2 (1975), pp. 165–89

Lubin, Nancy, *Calming the Ferghana Valley: Development and Dialogue in the Heart of Central Asia* (New York, 2000)

Naby, Eden, 'Ethnicity and Islam in Central Asia', *Central Asian Survey*, XII/2 (1993), pp. 151–68

Onaran, Yalman, 'Economics and Nationalism: The Case of Muslim Central Asia', *Central Asian Survey*, /4 (1994), pp. 491–506

Quelquejay, Chantal Lemercier, 'From Tribe to Umma', *Central Asian Survey*, III/3 (1984), pp. 15–26

Rakowska-Harmstone, Teresa, *Russia and Nationalism in Central Asia: The Case of Tadzhikistan* (Baltimore and London, 1970)

Roy, Olivier, *Central Asia: The Creation of Nations* (New York, 2000)

Wasilewska, Ewa, 'The Past and the Present: The Power of Heroic Epics and Oral Tradition – Manas 1000', *Central Asian Survey*, XVI/1 (1997), pp. 81–96

Williams, Brian Glyn, 'Jihad and Ethnicity in Post-Communist Eurasia: On the Trail of Transnational Islamic Holy Warriors in Kashmir, Afghanistan, Central Asia, Chechnya and Kosovo', *Global Review of Ethno-Politics*, II/3–4 (2003)

Wimbush, S. Enders, 'The Politics of Identity Change in Soviet Central Asia', *Central Asian Survey*, III/3 (1984), pp. 69–78

Winrow, Gareth, 'Turkey and the Former Soviet Central Asia: National and Ethnic Identity', *Central Asian Survey*, XI/3 (1992), pp. 101-12

Yavuz, M. Hakan, 'The Patterns of Political Islamic Identity: Dynamics of National and Transnational Loyalties and Identities', *Central Asian Survey*, XIV/3 (1995), pp. 341–72

Islam and Islamism

Akbarzadeh, Shahram, 'Political Islam in Kyrgyzstan and Turkmenistan', *Central Asian Survey*, XX/4 (2001), pp. 451–66

Akcali, Pinar, 'Islam as a "Common Bond" in Central Asia: Islamic Renaissance Party and the Afghan Mujuhidin', *Central Asian Survey*, XVII/2 (1998), pp. 267–84

Al-Azmeh, Aziz, *Islams and Modernities* (New York, 1993)

Anderson, John, 'Social, Political, and Institutional Constraints on Religious Pluralism in Central Asia', *Journal of Contemporary Religion*, XVII/2 (2002), pp. 181–96

Arabov, Oumar, 'Religion in Tajikistan: A Decade after the Break-Up of the USSR', *Central Asian Survey*, XX/2–3 (2003), pp. 339–42

Babadzhanov, Bakhtiar, 'On the Activities of Hizb at-Takhrir al-Islami in Uzbekistan (O Deatel'nosti Khizb at-Takhrir al-Islami v Uzbekistane)', in Aleksei Malashenko and Martha Brill Olcott, *Islam in Post-Soviet Space: A View from Within (Islam na Postsovetskom Prostranstve: Vzglad Iznutri)* (Moscow, 2001)

Deweese, D. A., *History of Islam in Central Asia* (Leiden and New York, 2000)

d'Encausse, Hélène Carrère, *Islam and the Russian Empire: Reform and Revolution in Central Asia* (London, 1988)

Dragadze, T., 'The Domestication of Religion under Soviet Communism', in C. M. Hann, *Socialism: Ideals, Ideologies and Local Practice* (London, 1993)

Emadi, Hafizullah, 'State, Ideology and Islamic Resurgence in Tadjikistan', *Central Asian Survey*, XIII/4 (1994), pp. 565–70

Fletcher, Joseph, and Boris Sergeyev, 'Islam and Intolerance in Central Asia: The Case of Kyrgyzstan', *Europe-Asia Studies*, LIV/2 (2002), pp. 251–76

Gross, Jo-Ann, ed., *Muslims in Central Asia: Expressions of Identity and Change* (Durham, NC, 1992).

Hagheyeghi, Mehrdad, *Islam and Politics in Central Asia* (New York, 1996)

Hetmanek, Allen, 'Islamic Revolution and Jihad Come to the former Soviet Central Asia: The Case of Tajikistan', *Central Asian Survey*, XII/3 (1993), pp. 365–78

International Crisis Group, *Central Asia: Islam and the State* (Osh and Brussels, 2003)

—, *Central Asia: Islamist Mobilisation and Regional Security* (Osh and Brussels, 2001)

—, *The IMU and the Hizb-ut-Tahrir: Implications of the Afghanistan Campaign* (Osh and Brussels, 2002)

—, *Is Radical Islam Inevitable in Central Asia? Priorities for Engagement* (Osh and Brussels, 2003)

Ilkhamov, Alisher, 'Uzbek Islamism: Imported Ideology or Grassroots Movement?', *Middle East Reports*, CCI (2001), pp. 40–46

Keller, Shoshana, 'Islam in Soviet Central Asia, 1917–1930: Soviet Policy and Struggle for Control', *Central Asian Survey*, XI/1 (1992), pp. 25–50

—, *To Moscow, Not Mecca: The Soviet Campaign against Islam in Central Asia* (New York, 2001)

Malashenko, Aleksei, and Martha Brill Olcott, eds, *Islam in Post-Soviet Space: A View from Within (Islam na Postsovetskom Prostranstve: Vzglad Iznutri)* (Moscow, 2001)

Mesbahi, Mohiaddin, 'Tajikistan, Iran, and the International Politics of the "Islamic Factor"', *Central Asian Survey*, XVI/2 (1997), pp. 141–58

Naby, Eden, 'Ethnicity and Islam in Central Asia', *Central Asian Survey*, XII/2 (1993), pp. 151–68

Naumkin, Vitaly, *Radical Islam in Central Asia: Between Pen and Rifle* (Lanham, MD, and Oxford, 2005)

Rashid, Ahmed, *Jihad: The Rise of Militant Islam in Central Asia* (New Haven, CT, 2002.

Ro'i, Yaacov, *Islam and the Soviet Union* (New York, 2000)

Sagdeev, Roald, and Susan Eisenhower, eds, *Islam and Central Asia: An Enduring Legacy or An Evolving Threat?* (Washington, DC, 2000).

Simpson, E. Sapper, 'Islam in Uzbekistan: Why Freedom of Religion is Fundamental for Peace and Stability in the Region', *Journal of Arabic and Islamic Studies*, II (1998–9), pp. 111–50

Walker, Edward W., 'Islam, Islamism, and Political Order in Central Asia', *Journal of International Affairs*, LVI/2 (2003), pp. 21–42

The Economies of the Republics

Abazov, Rafis, 'Policy of Economic Transition in Kyrgyzstan', *Central Asian Survey*, XVIII/1 (1999), pp. 197–224

Aslund, Anders, 'Sizing Up the Central Asian Economies', *Journal of International Affairs*, LVI/3 (2003), pp. 75–88

Bartlett, David, 'Economic Recentralization in Uzbekistan', *Post-Soviet Geography and Economics*, XL/2 (2001), pp. 105–21

Becker, Charles, Erbolat Musabek and Ai-Gul Seitenova, 'Short-term Migration Responses of Women and Men during Economic Turmoil: Lessons from Kazakhstan', *Post-Soviet Geography and Economics*, XLIV/3 (2003), pp. 228–43

Blank, Stephen, 'Energy, Economics, and Security in Central Asia: Russia and Its Rivals', *Central Asian Survey*, XIV/3 (1995), pp. 373–406

Brown, Andrew, 'Taking Shelter: The Art of Keeping a Roof Overhead in Post-Soviet Almaty', *Central Asian Survey*, XVII/4 (1998), pp. 613–28

Butler, Brian, and John Matzko, 'ICBMS and the Environment: Assessments at a Base in Kazakhstan', *Post-Soviet Geography and Economics*, XL/8 (1999), pp. 617–28

Cevikoz, Unal, 'A Brief Account of the Economic Situation in the Former Soviet Republics of Central Asia', *Central Asian Survey*, XIII/1 (1994), pp. 45–50

Chen, Chien-Hsun, and Hsiu-Ling Wu, 'The Prospects for Regional Economic Integration Between China and the Five Central Asian Countries', *Europe-Asia Studies*, LVI/7 (2004), pp. 1059–80

Cutler, Robert M., 'The Caspian Energy Conundrum', *Journal of International Affairs*, LVI/3 (2003), pp. 89–102

Dieter, Heribert, 'Regional Integration in Central Asia: Current Economic Position and Prospects', *Central Asian Survey*, XV/3-4 (1996), pp. 369–86

Ebel, Robert, and Rajan Menon, eds, *Energy and Conflict in Central Asia and the Caucasus* (New York, 2000)

Gleason, Gregory, 'Inter-State Cooperation in Central Asia from the CIS to the Shanghai Forum', *Europe- Asia Studies*, LII/7 (2001), pp. 1077–95

—, *Markets and Politics in Central Asia: Structural Reform and Political Change* (New York, 2003)

Haghayeghi, Mehrdad, 'Politics of Privatization in Kazakhstan', *Central Asian Survey*, XVI/3 (1997), pp. 321–38

Heinen, Joel, Chinara Sadykova and Emil Shukurov, 'Legislative Policy Initiatives in Biodiversity Conservation in Kyrgyzstan', *Post-Soviet Geography and Economics*, XLII/7 (2001), pp. 519–43

Iwasaki, Ichiro, 'Observations on Economic Reform in Tajikistan: Legislative and Institutional Framework', *Post-Soviet Geography and Economics*, XLIII/6 (2002), pp. 476–92

Kandiyoti, Deniz, 'Modernization without the Market? The Case of the "Soviet East"', *Economy and Society*, XXV (1996), pp. 529–42

Kaser, Michael, 'Economic Transition in Six Central Asian Economies', *Central Asian Survey*, XVI/1 (1997), pp. 5–26

Lipovsky, Igor, 'The Central Asian Cotton Epic', *Central Asian Survey*, XIV/4 (1995), pp. 529–42

Mars, Gerald, and Yochanan Altman, 'A Case of a Factory in Uzbekistan: Its Second Economy Activity and Comparison with a Similar Case in Soviet Georgia', *Central Asian Survey*, XI/2 (1992), pp. 101–12

McAuley, Alastair, 'Economic Development and Political Nationalism in Uzbekistan', *Central Asian Survey*, V/4 (1986), pp. 161–82

Melet, Yasmin, 'China's Political and Economic Relations with Kazakhstan and Kyrgyzstan', *Central Asian Survey*, XVII/2 (1998), pp. 229–52

Micklin, Philip, 'Water in the Aral Sea Basin of Central Asia: Cause of Conflict or Cooperation?', *Post-Soviet Geography and Economics*, XLIII/7 (2002), pp. 505–28

O'Hara, Sarah, and Bob Hudson, 'Agricultural Decline in Uzbekistan: The Case of Yazyavan Region', *Post-Soviet Geography and Economics*, XL/6 (1999), pp. 440–52

Onaran, Yalman, 'Economics and Nationalism: The Case of Muslim Central Asia', *Central Asian Survey*, XIII/4 (1994), pp. 491–506

Pannell, Clifton, and Philip Loughlin, 'Growing Economic Links and Regional Development in the Central Asian Republics and Xinjiang, China', *Post-Soviet Geography and Economics*, XLII/7 (2001), pp. 469–90

Peck, Anne, 'Foreign Investment in Kazakhstan's Minerals Industries', *Post-Soviet Geography and Economics*, XL/7 (1999), pp. 471–518
—, 'Privatization and Foreign Investment in the Utilities Industries of Kazakhstan', *Post-Soviet Geography and Economics*, XL/6 (2000), pp. 418–47
Saltmarshe, Douglas, 'Civil Society and Sustainable Development in Central Asia', *Central Asian Survey*, XV/3–4 (1996), pp. 387–98
Sievers, Eric, *The Post-Soviet Decline of Central Asia: Sustainable Development and Comprehensive Capital* (London and New York, 2003)
Tang, Shiping, 'Economic Integration in Central Asia: The Russian and Chinese Relationship', *Asian Survey*, XL/2 (2000), pp. 360–76

Energy and Natural Resources

Ebel, Robert, and Rajan Menon, eds, *Energy and Conflict in Central Asia and the Caucasus* (New York, 2000)
Kleveman, Lutz, *The New Great Game: Blood and Oil in Central Asia* (London, 2003)
Olcott, Martha Brill, 'The Caspian's False Promise', *Foreign Policy*, 111 (1998), pp. 94–113
Simonian, Hovann, and R. Hrair Dekmejian, *Troubled Waters: The Geopolitics of the Caspian Region* (London, 2003)

International Relations and Foreign Policy

Ahrari, Ehsan, 'The Strategic Future of Central Asia: A View from Washington', *Journal of International Affairs*, LVI/3 (2003), pp. 157–70
Ahrari, M. E., 'The Dynamics of the New Great Game in Muslim Central Asia', *Central Asian Survey*, XIII/4 (1994), pp. 525–40
Allison, Roy, ed., *Central Asian Security: The New International Context* (London, 2001)
Aydin, Mustafa, 'Turkey and Central Asia: Challenges of Change', *Central Asian Survey*, XV/2 (1996), pp. 157–78
Blank, Stephen, 'Energy, Economics, and Security in Central Asia: Russia and Its Rivals', *Central Asian Survey*, XIV/3 (1995), pp. 373–406
Bunce, Noah, and Ian Small, 'The Aral Sea Disaster and the Disaster of International Assistance', *Journal of International Affairs*, LVI/3 (2003), pp. 59–74
Chen, Chien-Hsun, and Hsiu-Ling Wu, 'The Prospects for Regional Economic Integration Between China and the Five Central Asian Countries', *Europe-Asia Studies*, LVI/7 (2004), pp. 1059–80
Dieter, Heribert, 'Regional Integration in Central Asia: Current Economic Position and Prospects', *Central Asian Survey*, XV/3–4 (1996), pp. 369–86
Ebel, Robert, and Rajan Menon, eds, *Energy and Conflict in Central Asia and the Caucasus* (New York, 2000)
Gleason, Gregory, 'Inter-State Cooperation in Central Asia from the CIS to the Shanghai Forum', *Europe-Asia Studies*, LIII/7 (2001), pp. 1077–95
Hansen, Flemming Splidsboel, 'A Grand Strategy for Central Asia', *Problems of Post-Communism*, LII/2 (2005), pp. 45–54
Horsman, Stuart, 'Uzbekistan's Involvement in the Tajik Civil War 1992–1997: Domestic Considerations', *Central Asian Survey*, XVIII/1 (1999), pp. 37–48
Hunter, Shireen, 'Iran's Pragmatic Regional Policy', *Journal of International Affairs*, LVI/3 (2003), pp. 133–48
Hyman, Anthony, 'Moving out of Moscow's Orbit: The Outlook for Central Asia', *International Affairs*, LXIX/2 (1993), pp. 288–304

International Crisis Group, *Central Asia: Islamist Mobilisation and Regional Security* (Osh and Brussels, 2001)

Israeli, Raphael, 'Return to the Source: The Republics of Central Asia and the Middle East', *Central Asian Survey*, XIII/1 (1994), pp. 19–32

Kazemi, Leila, 'Domestic Sources of Uzbekistan's Foreign Policy, 1991 to the Present', *Journal of International Affairs*, LVI/3 (2003), pp. 205–20

Kirimli, Meryem, 'Uzbekistan in the New World Order', *Central Asian Survey*, XVI/1 (1997), pp. 53–64

Kubicek, Paul, 'Regionalism, Nationalism, and *Realpolitik* in Central Asia', *Europe-Asia Studies*, XLIX/4 (1997), pp. 637–755

Legvold, Robert, ed., *Thinking Strategically: The Major Powers, Kazakhstan, and the Central Asian Nexus* (Cambridge, 2003)

Melet, Yasmin, 'China's Political and Economic Relations with Kazakhstan and Kyrgyzstan', *Central Asian Survey*, XVII/2 (1998), pp. 229–52

Menon, Rajan, 'In the Shadow of the Bear: Security in Post-Soviet Central Asia', *International Security*, XX/1 (1995), pp. 149–81

Mesbahi, Mohiaddin, 'Russian Foreign Policy and Security in Central Asia and the Caucasus', *Central Asian Survey*, XII/2 (1993), pp. 181–216

—, 'Tajikistan, Iran, and the International Politics of the "Islamic Factor"', *Central Asian Survey*, XVI/2 (1997), pp. 141–58

Micklin, Philip, 'Water in the Aral Sea Basin of Central Asia: Cause of Conflict or Cooperation?', *Post-Soviet Geography and Economics*, XLIII/7 (2002), pp. 505–28

Misra, Amalendu, 'Shanghai 5 and the Emerging Alliance in Central Asia: The Closed Society and Its Enemies', *Central Asian Survey*, XX/3 (2001), pp. 305–22

Olcott, Martha Brill, *Central Asia's New States: Independence, Foreign Policy, International Security* (Washington, DC, 1996)

Pannell, Clifton, and Philip Loughlin, 'Growing Economic Links and Regional Development in the Central Asian Republics and Xinjiang, China', *Post-Soviet Geography and Economics*, XLII/7 (2001), pp. 469–90

Peck, Anne, 'Foreign Investment in Kazakhstan's Minerals Industries', *Post-Soviet Geography and Economics*, XL/7 (1999), pp. 471–518

—, 'Privatization and Foreign Investment in the Utilities Industries of Kazakhstan', *Post-Soviet Geography and Economics*, XL/6 (2000), pp. 418–47

Rumer, Boris, ed., *Central Asia: A Gathering Storm?* (Armonk, NY, 2002)

Sestanovich, Stephen, 'Promoting Democracy', *Journal of International Affairs*, LVI/3 (2003), pp. 149–56

Simonian, Hovann, and R. Hrair Dekmejian, *Troubled Waters: The Geopolitics of the Caspian Region* (London, 2003)

Tang, Shiping, 'Economic Integration in Central Asia: The Russian and Chinese Relationship', *Asian Survey*, XL/2 (2000), pp. 360–76

Trenin, Dmitri, 'Southern Watch: Russia's Policy in Central Asia', *Journal of International Affairs*, LVI/3 (2003), pp. 119–32

Vaughn, Bruce, 'Shifting Geopolitical Realities between South, Southwest, and Central Asia', *Central Asian Survey*, XIII/2 (1994), pp. 305–16

Walsh, J. Richard, 'China and the New Geopolitics of Central Asia', *Asian Survey*, XXXIII/3 (1993), pp. 272–84

Weinthal, Erika, *State Making and Environmental Cooperation: Linking Domestic and International Politics in Central Asia* (Cambridge, MA, 2002)

Winrow, Gareth, 'Turkey and the Former Soviet Central Asia: National and Ethnic Identity', *Central Asian Survey*, XI/3 (1992), pp. 101–12

Zardykhan, Zharmukhamed, 'Kazakhstan and Central Asia: Regional Perspectives', *Central Asian Survey*, XXI/2 (2002), pp. 167–84

The Environment

Butler, Brian, and John Matzko, 'ICBMs and the Environment: Assessments at a Base in Kazakhstan', *Post-Soviet Geography and Economics*, XL/8 (1999), pp. 617–28
Micklin, Philip, 'Soviet Water Diversion Plans: Implications for Kazakhstan and Central Asia', *Central Asian Survey*, I/4 (1983), pp. 9–44

Narcotics

Barsegian, Igor, Alex Klaits and Nancy Lubin, *Narcotics Interdiction in Afghanistan and Central Asia: Challenges for International Assistance* (New York, 2002)
International Crisis Group, 'Central Asia: Drugs and Conflict', International Crisis Group Asia Report 25 (2001).
Makarenko, Tamara, 'Drugs in Central Asia: Security Implications and Political Manipulations', *Cahiers d'éétudes sur la Mediterranéée orientale et le monde turco-iranien*, 32 (2001), pp. 87–115
Mansfield, David, *Coping Strategies, Accumulated Wealth and Shifting Markets: The Story of Opium Poppy Cultivation in Badakhshan 2000–2003*, Agha Khan Development Network Report, January 2004

The Caucasus Conflicts

Chenciner, Robert, *Daghestan: Tradition and Survival* (London, 1997)
Roberts, Elizabeth, *Georgia, Armenia, and Azerbaijan* (Brookfield, CT, 1992)
Ro'i, Yaacov, *Muslim Eurasia: Conflicting Legacies* (Portland, OR, 1995)
Rosen, Roger, *Georgia: A Sovereign Country of the Caucasus* (Hong Kong, 1999).
Altstadt, Audrey L., *The Azerbaijani Turks: Power and Identity under Russian Rule* (Stanford, 1992)
Baumann, Robert F., *Russian-Soviet Unconventional Wars in the Caucasus, Central Asia, and Afghanistan* (Ft Leavenworth, 1993)
Blank, Stephen, *Russia's Invasion of Chechnya: A Preliminary Assessment* (Carlisle, PA, 1995)
Conquest, Robert, *The Nation Killers: The Soviet Deportation of Nationalities* (London, 1970)
Ebel, Robert E., *Energy and Conflict in Central Asia and the Caucasus* (Lanham, MD, 2000)
Ekedahl, Carolyn McGiffert, and Melvin A.Goodman, *The Wars of Edouard Shevardnadze* (University Park, 1997)
Hopkirk, Peter, *Setting the East Ablaze: On Secret Service in Bolshevik Asia* (Oxford, 1984)
Van der Leeuw, Charles, *Azerbaijan: A Quest for Identity* (New York, 2000)
Rosen, Roger, *The Georgian Republic* (Lincolnwood, IL, 1992)
Schweitzer, Glenn E., *Swords into Market Shares: Technology, Security, and Economics in the New Russia* (Washington, DC, 2000)
Souceck, Svat, *A History of Inner Asia* (Cambridge, 2000)
Suny, Ronald Grigor, *The Making of the Georgian Nation* (Bloomington, IN, 1994)

Contemporary Politics and External Intervention

Anderson, John, *Kyrgyzstan: Central Asia's Island of Democracy?* (Amsterdam, 1999)

Bertsch, Gary K., Cassady B. Craft and Scott A. Jones, eds, *Crossroads and Conflict: Security and Foreign Policy in the Caucasus and Central Asia* (New York, 1999)

Brook, Stephen, *Claws of the Crab: Georgia and Armenia in Crisis* (London, 1992)

Chorbajian, Levon, Patrick Donabedian and Claude Mutafian, *The Caucasian Knot: The History and Geo-Politics of Nagorno-Karabagh* (London, 1994)

Crichtlow, James, '*Punished Peoples' of the Soviet Union: The Continuing Legacy of Stalin's Deportations* (New York, 1991)

Dale, Catherine, 'Georgia: Development and Implications of the Conflicts in Abkhazia and South Ossetia', in *Conflicts in the Caucasus Conference* (Oslo, 1995)

Dunlop, John B., *Russia Confronts Chechnya: Roots of a Separatist Conflict* (Cambridge, 1998)

Edmunds, Timothy, 'Power and Powerlessness in Kazakstani Society: Ethnic Problems in Perspective', *Central Asian Survey*, XVII/3 (1998), pp. 463–70

Ertuk, Korkut A., *Rethinking Central Asia: Non-Eurocentric Studies in History, Social Structure, and Identity* (Reading, 1999)

Ehteshami, Anoushiravan, *From the Gulf to Central Asia: Players in the New Great Game* (Exeter, 1995)

Funch, Lars, and Helen Krag, *The North Caucasus: Minorities at a Crossroads* (London, 1994)

Goldenberg, Suzanne, *Pride of Small Nations: The Caucasus and Post-Soviet Disorder* (London, 1994)

Herzig, Edmund, *The New Caucasus: Armenia, Azerbaijan and Georgia* (London, 1999)

Hunter, Shireen T., *The Transcaucasus in Transition: Nation-Building and Conflict* (Washington, DC, 1994)

Jonson, Lena, *Russia in Central Asia: A New Web of Relations* (Washington, DC, 1998)

Karimov, Islam A., *Uzbekistan on the Threshold of the Twenty-First Century: Challenges to Stability and Progress* (New York, 1998)

Libaridian, Gerard, *The Challenge of Statehood: Armenian Political Thinking since Independence* (Watertown, MA, 1999)

Lynch, Dov, *Russian Peacekeeping Strategies in the CIS: The Cases of Moldova, Georgia and Tajikistan* (New York, 2000)

MacFarlane, S. Neil, Larry Minear and Stephen D. Shenfield, 'Armed Conflict in Georgia: A Case Study in Humanitarian Action and Peacekeeping', Occasional Paper, Brown University, Watson Institute (Providence, RI, 1996)

MacFarlane, S. Neil, *Western Engagement in the Caucasus and Central Asia* (Washington, DC, 1999)

Menon, Rajan, and Ghia Nodia, eds, *Russia, the Caucasus, and Central Asia: The 21st Century Security Environment* (New York, 1999)

Nasmyth, Peter, *Georgia: A Rebel in the Caucasus* (New York, 1992)

Olcott, Martha Brill, *Central Asia and China* (Washington, DC, 2001)

—, *Central Asia's New States: Independence, Foreign Policy, and Regional Security* (Washington, DC, 1996)

Peimani, Hooman, *Regional Security and the Future of Central Asia* (New York, 1998)

Rashid, Ahmed, *Taliban: Militant Islam, Oil, and Fundamentalism in Central Asia* (New Haven, CT, 2001)

Rubinstein, Alvin Z., and Oles M. Smolansky, eds, *Regional Power Rivalries in the New Eurasia: Russia, Turkey, and Iran* (New York, 1995)

Rumer, Boris Z., *Central Asia and the New Global Economy* (Armonk, NY, 2000)

Saltmarshe, Douglas, 'Civil Society and Sustainable Development in Central Asia', *Central Asian Survey*, xv/3–4 (1996), pp. 387–98

Smith, Sebastian, *Allah's Mountains: Politics and War in the Russian Caucasus* (London and New York, 1998)

Swietochowski, Tadeusz, *Russia and Azerbaijan: A Borderland in Transition* (New York, 1995)

Vassiliev, Alexei, *Central Asia: Political and Economic Challenges in the Post-Soviet Era* (London, 2001)

Walker, Christopher J., *Armenia and Karabagh: The Struggle for Unity* (London, 1991)

Winrow, Gareth, *Turkey and the Caucasus: Domestic Interests and Security Concerns* (Washington, DC, 2001)

Afghanistan

Amin, S. H., *Law, Reform, and Revolution in Afghanistan: Implications for Central Asia and the Islamic World* (Glasgow, 1993)

Bodansky, Yossef, *Bin Laden: The Man Who Declared War on America* (Rocklin, CA, 1999)

Borovik, Artem, *The Hidden War: A Russian Journalist's Account of the Soviet War in Afghanistan* (New York, 1990)

Bradsher, Henry S., *Afghan Communism and Soviet Intervention* (Oxford, 1999)

Cordovez, Diego, *Out of Afghanistan: The Inside Story of the Soviet Withdrawal* (New York, 1995)

Ewans, Martin, *Afghanistan: A New History* (London, 2001)

Goodsen, Larry P., *Afghanistan's Endless War: State Failure, Regional Politics, and the Rise of the Taliban* (Seattle, 2001)

Gohari, M. J., *Taliban: Ascent to Power* (Oxford, 2001)

Griffin, Michael, *Reaping the Whirlwind: The Taliban Movement in Afghanistan* (London, 2001)

Kakan, Hassar, *Afghanistan: The Soviet Invasion and the Afghan Response, 1979–1982* (Berkeley, 1995)

Marsden, Peter, *The Taliban: War, Religion and the New Order in Afghanistan* (London, 1998)

Matinnudin, Kamal, *The Taliban Phenomenon: Afghanistan, 1994–1997* (Oxford, 1999)

Mayley, Richard, *Fundamentalism Reborn? Afghanistan and the Taliban* (New York, 1998)

Urban, Mark, *War in Afghanistan* (New York, 1988)

Warikoo, K., *Afghanistan Factor in Central and South Asian Politics* (New Delhi, 1994)

Index

Uzbekistan and 13, 42, 74–5
hydrocarbons *see* oil *and* gas

ijtihad 29, 69
Ili
  rebellion (1944) 179
  riots (1959) 184
  River 213–14, 215
Imam Shamil 24
Ingushetia 138, 141, 145, 154, 160–61
insurgency 16, 21, 31, 85–6, 126, 130, 145–6, 218–19, 230
  Abkhazia 169
  Afghanistan 96, 99–100, 102, 112
  Chechen 143–6, 152–3, 159, 161, 166–7
  China 192
  Hizb ut-Tahrir 73, 75, 77, 79, 76–8
  Iraq 217
  Kashmir 105
  Russia calculations on 87
  Tajikistan 84–5, 94
  Uzbekistan and Kyrgyzstan 44, 114, 119–20, 127, 131–2, 137
International Islamic Front 115
International Monetary Fund (IMF) 38, 49, 135
International Security and Assistance Force (ISAF) 110
investment
  China 191, 222, 224–5
  Iran 204–05
  Kazakhstan 34, 37–9, 40
  oil and gas 198–201, 205, 209–10, 214, 221, 237
  Turkey 235
  Uzbekistan 43
Iran
  Azerbaijan supported by 169
  China relations 198, 223
  drugs 239
  ending the Tajik Civil War 89–91
  energy crisis 204–5
  flight of Turanzoda 83
  IMU opposition to 115
  investors deterred by 200
  IRP lobbyists 84
  Kazakh cooperation 40, 208
  oil industry 202–6, 208–10
  regional influence of 32, 46, 54, 104, 137, 194, 233–4, 237

Revolution (1979) 23, 58, 64–6, 98, 117, 231, 234, 241
Shia Afghans and 28, 101, 102, 104
Turkmenistan 221
United States 32, 40, 97, 137, 204, 207–9, 214, 218, 234
Yuldeshev and 118
Islam
  Deobandi
  focus against Soviet Union 46, 63–4
  growth of (post 1991) 25
  Islamism 13–15, 27–8, 58, 64, 67–9, 71, 74–5, 77–9, 83–4, 88–92, 94–5, 98, 102, 105, 115–19, 121, 123–4, 132–5, 139, 148, 160, 166, 180, 194, 215, 217, 225, 231–2, 234, 236, 241–2
  reforms in China 185
  Salafi or Wahhabi
  Shia
  Solidarity 72, 107–08, 229
  Soviet techniques against 25–7
  Sufi
  Sunni
  suppression in China 184–190, 194–6, 222
  underground move-ments of 27, 64, 72, 91–2, 119, 123–4
  Uzbek suppression of
Islam Lashkarlary 66, 117
Islamabad 54, 89, 104–5, 133, 194
Islamic Directorate for Central Asia and Kazakhstan 26
Islamic Movement of Turkestan (IMT) 114–37
  see also Jihadism *and* terrorism
Islamic Renaissance Party (IRP) 91–5
Islamic state 59, 66, 68–70, 83, 93, 102, 106–7, 112–13, 115–17
IMU (Islamic Movement of Uzbekistan) *see* IMT
Islamisation 162, 166

Jadidism 23
Japan 34, 39, 62, 94, 125–6, 178–9, 206–7, 226
Jihad 14, 28–9, 64–5, 67, 69, 73, 76, 93, 102, 106–7, 115–16, 119, 124–5, 136,

139, 144, 148–9, 187, 229
Jihadism 25, 29–30, 34, 42, 44, 69–70, 78, 94–6, 101, 106–8, 113–16, 118–20, 123, 128, 130–31, 136, 139, 145, 147–9, 155, 157, 159, 163, 174, 190, 195–6, 216–19, 225, 230, 232, 235–6, 241–2
Jamaat Sharia 160

Kadyrov, Akhmad 144, 154, 156, 161
Khadyrov, Ramzan 162–3
Karabakh 15, 82, 139, 167–9, 216, 238, 242
Karimov, Islam
  government of 41–2, 44–5, 117, 119, 121, 123–4, 126, 134
  IMT view of 71, 78, 116–18, 122
  regional policy of 85, 87–8, 120, 122–3, 134, 200
  views of 13–14, 42, 67, 88, 119, 121–3, 133, 137, 220, 233
  US view of 131
Karmal, Barbak 58–9, 98–9, 102
Karzai, Hamid 58, 61, 99, 109–10, 112
Kasimov, Ahmedjan 180
Kazakhstan
  allegations of corruption 38–9
  China relations 193, 206, 213–14, 221–3
  conquest 19, 35
  economy 34–40, 198, 201, 205, 207–8, 218, 237–8
  environment 211–13, 215
  Hizb ut-Tahrir in 76
  Iran and 208
  IRP in 66
  Islam in 23
  operations in Tajikistan 86
  policing 31
  Russian migration into 20, 35, 36
  Russian relations 203, 205, 220, 225, 236–7
  US relations 134, 203, 207–8, 218–19, 221, 236–7
  Uzbekistan compared 44
KHAD 24, 59, 100, 102
Khalidi, Noor Ahmed 16
Khalq 57–9, 97–8
Khasavyurt Accords 146, 147, 148
Khasbulatov, Ruslan 140